JIMMY'S HOME

NANCY J. SELL

Copyrighted Material

Jimmy's Home
2020 by Nancy J. Sell. All Rights Reserved.
No part of this publication may be reproduced, stored in a retrieval system or transmitted, in any form or by any means—electronic, mechanical, photocopying, recording or otherwise—without prior written permission from the publisher, except for the inclusion of brief quotations in a review.

For information about this title or to order other books and/or electronic media, contact the publisher:
Nancy J. Sell
Nancy.Sell@aol.com

Scripture quotations are from the King James Version of the Bible

Brand names are used only for clarity of the story and are not an endorsement of products

ISBN: 978-1-7360265-0-2 (softcover)
       978-1-7360265-1-9 (hardcover)

Printed in the United States of America

DEDICATION

*To My Children
Ruth, Janet and Daniel*

*. . . and my sincere appreciation to my daughter
Janet for her help and encouragement.*

CHAPTER ONE

Still holding the phone receiver to her ear, Elizabeth Markham dropped her head to her folded arms. Her dark brown hair, rumpled and uncombed except for restless fingers frequently running through it, fell softly around her face and hid the tears spotting the sleeve of her mauve velvet robe. A sob escaped from deep in her being, and her shoulders shook. At the far end of the line, the phone rang in Rand's office for the tenth time. She had counted the rings: ten. Now eleven, twelve . . . fifteen, sixteen . . .

"Where are you, Rand?" she silently questioned the thing in her hand as if it had the power to reason, the ability to communicate as well as to transmit communication. She closed her eyes and envisioned her husband's dark office, eerily soundless but for the ringing telephone on his neat desk, shapes and shadows turned monsters in the silent night. But empty, she conceded. Uninhabited by anything human.

Nineteen, twenty . . .

"Oh, Randy." She grabbed a tissue and took a deep breath. "Where are you?"

For the fourth or fifth time she had tried to call his cell phone. She couldn't leave a message because his voicemail was full.

The last time she had looked at the clock on the night table it was just past midnight, and that must have been hours ago; she had not allowed herself to look at it again. "If not at the office, then where *are* you? And," the next thought came, undesired, unbidden, like unexpected pain in the quietness of a restful, peaceful night, "with whom?" Her heart hurt. That unwelcome possibility of his not being alone inferred not only the breaking of promises, civil and sacred, but also the intrusion of a third party into their most private world. She shoved that thought away. It was intolerable and unfathomable.

She sniffled as fresh tears moistened her lashes.

No, Rand would not betray her. She refused to ponder that thought. But the possibility turned in her mind to a probability, and her hurt turned to anguish. "Stop it, Liz," she accosted herself, "and stick to the known, the positive."

Too numb to move, Liz let the phone go on ringing and welcomed the monotony of it. She lost count of the rings. Ennui, coupled with her anxiety, caused a troublesome restlessness that manifested mentally rather than physically. She sat up at her dressing table, however, and peered into her mirror, avoiding eye contact with herself. In her innermost being, she was terrified. The stakes were high, and she had too much to lose, too much she couldn't lose. Still avoiding her own eyes in the reflection, she set her gaze adrift around the familiar room via the mirror, her warm secure place that now bore the mien of a stranger. Her heavy walnut dresser, topped by a portrait of a uniformed Rand and strewn with makeup, jewelry, perfume, and store receipts, was half visible on her immediate right. She was a clutterer. She wished she could be neater.

Nancy J. Sell

Her eyes rested on young Rand in the brass frame: her love, her lover, her friend, and sometimes her adversary, and she willed him to hear her call wherever he happened to be. His presence in her world, no matter their conflict, lent stability to her life, strength to her weaknesses, fire to her emotions; she wanted, demanded, that he respond to her bidding. "Answer that phone!" she ordered furiously, then cursed inaudibly. She always swore silently so no one, especially the children, would hear, and she did so now from habit. Hurt was swelling to irritation, and soon anger would erupt into a full-blown fit. She swallowed hard and, with feigned disinterest, continued her study of the room, as if seeing it for the first time, or through someone else's eyes.

Next to the dresser stood her secretary desk with its twelve convex windows, each glass seeming to have one tiny eye to ogle her in the dim reflected light of the room. She hastily looked away, tearing herself from their spooky stare.

Liz hung up the phone, waited briefly, then redialed.

"Answer the *phone*, Rand!" she demanded again, pummeling her fist in rapid staccato movements on the glass top of the dressing table. "I hate you for doing this! You are an arrogant, inconsiderate boor!" She bit the inside of her lower lip and closed her eyes to squeeze back tears that insisted on escaping. She had lost count of the rings. It didn't matter; there were too many.

The king-size bed, on the wall opposite the dressing table, offered rest, but sleep was far from her weary brain and body. Hanging on the wall over the bed, and partly obscured in its reflection by her own head, was a large tapestry depicting a snowy mountain wilderness complete with sled and team of huskies, log cabin, and cache. Rand had brought it when he returned from Alaska where he had been stationed with the military. That was before they were married, before she knew him, and someday he planned to return and take her with him, or so he said. She had no doubt it would happen. Someday.

The hall door next to Rand's side of the bed was closed and locked: The children must not walk in on her unannounced.

Rand's highboy with a portrait of her, a jewelry case of manzanita wood from the West Coast, and an antique brass lamp were on the adjacent wall. It was neat. He was always neat. His orderliness, his extreme impeccability, sometimes bothered her when she allowed them to, but her clutter didn't bother him. His socks were lined up in the drawer according to color, as were the handkerchiefs and shirts; suits, trousers, sport coats, and jackets were arranged in the closet in systematic groups, ready for occupancy and action.

From Rand's dresser the mirror's-eye view was inadequate to complete the pan. Liz adjusted her vision to continue without the aid of the mirror. Her eyes rested one by one on the children's portraits that hung between the bathroom door and her mirror.

Liz ended the call, having little hope of a response. Then, as if needing a connection to a world outside her domain, she redialed then returned to the photographs.

Jeffrey Randolph III, almost sixteen, was less rugged than Rand but just as good-looking. He had his father's wide grin and deep-set brown eyes that sparked or sparkled without warning, a picture that belied the true, confused, angry Jeff of the moment; he also lacked Rand's quiet elegance. Maybe it would come with maturity. She was hopeful. But for now she had to endure his noisy exuberance, or sometimes unexpected silence.

Jeff claimed to hate academics, thus Rand believed he would fail at living up to his potential if he weren't continually pushed. Liz suspected Rand of seeing too much of himself in his son. The girls flocked after Jeff, calling on the phone from early morning until late at night, and so she and Rand had established a rule: no evening calls before eight or after nine, except for emergencies. During the remaining hours, Rand activated the answering machine with his own message that began, "This is J. Randolph Markham Jr. If you're a female calling for my son, Jeffrey Randolph Markham, the Third, you can hang up now . . ."

Pam, pretty Pam, also with her father's dark good looks, brown eyes flecked with gold, and no-nonsense approach to life, was a twelve-year-old planner, an organizer; she was the epitome of adolescent ambivalence with accompanying agonies and ecstasies. An honor student, her diligent pursuit of education was impressive but sometimes frightening. "Don't worry. She'll get over it," Rand comforted. But she didn't. She kept plugging along. "Maybe some of it will rub off on Jeff," he grimaced. Rand's phone message would soon be changed to screen her calls too, as they gradually increased in frequency.

And their Charlotte, or Charie, four, a mixture of *giggles and grumps,* as Jimmy so aptly put it and which described himself perfectly, was her mother's girl, with blue eyes and highlights of rust in brown curls, a throwback from the distaff side of Liz's grand-parentage. She was named for Charlotte Charles, Liz's Great-Aunt Lottie, her father's aunt who had never married but who had cherished and nurtured and doted on all the children of the family as well as any others who had appeared in her range of activities. Aunt Lottie played softball with them, water-skied, jumped rope, played hopscotch, built and destroyed snow forts. When she went sledding, she belly-flopped onto her saucer sled along with the rest of them. She had been accused of spoiling them all, but as Liz remembered her, she was a tough old bird who made them hop to it with a scowl and a smack on the rump. The children of Liz's generation had idolized her, and she had been a welcome addition to any picnic or party. One on one, she was a gem of wisdom and enjoyment. The next generation had been cheated: The year before Jeff was born, Aunt Lottie had dropped dead. Charlotte loved Aunt Lottie, if ever a dead person whom you had never met could be loved, and she talked of her constantly as if she were a living companion.

"Mommy," Charlotte complained, not for the first time, and with an exaggerated pout, "Jeffy says Charie is a boy's name. Tell him it's not, Mommy!"

"Well, honey, you know he's teasing. That's what big brothers do."

"But I don't like it. Tell him it's not!"

"You tell him, Charie. You know it's a boy's nickname if the boy's name is Charles, pronounced Charlie. Like chair, church . . ."

"Chip. Cheese . . ."

"There you go. But if you want a nickname for Charlotte, it's pronounced Charie, with a *sh* sound like . . ."

"Like what?"

"Like charades. You know the game we play sometimes. Chandelier. That's a big one. Let's think of some more." And so Charie was appeased once more.

Five-year-old Jimmy was a summer day with his straw-colored, thick straight hair, cowlick, and big dark-brown eyes that glistened with animation; he was a winter storm when those same eyes glinted with anger. No spring or fall, he was either cold or hot, up or down. He was an enigma. In the space where Jimmy would go, Charie had taped an eight-by-ten sheet of typing paper on which she had drawn, with her typical genre for simplicity, a scrawny stick figure beneath which she had carefully lettered the name, "Jimmie." If *Charie* ended in *ie*, so should *Jimmie*.

Jimmy was a handsome boy. His eyes were so dark, they often appeared black. He had clear skin and a beautiful, expressive face that blossomed without a second's notice. Basically good-natured, he was usually happy for all his being shuffled from place to place, and Liz was sure his damaged personality could be repaired with a consistent mixture of discipline and love.

His mother didn't want him, yet she would not sign a release for his adoption. So as a ward of the state, he had been placed and re-placed in foster homes, finally finding his way into the home of the Markhams' neighbors, Don and Jennie Blair, where he had spent the last two years. It was then he had made his first visit to the Markhams' home. Jimmy was a visitor, according to Rand, not permanent, and contrary to Liz's plans.

Thankfully, all four of them were quiet and probably asleep; Liz had been unable to cope with a major trauma this evening, and although Jimmy had presented a serious attempt at annoying her, he had finally settled in. She had wanted, no, *needed* solitude.

"J. Randolph Markham Jr. speaking."

She started, her flesh prickling with an awareness that she was no longer alone. The unexpected response to her call activated every nerve. Her husband's voice was thick, apparently with sleep, but she recognized an undefined added note: Was it annoyance? Liz sat up straight again and stared blankly at her teary swollen face in the mirror, hardly knowing the person who, in the subdued light, stared back at her. *That is you, Liz,* she informed the caricature whose eyes met hers. *That is you. You are real. A real mess. And that is really your husband on the line.*

"Where are you, Rand?" she demanded with a lame attempt to mime her normal voice, then shook mental cobwebs from her brain. She was elated to hear his voice. Her world, though still in chaos, was in focus again. "Oh, of course. I know where you are." She chuckled lamely, meeting his silence. "At the office. But I've been so worried. You didn't come home . . ." Why was she blubbering?

"Obviously."

Rand's one-word comment took her from zenith to nadir in a single breath. A smarting in her throat made her voice tremble. "Randy..." The word hung there, unsupported.

"I'm sorry, Liz." His voice was curt. "It's late."

"It's late. I know that."

"You woke me out of a sound sleep. I didn't mean to snap."

"I've been trying to call for..." She hesitated. "I wish you had called. I was worried..."

"I should have. I worked for hours. Then I fell asleep."

"Are you coming home?"

"No."

Silence.

"I wish you would. Rand..."

"No." His reiteration was followed by an interminable pause. Finally he went on, his voice softening considerably. "I'll finish these reports. I should have been working on them, instead of sleeping."

"You need to sleep," she interjected, but he continued as if she had not spoken.

"Then I'll try to sleep until the office opens in the morning."

Liz tried to hide disappointment mingled with annoyance that he had no trouble sleeping. "I'm glad you can sleep." She spoke gently and moderated the words carefully.

"So can you. Go to bed."

"No, I can't. I'm sorry I swore at you."

"Really?" He sounded doubtful, disinterested. He knew her too well.

"I love you, Rand."

There was no reply, only the click of the phone at his end. "I love you," she repeated, this time to the dial tone, then replaced the receiver. Both hands lingered on it as if she were reluctant to let go, to release his touch. Her head found a resting place on her folded hands. Her shoulders shook with silent sobs.

Eventually she rose and moved about the room languidly, pausing to peer out the dark window at a distant dim light here and there through the trees at the neighbor's: a car pulling into the drive at the Trents': Bud was finally home, probably drunk. How did Ceil put up with his monkeyshines? A kitchen light on at the Dudleys', then a few minutes later, off again: the baby awake early for his 3:00 a.m. feeding. A spotlight on at Morrisons': no doubt a sensor light activated by a passing deer.

Liz touched the jewelry case on Rand's dresser, then picked up his picture from her dresser and caressed his face with her eyes. She ran her fingers along the kaleidoscope he had bought her for her last birthday.

From her childhood Liz had always held a special fascination for kaleidoscopes, tirelessly watching the colors slip into their ever-changing, never-the-same patterns. How like life, she mused. How changing. How unpredictable. How deceptive. How beautiful. Sometimes.

When it worked. This one was broken.

Last week Charie had taken it from her dresser and held it to her eye, turning it slowly as Liz had previously demonstrated to her, watching the multicolored fragments rearrange themselves. "Don't drop it," Liz had warned.

"I won't," she had responded impatiently, continuing to turn the kaleidoscope without removing it from her eye as she twisted from Liz's protective hands.

"I want to see," Jimmy pressed. He reached for it and, because Charie tried to hold on tenaciously, it dropped to the floor.

"You did it, Jimmy. You stupid head! Why didn't you wait your turn?"

"I did *not* do it! *You're* the stupid head! You hung on and wouldn't let me have a turn."

"I did *not!* It's all your fault! You couldn't wait, could you? You make me so mad!"

Back and forth they had gone until a distressed Liz had intervened. The mirrors inside were dislodged and no longer reflected light and colors, and it was still sitting on her dresser because Rand was going to fix it. "What year?" she had asked him. *Anyway, I don't have to waste my time on that anymore,* she thought, berating herself. She resisted an impulse to throw it, then placed it gently into the trash can. She crawled into her side of their king-size bed with tears blurring her vision as she reached for the lamp switch, but she saw the digital clock: 1:38 . . . 1:39.

"I love you," he was usually quick to answer, and sometimes he added, "and I like you, too."

What had happened to them, to this marriage voted most likely to succeed by so many who knew them? The first year was supposed to be the hardest. Just the first, they said. Well, the first twenty hadn't been too easy.

"I love you so much, Randy. Isn't that enough? I thought it would be." But the argument that morning before he left for work had shattered her, and Jimmy was the question.

"The answer is no!" he had bellowed. "No!" he repeated when she tried to speak. "I mean NO! You're a manipulator, Liz," he stormed.

"Shut up and let me talk!"

"It's all been said! You're a conniver! A schemer! And *don't* ever tell me to *shut up!*"

"I'll tell you anything I please!" She swore at him, this time loud and clear, calling him names she never verbalized, ones she modestly tried to skip over when reading. Amazed at her own daring, she applauded herself.

"*Tsk, tsk, tsk,*" he embellished with an audacious grin.

"Shut up!"

"I've had it with you!"

"Good. Then get out!"

He pulled the door shut behind him, and it slammed with a vengeance. Why had he been so cold and cruel? She didn't know, but she had been almost ready to forgive him when he returned from work. Almost. But he had not returned. He had not called to explain. Didn't he know her heart was breaking, causing her to say the things she said to him? And he was breaking it. She would not tolerate this kind of treatment.

The long day was followed by a painfully empty evening, especially desolate because she had not anticipated facing it alone. So much had been left hanging . . .

It was then, after the children had gone to bed, that she had to stop pretending. She tried to write letters, tried to watch TV, tried to read, but the hurt when she returned to reality was too overwhelming. No, this kind of treatment was unacceptable.

Now as she lay in bed, sleep was elusive. She twisted and tossed and flopped as she mentally rehearsed and rehearsed again this most recent interchange with Rand, and each time she felt renewed turmoil. She made a fist and punched his pillow as angry tears surfaced. What a fool she was! She had planned to put her arms around him to assure him that all was forgiven, forgotten. Well, it won't be that easy now, J. Randolph Markham Jr! Rand had changed. She didn't like what was happening to him, and consequently to them. Her tired mind tried to file its jumbled thoughts.

Suddenly her alarm was ringing, jolting her awake. She groaned wearily. *I'm so tired!* Knowing she would be asleep again, however, if she allowed herself the luxury of a few more minutes in bed, she hauled herself to the edge and then to her feet.

What would she tell the children? Their father was sick in bed? No, the truth, of course. Dad was so bogged down with work, he decided to stay at the office. *It was the truth. Sort of.* Would they believe her, knowing his office was just over the line in White Plains, New York, a mere twenty-five miles from their Connecticut home? She would offer no more. They would have to believe it.

Liz turned on the light in the quiet kitchen and started the coffee, a smaller pot than usual, and sighed. Disintegrated marriages these days were the rule rather than the exception. Not theirs. It couldn't happen. Stormy weather made you tough, and, toughened, you survived. She needed Rand; she didn't want to lose him. She couldn't. She loved him. She loved him deeply in the quietness of their own solitude when conversation was unnecessary; she loved him openly in the presence of crowds as she reveled in his graceful interaction with others, which never seemed to impede his constant awareness of her; she loved him in his interaction with their own children as she marveled at his wisdom and patience; she loved him passionately in the privacy of their most intimate moments. She loved him. That was the bottom line. She *loved* him.

The damp early morning fragrance of hyacinth and magnolia blossoms reached her nostrils as she opened the window. The moment seemed untouched, uncluttered, almost holy in its beauty. If only she could hold on to it. An ovenbird sang his *teacher-teacher* song high in the big blue spruce; a squirrel scrambled in the magnolia tree, and in the movement the pink-white satiny blossoms released a fresh waft of fragrance. A bluebird flew defensively at a squirrel to protect his nest.

Nancy J. Sell

Her thoughts were mechanical: *Before Randy finishes breakfast and the newspaper, the children will be down to disrupt his routine. Then the mad scramble for books, for lunches, for sweaters . . .*

She winced. J. Randolph Markham Jr. would be getting coffee and Danish to-go from The Corner Deli this morning. The predictably hectic eight-legged race before her family went their separate ways would be reduced by one-quarter. Jeff, Pam, and Jimmy would leave on three different school buses for three different schools. Then Liz and Charlotte would be alone for a few hours. Jimmy, the kindergartner, attended for just the morning session, and Charie anxiously awaited his return each day at noon.

Their big dog, Mini, passed beneath her kitchen window, sniffing randomly before lifting his leg to the ten-foot saguaro-like tree stump from whose naked branches hung Liz's bird feeders in winter and flower pots in summer. Mini was a huge mongrel. "Yes, Minnie is a girl's name," she had to explain repeatedly, "but this one is spelled *M-I-N-I*, meaning small: dwarf." Then sensing a deepening puzzlement, she always added, "As in Petite Pup." She had tried to rename him Maxi when it became apparent the tiny homeless ball of fur from the pound would become a large, loping, horse-like member of their ranks, but she had been outvoted.

Sneakers, Pam's pet, blinked at Mini in snobbish boredom from the shadows of the mulberry tree, his white paws set daintily in front of him. A stray, Sneakers was a docile black beauty with pretty white face and feet. He had been dropped, quite literally, on their doorstep the previous summer when Rand and Pam had come home from a local nursery with plants and garden supplies. A dreadful looking creature had fallen from under the front end of the car, right at the front steps.

Pam shrieked, *"It's alive!"*

Jimmy's Home

"Wait, Pam! Don't touch it. Don't go near it until we figure out what the durn thing is!"

The durn thing was the cat. His coat was mangled and seared, his eyes glazed and unfocused. He was unsteady and confused. They ignored him for a whole week hoping he would go away, but strangely his condition improved daily. Then they learned why: Pam had been feeding him. As a result of Pam's long-term loving care, he was now her beautiful Sneakers. He had become a member of the Markham domain, despite Rand's dissenting vote, because he had been a good mouser; now he was Pam's loyal and devoted follower, fat and no longer interested in chasing mice. Liz never could turn her back on a homeless critter either, and Sneakers was here to stay.

"Mom, I just put Mini out." The voice was Charlotte's. Liz didn't look at her, but she knew she was carrying Bearsh, her favorite of all beings. Charie's short brown hair, the color, Rand said, of autumn leaves—dead ones—would be matted against her head from her pillow, and her lovely blue eyes narrowed to slits as if unable to tolerate the morning light. The freckles across her cheeks, barely visible all winter, were becoming more pronounced. When Jeff was in an amiable mood, which was less and less of late, he tried to count them, to her frustration, but lost count when he reached one hundred ninety-one, or so he said.

Charlotte, thumb in mouth, would curl up in the big chair by the fireplace in the family room where she and Bearsh, her fuzzy worn teddy, would commune silently until Charie was called to breakfast. Jimmy had wanted to name his teddy Bearsh too, but Charie said no—Bearsh had had that name for *years*. So Jimmy had conceded unwillingly and retained the name Tedley, his original choice. Bearsh and Tedley were people in their own right.

Putting school lunches together, Liz watched Charie from over the kitchen counter, which opened into the family room.

The room had been planned in this way, by Liz and Rand, to give the feeling of space, but it was doing much more: It was creating for them a family unit. The kitchen and the family room, including an eating area, were their life center. The casual setting, Liz and Rand had hoped, would always be a retreat, a place to be yourself, to put aside the outside world, to absorb stability, reality, warmth. Their living and dining rooms were a decorator's delight, but only because they were ignored except for the more formal entertainment of guests.

"The President's coming to dinner," someone would usually expound when seeing the dining room table set with linen cloth, fine china, and crystal. The Markhams often entertained, but the observation was forthcoming nevertheless. Liz loved the look of her beautiful table, the lighted breakfront displaying treasured pieces that had once belonged to her grandparents and to Rand's. She had placed a silk red rosebud with baby's breath in a small fine porcelain vase on the silver tea service tray.

Why is Charie always up so early? Liz wondered. She would so enjoy a few minutes to herself to read the newspaper over a second and third cup of coffee after the others had gone. Or go back to bed, she thought wearily with hurting head and burning eyes. So much for serenity and silence, she sighed as Jimmy's footsteps thumped down the stairs. Pam entered ahead of Jimmy; Jeff would follow.

"Where's Dad?" Pam queried, glancing briefly with only perfunctory interest to Rand's empty chair, her big round eyes momentarily opening in surprise to see her father's empty place. Her long dark brown hair fell straight and beautiful, framing her pretty, expressive face. In spite of Pam's adolescent confusion and contrariness, she was a dear heart. Draping an arm across her daughter's shoulders, Liz hugged her, then explained Randy's presence at his office to finish some important work. Pam's attention immediately shifted to food and to the schedule.

Jimmy caught the tail end of the story when he entered the kitchen, so she explained it to him. She wondered if they believed her; they seemed to silently accept her story.

But not Jeff. "Why didn't Dad come home last night?" he asked as he plunked his schoolbooks on the table. When Jeff entered a room, he was a presence to be reckoned with, an entity not to be ignored. Liz fumbled at her son's bluntness, his intimidation, then recovered enough to give him the same report. "Yeah," he said, giving her a there's-more-to-it-than-that look. He drank his orange juice without sitting down, filled a paper cup with Honey Nut Cheerios®, and left, calling an impersonal goodbye to the universe.

"Lunch!" Liz shouted. He returned and sheepishly snatched his brown bag from the counter, knowing that hot lunch from the school cafeteria would come out of his own pocket, in reality his car fund, in the event his prepared lunch was left at home.

CHAPTER TWO

J. Randolph Markham Jr. made it a practice not to lie to his wife. Especially not to his wife. He was honest, forthright, sincere, and faithful, if not always in thought, then certainly in deed. Rand never, ever forgot his anniversary or his children's birthdays. He often sent Liz a dozen roses—just because. Moreover, he expected everyone else to be that honest, thoughtful, and considerate as well.

He was meticulous in his business and had a reputation for being too unyielding, too unwilling to compromise for the sake of convenience or for the sake of a profit. Yet amidst a contingency promoting chicanery and subterfuge, he was respected; he was known as a person to be trusted, and he valued that trust. He was a moral man.

He was meticulous in his home life for the same reasons, always trying to be the best husband, father, friend, and person he could possibly be.

He pushed away an ashtray Max, his boss, had half-filled that afternoon with partially smoked cigarillos. Rand had an aversion to human chimneys who blew their billowing haze skyward and fogged up a room. He rose, emptied the ashtray into the garbage, then washed it, hoping to remove the last trace of odor from his immediate environment. In fact, he disliked the habit so much he had given up smoking cigarettes before he met Liz. It was tough, but he was glad he had been able to do that. He didn't want to continue polluting his lungs or anyone else's air, and she would have rejected him. On the spot.

He was scrupulous.

But his conscience pricked him only slightly as he stretched out again on the uncomfortable sofa in his office, his long legs propped on one arm, his head on the other. His reports almost finished, he was trying to sleep when the phone had started ringing. He knew it was Liz and tried to ignore it, her. It was an everyday, common white lie, this story he had told her about his unfinished work. Rationale: He didn't want to explain his long delay in answering the telephone. He quickly realized, however, that if he didn't answer it at all, she would say, "You weren't at the office. I tried to call you. So where were you?" White lie number two: He didn't tell her he couldn't sleep either. A lie is a lie, he reminded himself. White, black, or anything in between. He would confess.

He was relieved when the phone stopped ringing. Briefly relieved, because it started ringing again. He went to the men's room outside his office to block out the sound.

There were changes in their relationship, changes in her, that he didn't like. Rand loved her. He revered his home, honored his marriage, usually liked his kids. Sometimes went to church. So what was wrong? He wasn't a quitter, but was it worth the strain, the pain?

He had always tried to be a worthy husband; he was a man with a commitment, a dedication. That was the only way a marriage could work, he had been advised early on: *Be committed to one person. Be dedicated to that one person in your life. All your life.*

But lately, the unbidden, unintentional thought was, *WHY? Why bother?* Two reasons, he knew: First, *he did love her,* and second, he was afraid of guilt he couldn't live with, not to mention the risk of disease. The first reason outweighed the second by so much that the second had been no concern whatsoever. Liz was all he wanted or needed. Now, however, certain female employees leaning over his desk were causing some unplanned, not-too-unpleasant feelings. There was Bebe, he thought, the worst offender.

And there she had been. It was still early evening when she had offered in a silky voice, "I'll be glad to type those reports for you as you finish them, Rand." She was a dark, buxom Mediterranean girl with impish dark eyes and full, moist red lips. She wore a low-cut red satin blouse under a black blazer and a black skirt flecked tastefully with red and silver threads. Stunning, he mused. And expensive. Her gray designer purse that matched her shoes had cost almost a week's pay, he had heard her telling another secretary who had been duly impressed. She assured him coaxingly, enticingly, yet maintaining a businesslike tone, "I'd be glad to stay and help you." Her eyes held a natural sparkle, and she was pleasant company. And she always encouraged first names when they were alone.

Greek, he thought. That's what she was. He had always been partial to Greeks. He liked their pizzas, their olives, and their audacity. And he liked her perfume. It was already seven o'clock, and the office was empty but for the two of them. *Why not?* Rand asked himself. He knew she had a thing for him, and she was pretty easy to take. "Are you still here?" Witless question: Of course she was here. He was talking to her, looking at her, wasn't he?

"I had reports to finish for Max."

"I see. No, you go home. Type them in the morning." *She could have done Max's reports in the morning, too.* "You'd have hours to wait before they're ready for you."

"I don't mind. I've nothing else to do tonight."

Rand smiled in his quiet manner, seemingly unaware of the effect he produced. "I'll bet. Thanks anyway. I'll walk you to your car."

"I'd like to help. And I can get to my car just fine."

"I'll take a rain check on the help," he had told her as he donned his suit coat. "It's dark out there, and besides, I'm a chauvinist."

"You are that." Her tone conveyed the message that she was able to put up with that quite well, if only to extend the time with him. "Who's going to protect *you?*"

"I am." His eyes twinkled and his lips curved into a half smile as he looked into her dark eyes and felt a flush of pleasure at the response he found there. He forced himself to look away.

"I need to stretch."

They walked across the small parking lot toward her convertible, and he inhaled deeply of the redolent spring air. Cherry trees, illuminated by halos from street lights, lined the parking lot; the fragrance from the blossoms was intoxicating. No wonder people flocked to DC in the spring to see the famous cherry blossoms. Someday. Someday they would go.

When she pressed the remote she had removed from her pocket, the driver side door unlocked and the interior lights came on. She turned and kissed his cheek. It was a warm, slightly moist kiss and, embarrassed, he resisted an impulse to run his palm over the spot. *Are you wiping it off, or rubbing it in?* he always teased Charlotte. Now, unbidden, he silently asked himself the same question.

"Thanks for the chivalry. The devoted family man," she complained in a throaty voice. "I'll be available if ever you need me. To type," she added, and he felt awkward. She slid gracefully behind the wheel and started the engine, her movements deliberate and controlled.

You jerk, he berated himself. *You're so naive, so unsophisticated.* He was none of these. "Thanks." He closed the car door, and for lack of something better to say, just smiled again and said goodnight.

"Hold the pickle, Gertie. Easy on the onions." Stopping for coffee and a chef salad at The Corner Deli, Rand had wondered if he really wanted to eat. It was almost closing time, and Gertie threw in a large portion of bacon, cheese, egg, and ham. *Thanks for the extra cholesterol,* he groaned. But he was hungry, and he would enjoy it back in the quiet office.

He tried to evaluate this situation and his emotions as the elevator climbed back to his floor. Bebe was of no interest to him, but yes, he admitted to himself, he was pleased to know he was of interest to her; he could still cut it. The so-called male midlife crisis, he reflected. That's what caused it—the need to be needed, to be useful, to be wanted; yes, to be vulnerable. Nice to know you still had it. But he was not about to be hurt or to inflict hurt on anyone else. Rand had too much at stake for an involvement. What he had at home was enough—all he wanted. At least it had been under normal circumstances. And besides, life was much too complicated already without that added dimension, so he was not about to go shopping. He knew from experience what hell that could cause in a home.

He was just a young boy of seven when his mother had kicked his wayward father out, but he was old enough to be cognizant of her anguish. Rand had suffered too. He was old enough that he remembered the physical abuse, the emotional upheavals, the verbal pummelings. His father was a respectable alcoholic. He became an odious citizen every weekend when he started to imbibe. How could so many people have been so duped by him?

J. R. Markham Sr. was an egotistical, self-righteous slob of a man who held the impressive position of second vice president of a large New York City bank. He produced so accurately, efficiently, and sufficiently that few suspected one of the real loves of his life: drinking. Between his numb weekends, he was dapper and lovable, a distinguished representative of his profession. He possessed an uncanny ability, even in his pickled state, to know when to quit. He needed his well-paying job to support his high-cost lifestyle.

The other love of his life: women. Rand's father was a rake. Rand refused to allow him in his home out of fear for his wife and daughters. He would like to deny him, to disown him. This was a father? Did the uniting of sperm with ovum make a man a father? Rand forced him to stay in the City with the threat of a permanently severed tie if he as much as set foot over the Connecticut line. He knew his father's habits would eventually cause his ruination.

Rand still saw him on a regular basis, but really wanted nothing to do with him, yet continued a ridiculously unrewarding relationship out of necessity: This man was his father regardless of his minute qualifications. To be honored? Why? He could drum up nothing but negative feelings for him, and sometime, he knew, he would sever the final tie with him. *Honor thy father* . . . , his friend, Nick, told him. Honor? Why? he asked himself again. Even when he didn't deserve honor? Love him? Impossible.

Rand's mother had suffered, then been treated for emotional problems. Recovering quickly, she had remarried long ago and moved near Carlisle, Pennsylvania. Rand's phone call to her the first of every month with an occasional visit by her to see a new grandchild, or to check on the children's progress, seemed to satisfy her. They held no animosity toward each other, and also no deep affection. She had deserted him at a crucial time in his life. What Rand knew about warmth in a real family Liz had taught him. Yet there was a tie that bound them in this situation, too. Sometimes he sensed that his mother wanted to make up for her earlier failures. Rand blamed his father for all her—and their—problems.

More positive influences in his childhood had come from Aunt Matty and Uncle Sal, now deceased, who, strangely enough, had been connected to his parents, and who had taken charge of him and his younger sister, Theresa, when the senior Markhams had split up. They were related, Rand never knew quite how, and they had provided food, warmth, and shelter, three of his basic needs to survive; but Rand and Theresa often wished for more loving, stable people to cuddle up to on a cold night. Matty and Sal had supplied all of their needs and some of their wants, but one of Rand's and his sister's greatest needs, they had to daydream about: *love.* Matty and Sal did know the value of a firm hand in denying their every wish, in part because they had precious little goods to share. But if they felt love, they didn't show it. Or maybe they didn't know how. Or maybe they were afraid. That was it.

He would never be free of the heartaches he had caused them. *Like father, like son,* some had said when, as a thin, boyish high schooler, Rand also started to drink excessively. Matty and Sal suffered silently as they watched him go his father's way, helpless to intervene, sadly and patiently dealing with their sorrow and his waywardness.

One Christmas vacation Rand had grappled with the decision to spend dreary holidays with Matty and Sal there in Yonkers, a suburb of New York City, or accept his classmate's invitation to travel to his family's winter vacation condo in New Hampshire. The elderly couple had applied for an apartment in senior housing, and Rand was anxious for that to happen. He wasn't sure what

Jimmy's Home

he would do for a place to stay; the least attractive choice was to move back with his father. Rand had seen the hurt in Matty's and Sal's eyes when he had opted for the ski trip, but he had been presented with numerous enticements, many, he realized later, being family-oriented and promising sample tastes of that lifelong need. He also longed to see New England in its winter glory, with Christmas lights twinkling on and through the fresh clean snow instead of muddy, slushy streets. He wanted to learn to ski, have a rowdy snowball fight, drink hot chocolate by the fire, walk alone in the moonlight under trees heavy with snow, and the snow crunching under his feet. Nicholas, his classmate, had painted glowing word pictures for him, and Rand's appetite was whetted. He accepted the invitation.

Nick had warned him there would be no liquor available: His family were teetotalers. (What a dumb word, Rand thought. Didn't they drink coffee, soda pop, or beer? Certainly not just totally *tea!*) Rand couldn't imagine anyone's complete abstinence, but he would survive. He longed to go. He'd find some booze, or smuggle it in with him. Certainly not hard to do.

Nick had extended the invitation to include Rand's sister, Terry, but Rand had refused for his sister, not telling his friend he had not so much as mentioned it to her. The rationale for that was two-fold: One, she could be with Matty and Sal, and two, he didn't want Nick to become interested in her. Occasionally Rand worried about Terry. His own insecurity and instability, however, rendered him helpless to cope with her irresponsibility, her independent lifestyle.

On New Year's Eve a fire had consumed Matty's and Sal's third-floor walk-up. Rand was still in New Hampshire, and Terry, a struggling high school sophomore, had been with friends on an all-nighter when Aunt Matty and Uncle Sal died.

Rand had wrestled with guilt for a long time over the fire tragedy; he supposed Terry had too. If they had been there they might have prevented the holocaust, or at best rescued them. But what would have happened to the old folks? Where would they have gone? Maybe he and Terry would have perished, too. Rand was soon caught up in his studies, basketball, and his social life. He wanted to succeed, to conquer the world. He could not cope with death. He thought about the old folks; he missed them, but life had to go on, didn't it?

Miraculously, after a stint in the Army, then college under the GI Bill, and with three years of hard work behind him, a new Rand emerged. Finally, at age twenty-eight, he rounded a curve, got a grip on things, and straightened out. Matty and Sal hadn't lived to see the wonder of it.

Life had new meaning. Rand stood taller, walked straighter, and loathed the person he had almost become, a carbon copy of his father. In time he found it difficult to remember what he once had been. Another time, another place . . . The real Rand came out of the shadows. He had so much to thank Nick for, as well as Nick's family who had welcomed him, challenged him, as one of their own. He would always feel indebted to them for their input in his life, for their patience with him.

Then he met Liz. They literally bumped into each other as, beginning a new job, she entered the up elevator he had just come down. "Sorry!" he had exclaimed with a quick smile and a flip of his heart. She frowned. He turned and, facing her, he leaned against the elevator door to hold it open. "I said, 'I'm sorry.'"

"Hey," an occupant challenged him, "either in or out. Up or down. Some people are here to work."

She stared him down. ("I know I saw a smile trying to get out," he told her later.) They exchanged silent greetings, he with a smile, she with a cold, indifferent nod, each time they passed over the next two weeks. His persistence bordered on harassment, but he refused to let go. There was something special about her. He progressed to a "Hello," and a "Hi, there," and finally she smiled. *Finally*. At *him*. It was brief. Impersonal. Not just at her female companions, but *at him!* He asked her out to lunch and she finally agreed to a sandwich at a picnic table in a nearby park. He bought subs at a deli. "Hold the onions," he ordered. Too bad. She loved onions, she said. He was so nervous he almost spilled his hot coffee on her. Then it was a movie, dinner, and they soon became a couple. A couple of good friends. They talked. They laughed. He wanted more, but she kept her distance. But she was so good to be with he wondered why he had ever been nervous.

She was aloof, reserved. *Just friends*, she reminded him. And she didn't budge an inch. She was a stark contrast to most of the women he came in contact with. Be patient, he told himself. She was a challenge he had never had to face. On rainy days, and as the weather cooled, their occasional lunches relocated to a nearby coffee house, and they were often joined by other coworkers. Then finally, in November, he and Liz met for an actual date.

It was over a seafood dinner at an out-of-the-way restaurant near the shore in Cos Cob when, in their conversation, Liz asked him what his plans were for Thanksgiving.

He picked up his water glass and swallowed slowly to give himself time to consider a truthful response. Nick had given him a casual invitation to be with his family in New Hampshire, to which he had given a casual acceptance. "Is this an invitation?" he asked Liz. He hoped so.

She nodded. "If you want it to be." Across the table, she was stunning in a royal blue dress, the candlelight picking up the lights in her beautiful blue eyes. Around her neck she wore a fine pearl choker and around her wrist a bracelet to match, her only jewelry except for small pearl earrings. He had noticed heads turning as they were escorted to their table, not aware of his own fine appearance in his gray slacks, tweed sports jacket and black button-down shirt.

"I do. Want it to be," he explained. "Thank you. I accept." He knew Nick would understand. This was an opportunity he couldn't pass up, and he knew Nick would concur. *I can't imagine being included in such a large family holiday gathering,* he thought.

She lived in Connecticut, she had told him earlier at their first picnic table lunch. She and her sister shared an apartment that was connected to her parents' home.

"Thanks," he repeated. "Sounds great."

"Just a little warning. My family—actually my siblings, are kind of . . ." she hesitated, ". . . nuts. Especially Robert."

"But *family*. I never had much to speak of, you know. My longtime friend, Nick, and his family have been my family since forever. Since middle school."

"Just be warned."

"Tell me about them."

"Starting where? My parents are special: warm, welcoming. Very committed to each other. And to their kids. My dad and I did a lot of things together when I was growing up. Mom, too, but he took me lots of places."

"Like?"

"Fishing. Sometimes Mom went too. And the other kids."

"Did you bait the hooks?"

"Had to. Also had to take the fish off the hooks, and clean them, too. Rules, you know."

"That I've got to see. Didn't your brothers like to fish?"

"Oh, yes. We spent a lot of time at the shore, mostly Long Island Sound. But then the boys got involved in sports, summer baseball league, basketball, soccer, you know. Football, too."

"Same here. Really kept me out of a lot of trouble. I'd like to go fishing sometime. Your brothers?"

"Stephen is the oldest. Married to Stephanie. He's an accountant, like my dad. She's his secretary, and they work out of their home. At tax time he and my dad work together a lot. They have two boys and a girl, eight, six, and four, Stephen Jr., Mark, and Molly.

"My brother, Andrew, and his wife, Billy Jo are both teachers. Andrew is head of the high school math department. Billy Jo subs occasionally and also tutors. She really wants to be a stay-at-home mom. They have two boys, Andrew, eight, and John, almost seven, and a girl, Mary Beth, four. Another baby is due before Christmas. My sister, Cassie, is a senior in college and soon to be engaged. Robert, the youngest, is a junior. The twins are both in the military."

"And you went to the local community college and now work for Office Temps."

"I may not be in White Plains much longer. I'm replacing someone on maternity leave."

"Then where will you go?" He was disappointed, although he had known it was a temporary position.

Liz took a deep breath. "I'm not sure, but I may work at home. On the computer. Under contract." He tried not to look downcast. "Now it's your turn."

"Not much to tell. My mother moved to Pennsylvania, near Carlisle, after she remarried. We keep in close touch, get together now and then. I've been out to visit them. They seem happy, and I'm glad for her. My sister, Theresa, has pretty much disowned not just family, but anyone she ever knew. She's in Florida. Nick is my family. You'd like him. Nicest guy."

"Your father?"

"New York banker. Dishonest. Arrogant. Obnoxious. I went to live with him during my last year of high school. Very bad choice."

"Oh, really, it couldn't have been that bad."

"Yes, that bad. J.R. Markham Sr. Not to be confused with TV fame."

"Why did you go to live with him?"

"He insisted."

"Why was it a bad choice?"

"Too many of his friends to put up with. Too many parties. Too many women. Too much liquor available."

The waiter appeared and handed them dessert menus. "Just coffee for me," Liz said.

Rand ordered apple pie and coffee. "Just order vanilla ice cream," he addressed Liz. "I'll put it on my pie. If you're sure you don't want it."

Liz giggled. "You sound like my brother, Robert."

"I like him already."

As they left the restaurant, Rand handed the parking attendant his ticket. "How about if I take you home, and you leave your car at the parking lot?"

"Won't work. How will I get to work tomorrow?"

"I know. Just wishful thinking. But I could come back in the morning and get you. Not practical, right?" Rand reluctantly took her to the commuter lot where she had left her car. "Thanks for the invitation for Thanksgiving."

"Thanks for a lovely dinner. I enjoyed it, and the lovely evening."

Rand nodded in agreement, then waited for her to leave. He wasn't ready for the evening to end.

CHAPTER THREE

A light snowfall had begun when Rand rang the doorbell of Liz's parents' home late Thanksgiving morning. He wondered if he'd get snowed in. Pleasant thought. This was a milestone, and he didn't know what was in store for him, maybe his whole future. He just knew he had never before met anyone like Liz, and he was hoping this Thanksgiving Day would be a positive progression in what seemed at times like a shaky friendship.

One of Liz's brothers opened the door and stared blankly at him.

Rand introduced himself. "Randolph Markham." His extended hand was ignored. "Is Liz here?"

"Oh, wrong door. She lives next door."

This must be Robert, Rand thought.

"Robert!" Rand heard Liz's voice before she appeared. Robert smirked. "Don't say I didn't warn you," she said, addressing Rand and frowning at Robert. "He's nuts."

Rand handed her the single rose he had brought, then removed his coat.

"How nice."

"It's for your mother," he winked, taking in Liz's appearance. She was dressed in navy slacks with a white turtleneck sweater and a necklace of blue and orange entwined beads.

"I'll give it to her."

"Just kidding . . ." he began lamely as Liz's mother appeared, followed by her father, a very young-looking couple who appeared at the same moment.

"This is my mom, and also my dad. Mr. and Mrs. Cunningham."

"Randolph Markham," Rand said, completing the introduction and shaking their hands.

"He brought this for you, Mom." Liz handed her mother the rose.

"Thank you! And welcome, Randolph. Make yourself at home in this noisy place. Dinner will be ready in an hour or so."

"It smells wonderful."

"It was for you," Rand said after her parents disappeared. Liz's lips formed a hint of a smile—and did he hear a chuckle?—before she led him to the large family room where people of mixed ages were talking and watching the Macy's Thanksgiving Day Parade. Kids were on the floor, or on laps. The adult men were engrossed in several animated conversations. All ceased while she introduced Rand. Liz knew by the expressions on their faces that Robert had preceded them with choice comments.

The turkey dinner, complete with stuffing, mashed potatoes, and umpteen vegetables, was out of this world to a guy who ate in restaurants, or heated prepared meals in a microwave. And dessert was yet to come. Rand handled it well and thrived on the warmth, the contentment, of his initiation into Liz's family.

Later that same day, little Mary Beth, age four, came up to Liz and Rand where they were sitting alone after most of the big family had left. "Are you going to marry Aunt Lithebith?" Her big blue eyes stared at Rand.

Liz groaned.

Rand was surprised, but chuckled. "No, I'm going to marry *you*."

She squealed with delight. "You're too old! 'Sides, I have a boyfriend." She climbed onto Liz's lap and snuggled down comfortably. "You could marry Aunt Lithebith. She's old, too."

"She'll probably say no."

"No, she won't. She told me she wouldn't say no. She wants to get married."

Liz gasped. "Mary Beth, you've been taught not to lie!" She would be glad when this child went to bed.

She giggled. "I'm not lying. I made it up. That's different from lying. Besides, you told me you wanted to have a little girl like me. And you have to get married first."

"That's true," Liz conceded, "but the rest of it isn't."

"And you want another girl like me, and two boys."

Rand was charmed. "Let's table that one." It sounded like way too many kids. "What's your boyfriend's name?"

"Can't tell."

"Guess I can't know what the competition is then."

"I have Jesus in my heart. Do you?" she asked Rand.

His eyes widened. "Well, I guess I do," Rand assured her, momentarily stunned by the question.

"No, either you do, or you don't. You can't guess."

"Well, maybe we can talk about that another time," he responded.

Bless you, Mary Beth, Liz thought. He had told Liz of his visits with his skiing friend and family. Major changes had taken place in his life. A change of subject was in order at present, however; the subject would be taken up at a later time.

Mary Beth's parents, Andrew and Billie Jo, came in to say goodnight. "We'll see you soon, honey. Be good," her mother whispered. "And don't forget to go potty."

So, the pregnant one is Mary Beth's mom, Rand observed.

"Mommy, you always say that," she scolded, rolling her eyes toward Rand in embarrassment.

"I know," her mother smirked.

They chatted briefly, told Rand they hoped to see him again, and left.

Liz grinned at Mary Beth and said, "Tell this old man what you're getting for Christmas." She responded to the fake hurt on Rand's face. "*She* said you're old, *I* didn't."

"I don't think she likes you." This from Mary Beth.

"You're very observant for a four-year-old."

"I'm almost five."

"But she likes me. She pretends she doesn't."

"I know. She's a good pretender. We're getting a new baby."

"A doll?" he asked.

"No, a real baby, silly. She's a girl."

"And what's her name?" Liz prompted.

"Lily Ann."

"You mean Lillian?" he asked.

"No." Mary Beth faked annoyance. "I *said* Lily. Ann."

"Her mother's from the South," Liz offered. "You know, double names."

"I'm staying here until the doctor takes the baby out of Mommy's tummy," Mary Beth explained. "So are my brothers, John and Andrew."

"C-section on Monday," Liz explained.

Two boys first, then two girls, just like Liz's family. But then came Robert. So many kids. They gave him cause to wonder. *Too many,* he thought.

Liz and Rand talked softly for a while before Liz said, "She's fallen asleep."

Liz's dad appeared, ready to take his granddaughter from where she slept. His wife joined him and together they said goodnight to Rand first. "Nice to meet you, Randy. Do come again, won't you? Maybe next time we'll get to visit."

Rand stood and shook hands, then looked at Liz before answering. "It would be my pleasure, sir, ma'am. Thanks for today. The meal was superb, and so was the company."

Liz's dad lifted Mary Beth from Liz, and the child snuggled in his arms. "Grandpa, I don't have my jammieth on."

"Grandma will help you to bed, pumpkin."

"I'm not a pie, Grandpa." She giggled.

"Aren't you my sweetie pie? Hey, I thought you were asleep. So—you can walk to your bed."

"Unh uh," she answered sleepily. "I am. Asleep. Oh, but I have to give Aunt Lithebeth a hug." She wiggled out of her grandpa's arms and put her arms around Liz. "Give this one to him," she said, giving her aunt another hug.

"You owe me one," Rand said after Liz's father left with Mary Beth.

Rand was putting on his coat when Robert appeared. "Hey, Robert. Nice to meet you, even though you weren't going to let me in."

Robert laughed. "Good to meet you too, Randy. I'm sure you'll be around for a while. I know Liz, and believe me, she is *smitten!* Too bad for George," he added in a soft aside, referring to Liz's occasional date.

"Robert," Liz spoke to his back. "Why don't you go back to school."

"Soon enough, Sis, but you know you're going to miss me."

"Right. Like I miss a toothache."

He tried to kiss her cheek, but she ducked. He leaned toward her and said, supposedly confidentially, "You don't have a real one in your head. How could you have a toothache?"

She glared at him in silence, trying to keep from laughing. "You're as bad as Mary Beth, making up stories."

"Where do you think she gets it from? 'Unca Robert,'" he said in a little girl voice, "'tell me a story.' How does she say it? 'Thtory.' 'Tell me a thtory.' She and Molly, both of them."

"Don't make fun of the way she talks."

"Never! She's a sweetheart. They both are. Oh, and he's smitten too, Liz. I recognize these things. And why wouldn't he be? You're cute. You're intelligent. You're pleasant and polite. And," he went on in a conspiratorial whisper, "you have all the curves in the right places."

Liz gritted her teeth and groaned. *"OH, ROBERT!"*

"Bye, Randy. And goodnight, Liz. See you anon."

When Liz went out to Rand's car with him, he leaned on the door before getting in. "Don't let him bother you, Liz. He's a fun guy. I had a great time, and enjoyed every minute. Except for the first ten."

"You were nervous? Actually," she referred back to Robert, "I can't let him get away with *everything*, you know."

"Why not? You'd be better off if you did. Besides, I agree with him on all points but one."

Liz felt her cheeks flush.

"Cute," Rand continued. "Describes Mary Beth. Not you. Pretty, beautiful, yes. But not cute. Everything else is true." He shifted gears as he looked at the sky. "Too bad it stopped snowing."

"You like the snow?" Liz was glad for the change in subject. "So do I. I like to walk in it at night, when it's snowing hard."

"Sounds like a plan."

It was quiet while they both enjoyed the night air, the silence after a busy day.

"Guess I'll head out. But I have a question for you."

She looked at him inquiringly.

"Just promise me you won't laugh."

"I don't make promises I might not be able to keep."

"Aunt Lithebith," he paused dramatically, "will you marry me?"

She burst out laughing, a sound he was beginning to love. "Ask me again in about five years."

He smiled at her, enjoying the laughter. "At least that wasn't a no. That means there's hope, right? Thanks for a great day. Oh," he groaned, "five years!" He moved toward her to give her a quick hug, but she backed away. *Patience, Rand.* "You owe me one, you know," he reminded her. She ignored him.

It was quiet again. And Rand didn't move to get into his car. "What's Christmas like here?" he asked, changing the subject to prolong his departure.

"Similar dinner, many of the same people. My grandparents and Cassie and her boyfriend will be here. I think they'll be engaged by Christmas. They were at his house today. Friends. Ones who might be lonely, who have no family around."

"Like me?"

"Are you serious? After today? You'd venture back? But certainly you're invited."

"No, no, no. I wasn't looking for an invitation. My father made plans for me. Not a great Christmas to look forward to. I have no choice. I try to honor him, thinking maybe I'll have an influence on his ornery soul. But believe me, I'd rather be here." He slid behind the wheel.

"Bye," she offered. "See you next week. Let me know if your plans change."

"Thank you, I will."

Who's George? he wondered as he drove away.

Rand saw Liz only once during the weeks before Christmas, but he called her now and then between work and his evenings at the health club. He played racketball, sometimes basketball. And he always finished with eight or ten laps in the pool. He made one trip to New Hampshire to ski with Nick between the two holidays.

CHAPTER FOUR

Tracks in the snow were barely visible as the blizzard-like storm filled them in. Only occasional headlights gave evidence of other venturesome souls on the road. His SUV handled the road well, but he hoped he would eventually catch up to a snowplow and remain in its wake for the final ten or so miles to his exit.

He was headed east into Connecticut, after getting a call from New York City, a most welcome call which changed his whole day's plans: His father was sick and had to cancel their schedule. Rand wasn't sure he believed his father and didn't wish illness on anyone, but the timing couldn't have been more welcome.

Rand tried to contact Liz, or anyone who might answer her parents' phone, but apparently the area telephones were out with the storm. He wished he had her cell number. But of course he was invited, she had said. And by now Christmas gift-giving and dinner would be over, so he wouldn't be intruding. He had waited until early afternoon to leave.

He followed a snowplow into a commuter parking lot near the exit ramp, grabbed his gym bag which was stuffed with dry clothes, if he should need them, and a little gift for the love of his life; and then trudged the last distance to his destination. His thoughts were constantly on Liz, and somehow he would tell her—what? How much she meant to him? How he was falling in love with her? How could he tell her anything when he couldn't get near her? He trudged along the narrow country road in silence, his warm insulated snow boots making the only sound as they softly crunched in the snow, thinking about a walk later with Liz. He saw families trying to put up outside decorations, some shoveling snow in hopes of keeping their driveways passable, and some just playing in the snow.

He heard excited, animated voices before his destination came into view. Sure enough, the guys were playing . . . football in the snow! The game had the appearance more of keep-away, but this family was full of surprises.

"Who are you?" the big guy closest to him asked. Rand didn't recognize him and wondered if he was George.

"Leave him alone, Lenny," Robert spoke from behind a ski mask. "He's just Liz's latest victim, I mean boyfriend. C'mon, Rand, grab a spot on our team. We need an extra body."

Rand heard children's voices from around the corner, and knew that's where Liz would be. He had hardly joined the football game when suddenly five children appeared with Liz, running toward him with a large supply of snowballs.

"Get him, kids!" she shouted.

Rand headed for Liz, whirled her around in front of him, and pinned her arms in front of her. "Okay, kids. Let her have it!"

Instead of pelting Liz with the snowballs, the children turned on Rand. "You're counting on their loyalty, huh?" he challenged Liz. Suddenly all the guys joined the snowball fight, and a free-for-all ensued. The shouting almost drowned out the laughter. Liz tried to stuff snow down Rand's neck.

Mary Beth, with a bullhorn, called from the window. "Guyths! Guyths!" She rang a big dinner bell with her mother's help. "Grandma wanths you to come for dinner. She wanths you to come right away, and leave the snow outside!"

"Hey, I thought dinner would be over!" Rand looked at Liz in surprise.

"You lucked out. The power was off for two hours. We were wondering if we'd ever get the turkey cooked. The alternative menu was tuna fish sandwiches, or peanut butter and jelly, depending on your preference."

"I tried to call," Rand responded lamely.

"There's always plenty, Rand. I'm glad you came. Your place has already been set, I'm sure. You'll see."

"Do you want apple, pumpkin, or pecan pie?" Liz asked Rand after the wonderful main meal was finished and cleared. She had asked all around the table.

"Apple, pumpkin, and pecan. Yes."

A loud chuckle went around the table, from all but Robert, who guffawed loudly as he smacked the table. "You're in, Rand! Boy, are you in!"

Liz punched him in the shoulder. *"Robert!"*

"Yes?" he asked innocently.

"Did they ever teach you the meaning of, 'a time to speak; a time to keep silent' at that school of yours?"

"No, but Mrs. Jones taught it to us in Sunday School, same teacher you had."

"Then why don't you think before you speak so you know when to keep quiet?"

Jimmy's Home

"'Cause then the moment would be gone, and I'd always be sorry if I didn't seize it."

Liz looked at Rand, who seemed amused as he wondered where this was going.

"A little of each. Apple first," Rand said, unfazed. Liz brought him three dessert plates, each with a piece of pie. His eyes widened. "These are little? I think I'll need a doggy bag."

"I'll have apple too, Liz," Robert said.

"That was the last piece."

Rand, fork poised over the apple pie, slid it across the table to Robert.

"You're too nice," Liz commented.

"First time I've been told that."

"I'll bet."

"Well, you all know, except for Randy, of course," Robert said around a mouthful of apple pie, "that the guys do cleanup on Christmas. We'll even take care of leftovers, Mom. Yes, we'll save them." There was murmured assent. "That means you stay out of the kitchen. You and Dad can go have a snowball fight with the kids. Or make a snowman. And," Robert prepared for a big speech, "the new kid on the block gets to do the pots and pans."

"Who's the new kid?" Rand asked.

"The one who just asked a dumb question," replied Robert.

"Meaning me, I guess. I'm game," Rand put in. "But who gets off easy because I showed up?"

"Robert," Liz's brother Stephen put in. "He's a conniver."

Liz's father reached for his Bible as dessert and coffee were being finished. "Luke, chapter two, verses one through twenty. The story of Jesus' birth." All grew quiet in preparation for the reading. "'Now it came about in those days that a decree went out from Caesar Augustus that all the world should be taxed.'" When he finished, Molly, Stephen's daughter, climbed into his lap and exclaimed, "Oh, Grandpa, I love that thtory!" Mary Beth followed, also situating herself on her grandpa's lap opposite her cousin Molly.

"So do I, Molly," her grandpa responded. "Tell me, though, why do you love it?"

"It just," she thought seriously, "just warms my heart."

"And why do you think it warms your heart?"

"It must be because Jesus lives there."

"I think that's why my heart feels warm, too," Mary Beth spoke. "I just wish I could have helped His mommy take care of Him."

"Now you help your mommy take care of little Lily Ann. Let's thank God for the wonderful gift He gave us when He sent Jesus to be our Saviour."

Robert cleared his throat, indicating he had something to say. "Better keep it short, Dad. It's getting late, and the roads are bad for those who have to travel." His father met his gaze without words.

"Sorry," Robert said, backing off.

"Robert, would you pray first? I'll close."

Robert put his head down and closed his eyes. *Oh, my big mouth.*

"Robert?"

"Dear God," he finally began very softly. "Thanks for a great day with family and friends. Friend," he corrected. "Just one this time." He suppressed a chuckle and glanced up at Rand, who just happened to look up at the same moment. "Thanks for giving us Christmas. Amen." He wanted to laugh out loud.

His father paused briefly. "Lord, we really do thank You for Your blessings to us each day, so many we can't possibly count them. We thank You for the new baby You have brought safely to our home and hearts, and for each one gathered around this table. We pray for safekeeping as the travelers go home. And we thank You, Lord, that You enjoy our humor, too. Amen."

Jimmy's Home

The family dispersed amid many giggles and backslapping, and after cleanup was completed, most of them began to leave, packing up their leftovers and gifts.

"Come next door when you're done," Liz whispered to Rand. "Through the family room," she explained.

"Nice," he said when she came to the door in response to his knock. She had flicked the switch to start the gas fireplace.

"You probably should get going, since the roads are still bad."

"How about a walk in the snow? I thought that would be the plan."

"Well, sure. I'd enjoy that too. Are you sure?"

"Sure I'm sure! I thought about that walk in the snow all the way from New York!"

As they trudged to the commuter lot to check on Rand's car, he marveled at the beautiful Christmas lights decorating the homes along the way. "I like the all-white decorations. The candles in the windows, the trees and white lights . . ."

"Like ours?"

"Right. That's my choice if I ever have a place of my own."

When they reached his car, Liz cleaned the windows with a scraper while Rand shoveled around the tires. "Let's walk some more." He took her gloved hand and linked it over his arm, then kept his hand firmly over hers. "I need to catch you if you fall," he explained.

"Oh, really," she drawled. "Then if you fall, we both go down."

He leaned his head toward hers. "Sounds like fun."

"You are impossible."

"I'm not. Try me."

Nancy J. Sell

"Oh. I love the smell of the snow," Liz declared.

Rand chuckled. "Snow doesn't smell."

"Does too. And the quietness! Just listen!"

"I'm listening. I don't hear a thing. I don't smell anything, and I don't hear anything."

"You *are* impossible!"

"I'll quit while I'm ahead. But, hey, now I smell the smoke from someone's fireplace. That smell says something to me. Like the smell of turkey roasting. Like your parents' home."

"Forget I said something."

Finally they arrived back at Liz's apartment. "Want to come in for hot chocolate?" she asked.

"Hey, that sounds good!" Besides, he had to retrieve his gym bag. "Are you sure it's not too late?"

"No, of course not. We always have hot chocolate after a walk in the snow, and I don't want the day to end."

Rand sat on the floor, back against the sofa, while Liz headed for the kitchen after she assured him she didn't need help. He located his gym bag and retrieved the little gift he had brought for her. When she returned with two steaming cups of hot chocolate topped with marshmallows, he took his from her, then patted the floor next to him. She joined him on the floor, but left a wide space between them. He moved closer to her.

"The fire is great," he said. "I always wanted a house with a fireplace. Very nice."

"My mom fixed a doggy bag for you. Complete with a piece of apple pie."

"I thought it was all gone."

"She baked another one. She had one in the freezer."

"Wow! How did I rate?"

"She treats everyone the same, whether she likes them or not."

"Oh," Rand mulled that one over briefly. "I'm not sure where I fit in there. Anyway, tell her I appreciate her thoughtfulness, and will even more so when I eat it tomorrow! Maybe I could tell her myself."

"She's probably in bed. I'll tell her tomorrow."

When they finished the hot chocolate, Rand stood and took the cups to the kitchen.

Cassie came through from her parents' home, and exclaimed, "Liz! You're still up! What a day, huh? And what a hunk! Where did you find him?" She didn't stop to breathe. "He's a keeper. And he's so good-looking, and I don't think he even knows it!"

"He knows it," Liz replied, meeting Rand's eyes with a smirk as he stood leaning against the door jamb behind Cassie.

He scowled at Liz in denial. *What are you saying?*

"Oh, my gosh! He's standing right behind me, isn't he!"

Liz and Rand both laughed, then Rand put an arm across Cassie's shoulders. "That's okay, Cassie, I like you, too."

Embarrassed, she chatted briefly, then quickly said goodnight and retreated to her room.

Rand handed Liz the beautifully wrapped gift he had brought her. She shook her head from side to side. "You shouldn't have, you know."

"I knew you'd say that, but I wanted to."

"All I have for you are homemade Christmas cookies." She handed him the tin holding an assortment of homemade cookies.

"Great idea. Probably on a par with the apple pie."

"Oh, Randy, it's beautiful!" She lifted the rare, delicate Christmas angel from its wrappings. "How did you know? This is something I've been admiring."

"Good guess."

"No, someone told you. I can't imagine who. It will go right here, on the mantel. Thank you so much."

"You're so welcome."

He gathered his belongings together to leave. They stood at the door, and Rand reached for her. Immediately she put her hands against his chest with slight pressure to keep him at a distance. Rand took her wrists, then lifted her hands to his face.

"Just friends," Liz reminded him with a smile.

"Friends, yes, Liz. But that's not enough." He brushed her lips with his own. Rand's kiss was brief. Soft. Accepted. He put his arms around her and kissed her softly and longingly. Her hands moved from his face to his shoulders, then to his neck. "Liz, look at me. Open your eyes." They fluttered open, then shut. "Open 'em!" he growled with fake gruffness. She trembled slightly, and he wasn't sure if it was in amusement or nervousness. She opened her eyes ever so slightly. "Look at me, Liz. I want to tell you something. I can't leave until you do, until I tell you." She opened her eyes and looked at him, avoiding his gaze. "I love you, Liz." She closed her eyes, and then rested her head against his shoulder. He held her head against him and nuzzled his face in her hair. "I'm not going to wait five years, Liz. Maybe not even five months, but I want you to know now, I love you." She rested quietly in his embrace.

"You warm my heart, too. Goodnight," he finally whispered. "I really don't want to go, but I must." He held her close, then put on his coat and hat, picked up his belongings, held her head with his free hand, and then kissed her again.

"Thank you again for the beautiful gift."

"Thank you, too." He kissed her lightly and left.

Jimmy's Home

Her phone rang soon after she got in bed. Rand said he was on the Parkway, and the roads were passable and well plowed.

"Am I calling too late?"

"No." Liz tried to sound wide awake. "Thanks for coming, Rand. It was a pleasant surprise."

"I appreciate the invitation."

"You're always invited."

"You should look out the window, Liz."

She got out of bed, put on her robe, and gasped as she opened the blinds. The moon was out full and was unbelievably beautiful on the new snow. "The moon on the crest of the new-fallen snow," she whispered.

"It's the night after Christmas. Maybe I should come back for another walk in the snow!"

"Too late. You lost your opportunity." Liz left the blinds open and crawled back in bed. "Tell me about your father, Rand. I want to meet him."

"No, you don't."

"And your mother."

They talked for the hour it took him to get to White Plains, then said goodnight, but not before Rand said, "Thanks for a perfect day." Then he added, "with a perfect ending."

"It was . . ."

"What? Say it, Liz. It was . . ."

"You're bossy."

"Oh, Liz," he groaned. "You just blew me off of cloud nine. C'mon, what. Say it. It was . . ."

"Nice," she finished.

"Thanks. I'll have to be satisfied with that. For now."

She didn't tell him he warmed her heart too. Not yet, she told herself. He was upsetting her planned future. She knew he *was* warming her heart too, but she was not ready for a serious relationship. And down deep, was he the person she wanted? He wouldn't have had to tell her about his childhood, not yet.

CHAPTER FIVE

Rand stretched out beneath the covers with a contented smile on his face. What a day it had been. The most outstanding Christmas he had ever known. And some of them had been good in spite of his circumstances. He didn't know why Liz kept him at a distance, but it certainly increased his desire to be close, to close the gap. This day had definitely represented progress. He relived the feeling of her hands on his face, then the warmth he felt as she moved them to hold him close. Was it possible she was falling for him, too? *Lord, help me not to blow it.*

Rand didn't remember falling asleep but awakened in the morning thinking he must have the same smile on his face. Well, he had an important errand to run, so he stretched, got up, did his usual fifty push-ups, showered, and dressed. He stopped at the nearby Dilly's Doughnuts to get a large coffee and three apple-filled donuts on his way to the store. He sat at a little round table and ate them, got a refill on the coffee, and pulled out his phone.

"Hi, Liz," he spoke into his cell phone.

"Who is this?"

Jimmy's Home

He spoke softly to avoid being heard by other shoppers. "The guy who kissed you last night." Rand paused, chuckling to himself. "Listen, I talked with Nick last night. He tried to get me for an hour, while I was talking with you. I would have called you back, but I figured you needed some sleep." Rand grinned. "Well, I don't want to hold you up from shopping with your mom. Aren't you shopped out?"

"I am. And so is she. But we're off to sale shop for Christmas decorations, napkins, cards, and stuff. So what's up with Nick?"

"He's coming in for the weekend *with* his girlfriend. I suspect they have a big announcement to make. Anyway, he wants me to get tickets for the Christmas Show at Radio City Music Hall for New Year's Eve Day. He already has two reservations for a matinee."

"Are you serious? Do you really think you'll be able to get tickets for that day? They're probably sold out."

"Oh, you're right. But I'll try."

"I love the plan. Have them come here, and you, too. You and Nick can stay at my parents'. They have lots of room. And Meredith can stay here with me. Then we can do whatever we want from here."

"Sounds great. I'll talk to you later, after I talk to Nick."

Randy didn't go back to his apartment. He had a purchase to make, and he wanted to be there when the store opened. Sure enough, the matching angel was still in the case. He had the clerk gift wrap it, then jogged back home. He didn't know when he would give it to her. Valentine's Day? Her birthday? He'd have to find out when that was. Anyway, he was prepared. Just before leaving the store he had made an additional purchase. The small figurine of a young girl holding a plate with a piece of pie was something he couldn't pass up. Of course it was apple pie. Had to be.

New Year's Eve Day dawned bright and beautiful. A perfect day for a trip to the City.

At the ticket office of Radio City Music Hall they found that the matinee to the Christmas Spectacular was sold out. "If you come back about an hour before show time, you might find someone trying to sell their tickets. Someone whose party is incomplete because of illness or whatever."

"You two go. We'll find something to do for, what, three hours? Maybe find a show to go to. Someplace to get warm." Liz shivered.

Liz and Rand watched the skaters for a while, then toured a news studio. They found their way to the level of the ice rink and unbelievably found an empty table to sit and watch the skaters, most of whom were novices, including small children. After they finished their coffee and bagels, Rand was ready to move again. "Let's walk the streets. Or maybe we could rent skates."

"I was just beginning to get warm! And no thanks on the skate rentals."

"I'll keep you warm," Rand commented with a grin. "And we can walk fast."

Liz rolled her eyes, but stood and reached for her coat. Rand took it and held it for her. She welcomed his help.

"Besides, Nick should be calling soon. Then we'd better look over the situation in Times Square. You're not anxious to stay for the ball to drop, are you?"

She didn't answer right away. "Six hours," she said softly. "We'll be in that madness, in the cold—for at least six hours."

"We can probably leave if we want to, and reserve our spot."

"No, once you leave you can't get back in."

"It'll be fun, I promise, the time will fly."

An exuberant Nick and Meredith joined them a short time later.

Long past the dinner hour, and many blocks later, they still hadn't found a restaurant without a two-hour wait. By eight o'clock they agreed it was too late to join the projected one million people already in Times Square.

"We can always go home and watch the madness—I mean the fun—on TV, in front of a nice warm fire."

Once they were riding along the East River on the FDR Drive toward the Willis Avenue Bridge, Liz called her mother and asked her to take a casserole out of the freezer.

"Honey, we have lots of food left over. Yes, they brought enough for a small army. No, they're not staying for the midnight hour. They'll leave in time to watch it at home, probably soon so they can get the kids to bed."

Rand stole a glance at her after she disconnected, reached for her hand, and squeezed it. *What a gal,* he thought.

She told him about the food situation. "I don't know what we'll get. I should have asked."

"It'll be good. It'll be *food!*" he agreed as he took another bite of granola bar and sip of water, then reclaimed her hand. He tried to draw her closer to him but felt her resistance as she glanced at the back seat occupants. "Warm enough?" she asked them.

"We will be by the time we reach Connecticut," Nick answered.

Liz's brothers and their families were about to leave when they arrived, and the table had been reset for them. Her mother had the ham and scalloped potatoes warming in the oven, and the salad on the table.

"Come over and watch TV with us," Liz encouraged her parents as they cleared the table and put the remaining food away.

"Thank you, Liz, but we'll watch from the comfort of our bed. If I stay awake! Your dad will give me a shake at the right time."

The guests thanked the host and hostess profusely, not just for the meal, but for their wonderful hospitality.

After the ball dropped in Times Square, Randy channel-surfed until he found an old movie already in progress.

"Happy New Year, everyone. I'm going to bed," Liz declared. "Y'all can watch all night if you want to."

"I'm with you, Liz." Meredith roused herself from the comfort of the sofa and Nick's arm. He stood and drew her toward the connecting door. "Come say goodnight to me."

"It's been a memorable day, Liz. I can't remember a better one," Rand remarked when they were alone. "Happy New Year."

"It has, Randy. And same to you. Goodnight."

Rand chuckled, putting his arms around her. "I liked being with you all day," he whispered, then kissed her.

"Good morning, Randy."

"Mornin', sir. Don't let me keep you from your newspaper."

"You're not," Liz's father responded as he folded the paper and put it aside. "I'm just keeper of the door. We're not allowed in there," he indicated the door to Liz's apartment, "until the ladies summon us for breakfast."

"Nick will be down soon. He's a hard one to wake up."

"How was your trip to New York?"

Rand puffed out a breath as he spoke. "Beyond words. I'm sure you'll hear all about it. The Christmas Spectacular was outstanding, as usual, according to Nick and Meredith."

"It is magnificent. I take it you couldn't get tickets."

"No. But we had a great time watching the skaters. Then we toured a news studio. After Nick and Meredith joined us, we tried to find a place to eat. That was a bummer, but the company was wonderful. Lots of laughs."

"And where did you eat?"

"Fast food, believe it or not. Had to wait in a long line. And we were hoping for a steak dinner."

"Did you do anything else?"

"Walked. Boy, did we walk. To the Empire State Building, and window-shopped on the way. We took the elevator to the top."

"Awesome view, isn't it?"

"Then we walked back to Rockefeller Center and watched the skaters. We also walked to Central Park, and a short distance into the park. I thought the girls would fall asleep on the way home, but they laughed and chatted all the way back." Rand was pensive.

"Something on your mind?"

"Always." Rand chuckled. "But I've been wanting to tell you how much I admire your family. I guess I have a little envy there."

"You'll have to tell me about yours sometime. But you know, we're put in the place God wants us, to make us what He wants us to be, Rand. Don't nurture any regrets. God supplied a good friend for you in Nick, and I understand his family as well."

Rand nodded. "Yes. Nick really made me toe the mark when we started hanging out together. I almost ditched him. Things changed when he invited me to go skiing for a long weekend. I packed a few drinks without him knowing it. Boy was I in for it!"

"I'll bet. How did Nick find out?"

"I tried to share them with him."

Nick had come in and sat quietly listening.

All three men laughed.

With that, Liz's apartment door opened, and the subject was dropped for the moment. As Liz entered, the three men stood. She moved to the circle of her father's outstretched arm. She smiled up at him, then at the other two men. "You gentlemen are invited to breakfast."

"Something smells wonderful!" Rand exclaimed as they followed Liz to her little kitchen.

"It's going to be a little squeeze around the table, and you can't move once you sit," she giggled.

"Hey, who are we to mind a little squeeze?" Nick spoke as he embraced his bride-to-be. She returned his hug and patted his cheek.

"Nick, would you pray?" Liz asked.

"Sure. Father, thank you for your blessings. So many this weekend. For this family who encompass all they meet into their lives and home. Be with us as we travel. And yes, we thank you for the food that we are about to enjoy!"

Echoes of amens went around the group. They fixed their plates with the scrambled eggs, bacon, and toast. Then cinnamon rolls after Liz removed them from the oven.

"We thank you for your wonderful hospitality," Nick addressed Liz's parents. "You made us feel like old friends."

Breakfast over, Nick and Meredith were on their way with promises to get together for skiing, bowling, and racquetball.

Rand's memories of that time and his meeting Liz were special. That January was the snowiest month in years, many of which had seen no snow at all. Liz began working at home for the same company she had been working for as a temp. Rand had helped her set up her home office with new top-of-the-line equipment. Because of the weather and his busyness at work, they didn't see each other often that month. Their phones were connected at least once a day, however, and texts were frequent. "Love you. Love me?" was the last one. She deleted it without answering. "Hey," said the next one, "I asked you a question." The next one said, "Can't say it? Or won't? Or don't?" He called that evening to suggest a walk in the snow. "Can I come see you?" he asked. "I have a question for you."

"Maybe tomorrow. Call first. I am not feeling well. Just tired, I think."

She was up and dressed when he arrived the next evening. He looked at her apprehensively, then drew her close.

"I'll give you my sore throat," she warned as she buried her face in his chest.

"You can give me anything you want. On second thought, I don't want a sore throat."

"I do."

"You do what?"

"Love you."

"Oh, Liz . . ."

"My dad told me to tell you."

"What?"

She giggled, then put her hands on his face and kissed him lightly on the cheek, then drew him to sit beside her on the sofa.

"We talked last night, he, Mom, and I. He said, among other things, 'Liz, Rand is in love with you.' I said, 'I know.'"

"'Has he told you?' I nodded. 'Do you love him?' I nodded. 'Then tell him,' he said."

"And what were the other things?" Rand whispered as he drew her closer.

"He's a gentleman. A fine person."

"All the reasons you were afraid to commit to? Like the differences in our backgrounds?"

Liz put a finger to his lips. "Randy, that's only touching on it. I can't help wondering why you don't want me to meet your parents. You must be holding grudges against them. You dislike and distrust your father so much."

Rand was quiet, pensive; she knew he was hurt. He sat up abruptly and faced her. "I'm meeting him Sunday night. Will you go with me?"

Liz hesitated briefly, then got up to check her calendar. "I can rearrange my schedule. Are you afraid for me? Or afraid for him?"

"He'll charm the life out of you. You'll think I've been lying to you."

"I can be charming, too." She looked askance at him.

"Yeah, tell me about it."

"Tell me what's involved."

"Dinner. Usually a nice restaurant. That's all."

"I'll be nervous. But, yes, I'll go."

"I'll be there to hold your hand," Rand grinned as he took out his cell phone and speed-dialed his father's number, disconnected when there was no answer, then speed-dialed another. "My mom," he explained.

Liz looked at him with a frown that said, "Do not hand me that phone!"

"Hi Mom. Yes, I'm fine. No, I just wanted to say *hi*. Actually I'd like to see you, and sometime soon." Silence while he listened. Then he spoke. "Yes. Special friend."

Liz gave him a thumbs up.

"Two weeks," he said to her after terminating the call. "Saturday evening. We can meet them halfway."

The following months were filled with bridal plans for Cassie and Lenny, as well as for Meredith and Nick. The arrangements were endless and complicated for Rand because Liz had been dating Lenny's best man, Adam, who was also a fellow athlete in high school and friend of Liz's brother, Stephen. The best man and maid of honor were thrown together. Thus Rand felt left out, especially in the light of lack of progress in his and Liz's relationship.

As Nick's best man, however, Rand had added responsibilities. This required additional trips to Massachusetts. Rand didn't mind and actually enjoyed the activities, especially when Liz joined him to attend bridal showers, to assist in making favors, decorating, and whatever she could. She was an invaluable asset, and Nick's parents, as well as Merry's, loved her. So did Rand.

Liz and Rand were married two years later in a little church Liz had grown up in, and where her parents had been married forty-some years before. *Wow! This is my girl!* he marveled as a smiling and relaxed Liz came toward him on her father's arm. She was a dream, and Rand wondered what he ever could have done to deserve such a prize. And his wonder over the years had never ceased.

They had enjoyed the best of times, survived the worst. He loved her as much now as he had then. No, more. He had learned to know her, to appreciate her strengths and weaknesses, her sensitivity, her humor, her tenderness. And her stubbornness when she knew she was right, though she pushed him to the brink of frustration.

No, he loved her much, much more.

Rand's father had been invited to the wedding at Liz's insistence. He had had the effrontery to bring a lady friend, and the two of them had marched right up the aisle and seated themselves behind Rand's mother and her new husband. Had there been room, they would have squeezed into the same pew. That was before Rand had banished him from their lives, before his father had made passes at Liz. He tolerated him only at Liz's insistence.

Terry had refused Liz's invitation to be a bridesmaid, but she had come to the wedding. It was the first Liz had met her. That was the last they had seen her. In time she had moved to Miami with her third husband and three children, each of whom had been fathered by a different mate. Liz kept up a one-sided relationship with her, sending cards, little gifts, and notes for Christmas and birthdays.

Business had been stable when Rand and Liz bought the house in the suburbs. But now the uncertainty of the economy and the elimination of high-level positions—"the executive extermination," he called it—were weighing heavy on him. He liked to think he was indispensable. His position was secure, true, but one never knew. He was tired of a desk job anyway. He wanted to work outside with his hands, maybe construction.

Rand had a lot on his mind.

And then there were future college bills to think about. The price of education was becoming monumental, out of sight . . .

And what about their health?

What if he and Liz were to be involved in a serious accident, similar to that of their neighbors, the Blairs? What would happen to the children? What about this pain in his chest? There. He had put a face to this specter that periodically returned to haunt him, a shape to his fears. He had told no one, not even Liz. Not even himself. The pain was not constant, and when it was not there, he didn't think much about it. Maybe he should see Dr. Rinaldi—Steve—and have a complete physical. Maybe he shouldn't. He wasn't going to like what he knew he would hear, what he most feared.

What if he dropped dead?

Seated at his desk again, he picked up the five-by-seven photograph that faced him each day, his heart tender as he studied each one of his family. Spirited Liz with her lovely smile, bright eyes; she was a bundle of ambition and energy, a soft touch, a contradiction of pessimism and optimism. "But," he had addressed her angrily, "you're always biting off more than I can chew!"

"Then *chew* it," Liz admonished with a grin.

Rand tried to be understanding but was often impatient with her, with the children. He tried not to be.

He studied his children's faces. *Looking at their picture is like looking at them when they're asleep. You forget what pains in the neck they can be.*

But they were special, his cherished possessions, and they had a hold on his heart.

Charie with her arms around his neck, rubbing noses till he had to tickle her to get away. "Now, Daddy, I'm going to do *tickle, tickle on the knee*. Make a straight face and don't laugh! '*Tickle, tickle on the knee,*'" she spoke slowly and seriously. "'*If you laugh, you don't love me.*'" Before she finished she was laughing hysterically at Rand's contorted face. Over and over she would try to complete the ditty without laughing herself silly.

Pam, more quiet and reserved, slipping under his arm as he sat on the sofa and snuggling up to him as he read the paper. "Let's do the crossword puzzle, Daddy." She would surprise him with her knowledge. Or, "I need some help with my math, Daddy."

And Jeff, who used to sit on his lap until they both fell asleep. Sometimes he would say, "C'mon, Daddy, let's have a catch . . ." "Pitch me a few, Dad." Or, "Let's shoot a few baskets—a little one-on-one." Jeff had long ago outgrown the lap-sitting, and now he reveled in putting his father through the paces. Rand, doggedly determined, sometimes beat him on the court.

"I guess I *am* a devoted family man," he said aloud, warm with a fresh awareness of his abundance.

But they were more than he could handle, too, especially Jeff. Rand surveyed his son's darkly handsome face and wondered what had come between them, why he couldn't seem to reach him. Is it just that so-called generation gap? The adolescent stage? A girl? Drugs? Is he mixed up in something he can't negotiate alone?

Rand, experienced, saw none of the telltale signs. He had no answers, for he could relate little of Jeff's behavior to his own childhood and adolescence. He felt like a failure.

He had to say no to Liz. There was no alternative.

Jimmy would not become a permanent member of the Markham family.

CHAPTER SIX

Now, hours later, breakfast as well as lunch cleared away, Liz stood at the window. Instead of the fragrance of magnolia trees and hyacinth blossoms, the herb and spice aroma of spaghetti sauce filled the room. *The sacred replaced by the mundane,* she contemplated. But it did smell good. The aesthetic appreciation of her family would be dominated by the coordination of their stomachs with the clock. In the evening, after the supper smells had faded away, the floral fragrances would return. Liz could often smell the lilacs that bloomed beside the bedroom window as she lay in bed at night and drifted into sleep.

The day, like so many before it, passed too quickly with too few items being checked off her list. She often looked at a week in retrospect and saw the days as a blur of activity, each day with no seeming defining characteristics of its own. But they mattered. There was no doubt that each one mattered and was a significant block of time plus energy toward an important goal.

As the children grew, the magnitude of their problems also grew. Often she felt, and Rand agreed, that the mechanism to deal with teenagers had not been built into their machinery. How good it was that children weren't born teenagers. It gave parents time to build, to prepare, to adjust. And how hard sometimes to be a wife first, to not turn her back on her husband when he was tired and impatient. With all his shortcomings, he was still her solid ground. She had weaknesses too; she acknowledged them. All the more reason she needed him to lean on. Oh, she needed him all right!

Now, today, nothing seemed to matter except this weight on her chest, this breach in a supposedly stable relationship. What was ahead for them? What had *happened* to Rand?

"But," she exclaimed with a stamp of her sandaled foot, "I'm not a manipulator, a conniver! Rand is wrong about that!" Thus reassured, she was convinced he had been striking out at her in his accusations.

No matter what happens, she addressed him silently, *this is Jimmy's home, Rand. He needs a home. We're Jimmy's family, Rand. He needs a family.*

The children's voices, muffled in joint conspiracy, reached her ears, and Liz smiled as she stepped out onto the deck. She was content for the moment, having shoved her ever-present aggravations into the closet of her mind. It was an unfriendly closet, the contents of which would come crashing over her when the time came to open the door. Where was her happiness, that contentment that didn't depend on the beauty of the day, the sounds and smells of springtime, the sight of the bluebirds guarding their nest, or a savory dinner on the stove? Something had gone awry.

Somehow they would scale this mountain, which now resembled a dung heap. But would it be with or without casualties?

Liz Markham stepped to the railing of the deck to look again at her small assortment of tulips and daffodils gracing the path almost one story below. Liz thought, *I'll have to transplant them soon, too, before Mr. Stuart comes to excavate for the new addition.* She had to look at them often, for given many more warm days such as this one, they would not last long at all. Little four- and five-year-old faces looked up at her with an unmistakable you-spoiled-our-surprise look.

"Hi, Mom," Charie grinned. She was a dear, and Liz warmed to her.

"Hi," Jimmy, the problem child echoed, not for the moment being able to think of anything original to say. He wasn't often speechless.

The problem child, she said to herself. *Which are worse, his own problems, or the ones he's created for us?*

They held up fists tightly clenched around several daffodil and tulip stems, each flower with an approximate three-inch stub, and waited expectantly for her certain pleasure.

Liz's heart sank. "Where did you get those flowers?" she gasped, not certain she could cope with this in her distraught state. A quick inventory of her own precious assortment revealed no beheaded stems. She was only momentarily relieved that her own were intact, for the alternative brought a fresh wave of chagrin.

To add to her irritation, delight had not diminished from their faces. "Down in the woods," Charie declared with that now-don't-get-excited-everything's-all-right tone. "We found them down in the woods, Mom."

Looking her severest, Liz started down the few steps to face them on their level, calming herself with each step to be sure she would administer no judgment and condemnation before trial. She tried never to vocally doubt her child's word—*any* child's word—until all the facts were in and evaluated, but she knew that no one would ever bother to plant spring bulbs down in the vacant property which the children called The Woods.

"Don't tell me you found them in the woods. I happen to know there are no flowers like these down in the woods."

"Oh, we wouldn't pick *yours*, Mom!"

Jimmy's sudsy smile began to fade as his big brown eyes widened. They were in such contrast to the vivid blue of Charie's. "Oh, yes," he stated assuredly, sweetly excited, "we did find them in the woods."

He was such a dear boy when the sun shone on his world, but oh, the storms that brewed when the clouds came.

Before her mother could reply, Charie started leading the way. "Come on, Mommy. We'll show you!"

"Just what I was about to suggest," Liz acquiesced, wondering at the same time what type of discipline would fit this crime. She felt too weary to bargain.

They passed the rabbit hutch with the two adorable bunnies, Peter and Potter, that Liz's mother had given them as Easter gifts. Each of the children stopped to wiggle a finger through the wire at their new pets.

The path worn by dozens of little feet through the corner of the vacant lot adjacent to theirs led through thick trees into the yard of their neighbors, Bernard and Wendy Morrison. Elizabeth and Randolph Markham had been especially pleased when they bought their home twelve years ago. Due to property rezoning in this southern Connecticut town of Glendale, their property had been landlocked, giving them and their surrounding neighbors a measure of privacy without isolation.

The two little ones ran a few yards into the wooded area and paused, bewildered, their eyes searching for the proof that would exonerate them. Liz saw them first: the bare stems.

"Here!" Jimmy yelled, running to the spot, a loose bandage dangling from his dirty knee. "We told you we found them in the woods!" His shout was victorious, ringing with pride that proof had been produced and favor would be restored.

There, where Wendy Morrison had planted them, in full view from her kitchen window, at the very edge of the woods but hardly in it, were the bare supports for a dozen or so blossoms.

"Oh, no!" cried Liz. "Jimmy! Charlotte! Those were Mrs. Morrison's flowers! She has waited all winter for them to bloom, and now look what you've done! Oh, you naughty, naughty children!"

Now you shall have no pie! she reflected, and repressed an unbidden giggle. She felt not the least like laughing. Picked tulips and daffodils held no comparison to lost mittens, the one a voluntary disobedient action, the other probably accidental.

Looks of dismay clouded two small faces.

"What do you suggest we do about this?" Liz asked, wanting to march them right to Wendy's back door and let the chips fall. Knowing how she herself would feel had her valued annual blossoms been stripped, she dreaded the encounter.

Charie looked up at her first. "Mommy," she choked, "won't they get more flowers in a few days? You know, like those red ones you planted by the birdbath last summer?" Jimmy looked hopeful. Liz shook her head from side to side, knowing that Charie referred to the hardy geraniums that blazed with color from spring to fall, if the deer didn't eat them first. But Liz didn't mention that to the children.

"These flowers," Liz pointed to the ones they still held, "just bloom in the spring. There will be brand-new ones next year, but that's a long time to wait. Don't you think so? What are we going to do?"

"S'pose we save our 'lowance and buy Mrs. Morrison some new ones so she'll have twice as many next time," Jimmy offered thoughtfully, albeit reluctantly. Charie nodded a reticent agreement;

Jimmy's Home

she and her money were not soon parted either, especially if it meant spending it on someone else.

"What do you think about that, Char? Shall we go tell that to Mrs. Morrison?"

Charie nodded, again reluctantly. "Mommy," she spoke timidly as they walked the remaining distance to the Morrison's back door, "I'm scared."

"Do you think she'll forgive us?" Jimmy queried apprehensively.

"You'll have to ask her," Liz replied with a sternness she no longer felt. She wanted to hug them both. Later, she told herself.

From the ladder where he was painting the kitchen walls, Bernard answered the children's soft knock. "Hi, Liz." He looked over the anxious little faces, hardly acknowledging them, to greet Liz with a grin. "Wendy left for Philly this morning," he offered. "Guess her sister needed her pretty quick, what with four other kiddies to take care of. Baby girl, born about ten last night," he answered Liz's questioning look. He finished his tale. "All's well, even though she delivered about two weeks early."

Liz mentally jotted down the details of the baby's birth to pass on to Randy and their mutual neighbors, then abruptly brought Bernard's attention to the business at hand.

"That's all right, Liz," he assured her after hearing their tale. "They can pick all the flowers they want. They'll all be finished blooming by the time Wendy gets home anyway."

"Bernard!" She glared at him. "The children were disobedient! They knew they must ask first, before they pick *any* flowers!" Her eyes spoke volumes.

"Well, you really should have asked first, kids," he added sheepishly. "Don't do it again, okay? You're just lucky the wife isn't home, or you'd be catching holy catfish."

The Wife, Liz thought. Why did men refer to their spouses as *The Wife? The Missus?* Women didn't say, *The Husband. The Mister.* She hated to be a thing. "Wait until *The Husband* gets home," she tried it on for size. "I'd like you to meet *The Husband.*" She grimaced.

"No, take them home with you," Bernard continued. "No one here to enjoy them. I won't be home much."

As the children ran ahead of her to the path and past the defrocked stems, Liz's frustration at Bernard, at the children, suddenly dissolved. She could understand how they would think the flowers were wild. Perhaps she had been too hard on them, too hasty in her assumptions.

Charie ran ahead, shaken that her mother's love gift had not been fully appreciated, but ready for new adventure. Liz, remembering supper on the stove, hurried past Jimmy. Now she turned to watch him shuffle along behind her. His chin on his chest, his hands stuffed in his pants pockets, he had dropped the flowers in the path behind him.

This child whom she thought of adopting was a trial.

"Pick them up, Jim." Liz put her hand on his shoulder, but he wrenched away from her touch. She knew they were in for another session. The clouds had covered the sun. "Jimmy." He refused to look at her. "Jimmy, pick up the flowers and then tell me what's bothering you," she stated kindly with determined tolerance.

He sat down in the path and, ignoring her, he concentrated on slapping his bandage to his knee. "Leave me alone," he growled.

"Okay," Liz sighed. "I'll leave you alone. When you're ready to tell me what's wrong, pick up the flowers and bring them to me. After that you and Charie can have your cookies and milk."

She had gone but two or three steps when he shrieked, "You don't love me! You said you did, but you don't!"

Liz breathed deeply. "I never lied to you, did I, Jim? Why would you think I don't love you?" Her words were phlegmatic. She wanted to scream.

"'Cause you yelled at me!" he screeched. "You wouldn't get mad and yell at me if you loved me!"

"You must not love me either then, Jim. You're mad. You're yelling at me. You said you loved *me*."

"Well, I *don't!*"

Somewhere along the road of this child's short life his value system had been severely messed up.

"Do you think I don't love Charlotte either?" Liz went on evenly, ignoring his last remark. "I just got mad at her, didn't I? Do you think I don't love her?"

Looking at her angrily, he wiggled his loose tooth with his tongue. "Leave me alone!" he reiterated.

"We can't talk while you're mad. Tell you what, Jim. You stay here 'til you're ready to get *un*mad, then bring the flowers to me and we'll put them in water, okay? And I want to see a smile then, too."

"I'm not smiling," he warned, then snarled. "Not ever! Leave me alone!"

I will do just that. Just wait and see!

She returned to the kitchen and her supper preparations. The sauce was bubbly and fragrant with oregano and garlic. She was sampling a meatball, a thing she couldn't resist, when Charie came in, so Liz gave her one, lollipop-fashion, on a fork. As she cut the salad greens, Liz periodically went to the back door to check on Jimmy's progress. He had almost reached the deck.

Having had her cookies and milk long ago, Charie was sitting on the kitchen floor with Bearsh, out of the way, making a mess with scissors and paper. "Jimmy's a real fussmusser, isn't he, Mom?" she asked, using a favorite created-by-Charie word.

The back door squeaked open, then squeaked shut. Jimmy stood just inside, his thick hair glistening in the late afternoon sun which streamed through the screen door. He ran his finger along the upper edge of the screen, his face shadowed, his mood uncertain. Finally, he turned her way.

"Here," he said, not unpleasantly, thrusting the flowers toward her.

Liz arranged them as best she could in the jelly jar with Charie's and sat them in the center of the dinner table. "Thank you. Now you two scoot. Get washed up, and let's get the table set for supper."

"I want my cookies and milk. You promised."

"You missed your teatime, Jimmy. It's almost suppertime now."

He started to pout, but changed his mind. He was obviously not ready for renewed battle. Liz forked a meatball and handed it to him. When she heard the water running in the powder room off the front hall and Charie singing loudly to herself, she became aware of Jimmy's presence beside her. A warm hand slipped into her own. Liz turned and smiled into Jimmy's upturned, questioning face, then stooped down to hold him in a close embrace. His arms hung limp at his sides. Taking first one of his arms, then the other, she placed them around her neck.

Tickling his ribs, she kissed him on both cheeks, then sternly ordered, "Be off with you! Get those hands washed and get to work, or you shall have no pie!" She smiled to herself.

Jimmy giggled over the sheer joy of restored fellowship and ran off obediently.

Liz was putting the salad on the table when Jeff and Pam arrived with their usual gusto: Jeff from basketball practice, and Pam from her Friday afternoon swimming class at the Health Club. Both were superb at their chosen sport, and Liz often wondered what goals would be obtained: athletic scholarships? The pros? They didn't work at it hard enough. She tried to encourage them without being pushy. What would Charlotte choose? Roller skating. *If* it became an event by the time she reached an eligible age. And *if* her skeletal system survived her many crash landings. "Aunt Lottie likes to skate with me," she informed Liz. "She holds my hand, and sometimes I don't fall."

Thank you, Aunt Lottie!

Jimmy did much better, and the two of them skated around the basement when the outside weather was prohibitive. Liz feared for Charie's head. Jimmy will be a ball player, she decided. Probably football. He was built for it. But what's for Charie?

Liz dreaded the time when the children would be grown and gone. She was sure that she and the house, too, would shrivel up and die with no little ones around, no problems to solve, no clothes to launder and mend, no taxi runs to make. She was tired, but she needed to be needed.

She and Rand had talked of having another child, but it didn't happen. Liz bristled when she thought of her friend, Nina, and her comments, such as, "It's a shame you're so tied up at home, Liz. You would be ful*filled*, Liz, if you could go out to work. Why not use a daycare center, or hire a nanny, for the little ones? Jeff and Pam don't need you, they're capable of taking care of themselves. You must be absolutely frustrated, Liz."

"Nina, believe me," she had replied, "I'm not frustrated except when you talk like that. I am where I want to be. Contrary to what you may think, Jeff and Pam *do* need me. Maybe I'm just telling myself that, but I believe it. I am *not* frustrated, and I am abounding in fulfillment. If you want to work, that's fine for you. I *choose* not to at this point in my life. My *family* is my life, Nina, and as much as this may surprise you, I wouldn't mind having it increase in size!" Liz knew, in this day of vasectomies and tubal ligations, the Markhams were out of step with present trends.

And she was thinking of making up her own bumper sticker: *I am a liberated woman and I don't have to go to work to prove it.* She was also thinking maybe it was time to make some new friends.

Liz sensed that each one was as glad to be home as she was to have them, and Rand's arrival, especially now, was the final completing touch. "Dad's home," Jeff announced, but Liz had already heard his car coming up the drive: Her heart was attuned to the sound. She heaved a relieved sigh, as if she had been holding her breath all day. He was home. That was a good sign. But her usual sense of peace, of completeness when her family gathered around was now blighted by the harshness of an unsettled argument.

"How soon is dinner?" Randy asked. He looked worn out. Their glances met, mirroring two wounded spirits. He kissed her but there was no warmth in the touch, maybe even a slight chill, then picked up the evening newspaper.

"Fifteen minutes, maybe twenty." *What a performance!* she thought. *Well, I can do as well.* "Have a good day?" she inquired as he glanced through two days' mail.

He mumbled a reply before becoming absorbed in the reading material before him. When finished sorting through the mail, he scanned the front page of the newspaper, went through the usual motions of throwing envelopes and unwanted ads in the recycling bag and placing bills in a special place on his desk in the family room where he would review them later, then went to change his clothes. Returning in jeans and flannel shirt, he placed a lighted match to the ready-laid fire on the hearth, for the spring evening was turning typically cool and damp. As the paper and kindling sprang to life, he took a pillow from the wooden rocker and stretched

Jimmy's Home

out on the floor; he was almost immediately asleep, the newspaper under his arm. Before long Liz realized that Charie and Jimmy were enjoying their usual frolic with Rand without benefit of his participation, both of them sitting on his back and bouncing.

"Enough!" she spoke, her voice soft and stern. "Can't you see Daddy's sleeping? Let him rest a few minutes . . ."

"Leave 'em alone," Rand muttered without lifting his face from where it was almost buried in the pillow.

Liz returned to her work with a vengeance.

As she put the steaming bowls on the table, Jeff, the last one to arrive for dinner, seated himself across from Pam. "Hmmm. I *knew* I smelled spaghetti," he grinned, rubbing his stomach and wagging his tongue like a windshield wiper across his upper lip, anxious for the rote prayer to be said so he could dig in. Liz was glad for the distractions her family provided.

"Hats off during dinner, boys. Don't make me remind you at every meal," Rand spoke firmly. Jimmy looked at Jeff and waited for him to move, then removed his baseball cap.

"How could you *not* smell spaghetti?" asked Pam.

"I mean when I came out the gym door," he retorted.

"You lie."

"What's for dessert?" Jeff asked.

"Pie!" Jimmy answered.

"You have to say what kind. They're not all good."

"Are too. But it's apple. The kind with crumby stuff on top."

"You should give Jeffy just 'zert," offered Charie. Liz, too, wondered why she ever bothered with the unimportant main course of a meal when this question invariably preceded any intake of food.

"Hurry up and pass the spaghetti," Pam ordered her brother.

"Do you want it in your hand or in your face?" inquired Jeff, who then defiantly passed it to Jimmy. He turned to Charie. "Do you want some salad?"

Charie's response was loud and emphatic. "YUK!"

"No, thank you," her father corrected.

"No, thank you," she repeated sweetly.

"Yes, please," her mother restructured the situation. Charie didn't answer, and Liz reiterated, "Yes, please," locking glances with her youngest.

"But Mommy," she began, then sighed. "Yes, please. But I really mean no, thank you," she returned reluctantly. "*That's enough!*" she screeched at Jeff as he served her a minute portion. "Let me help myself!" She stood and stamped her foot. "That's too much!" she fussed loudly at him as he added to the serving. "No more! Take some *back!*"

"Mom says you have to have some."

"Some is some! Some isn't a *whole big plateful!*"

"Eat it," Jeff ordered.

"Let me take care of it, Jeff," Liz interrupted. *Every child needs only one mother and one father,* she almost reminded him, but she'd said it so often. "Charie," she said, turning from Jeff, "your brother didn't give you too much salad. Eat it up, honey."

"'Sides," Jimmy cut in, "you'll get syph'lis if you don't eat it." He never had to be coaxed to eat anything. His appetite was insatiable.

"Scurvy," Rand corrected above loud chuckles.

"Mind your business," Charie retorted to Jimmy.

"Yeah," Jeff echoed, belching loudly, "mind your business."

Liz wanted to look at her husband in exasperation but restrained herself. "Jeff—" he started to reprimand his son when Pam interrupted.

"Hey, Mom! How come you picked the posies so short?" Silence.

"How come you picked them at all?" Jeff asked in surprise, knowing from his own youthful hard times that FLOWERS WERE FOR LOOKING AT, NOT FOR PICKING. He recalled quite vividly, though he was only three, the day he had sat on the flagstone path and made a beautiful, multicolored pile of tiny hyacinth flowerets.

Two forks paused in mid-air, and two pairs of eyes found sudden interest in the contents of their dinner plates. Charie began working earnestly at her salad, appearing to enjoy it. The silence was brief but painful.

"Oh, I get it," Pam went on. "The little terrors got loose again. I'll just bet hailstones and hot lava rained on somebody's head this afternoon."

"*Two* somebodies," Jeff assisted.

Rand seemed to be, in spite of himself, suppressing a chuckle. "That's enough, Pam, Jeff. I imagine the punishment has already been administered and accounts have been settled. So let's all butt out."

"We didn't get spanked," Jimmy explained, looking up at him wide-eyed. He adored Rand. "We never get spanked here."

"Mommy thought they were in Mrs. Morrison's yard, but they were really in the woods," Charie offered, encouraged by Jimmy's bravery. "Aren't they pretty?" she cooed.

"Holy Mackerel!" Pam ejaculated. "You mean they picked the neighbors' flowers? Oh, agony!"

"But you won't pick any flowers again without asking, will you?" Liz addressed the little ones, ignoring Pam and trying, it seemed in vain, to end the discourse.

"Not ever," Charie stated emphatically. "At least I'll try not to."

Jimmy hastily added, "I won't. Never, never, never!"

Nancy J. Sell

Later Liz loaded the dishwasher while Jeff and Jimmy cleared the table. "Mom," Jeff implored, "would you please make Jimmy stop being a robot while he clears the table? I'm doing all the work while he beep-beeps along." He muttered in disgust, "This kid's got to go."

Jimmy, undaunted and rocking as he walked, answered him in a metallic, mechanical voice. "I - just - a - lit - tle - ro -bot - work - ing - as - fast - as - I - can. And - I - can't - go - any - fast - er - than - this!"

"Mom . . ." Jeff pleaded.

"I'm - just - a lit - tle - ro - bot . . ."

"Go, you little monster. Just make sure your batteries are charged, 'cause you're finishing the job yourself!" Jeff vanished before Liz could comment, but no doubt he had done more than his share.

Pam and Charlotte argued over pots and pans, Pam insisting that it was Charie's turn to wash. Eventually Liz convinced Pam that spaghetti pots were too tough for an almost-five-year-old. Charie gleefully disappeared.

Finally, with a sigh, Liz sat at her desk to write a letter and subconsciously, then consciously, she listened to the sounds of her house. It had been so quiet after the usual fuss over cleanup, but now it was beginning to hum comfortably again. Rand, in his basement workshop, was staining shelves for the laundry room. Through the floor she could hear the monotonous voice of the radio news commentator along with the irregular hammering, which would be Jimmy building some sort of sailboat or footstool or other monstrosity. Happy as could be when Rand was home, he became his constant shadow. Liz felt a twinge of antipathy for her husband at times like this. There was so much she could not understand nor rationalize. *Please love him, Randy. Please want him. He's mine; please make him yours, too.*

"And besides, Nina," she mumbled as she shut the drawer of her desk determinedly, "I wouldn't mind creating a little *more* fulfillment!"

The kaleidoscope had been replaced on the corner of her dresser, and as she went by, she put it to her eye. Finding it still broken, she leaned over and again placed it in the trash can, again resisting the impulse to throw it, or at best, drop it.

She listened to Charie, singing in her bubble bath, then trying to blow a whistle full of water. Charie fought getting into the tub until Liz forbade her to get into bed with dirty feet, then fought getting out. Squeezing a stream of water out of a rubber doll, she yelled, "Mommy, Lovely's going potty in the bathtub!" Then came the sound of kicking feet: She would be on her stomach with bubbles up to her chin, her neck strained to the extreme to keep the suds off her face. She would come out looking like a pink prune.

Pam was busy cleaning up her half of the bedroom she shared with Charie so she could go to the City with her friend, Millicent, and her family tomorrow. "Mom, I need a room of my own!" she argued relentlessly. Her mother agreed, but Pam knew it was unlikely until the addition was finished. Even then, the second floor of the addition was to be a small apartment for Liz's mother and would only be for temporary use of the family until Gran agreed to move in. According to Gran, Liz would be a great-grandmother before it happened.

Liz knew that, when this room-cleaning job was done, Pam's half would be neat, but Charie's would be a mess, and she mentally prepared herself for the wits-matching session ahead. "But it's just Charie's own stuff I threw on her side," Pam would maintain. "Can't she be responsible for her things?"

"Of course," Liz had to reply.

Nancy J. Sell

Jeff was in the garage working on an ailing minibike that had been given to him. He and his friend Shep were hoping to sell it, and now and then Liz heard them try to start it. Often he was in the cellar conferring with his father on his progress, or lack of it, or looking for a special tool. She was glad for this common interest between them; otherwise their conversations were often one-sided or monosyllabic. Sometimes she thought they were losing Jeff. *It's just the usual teenage rebellion,* she kept assuring herself, wishing there were no such term as "generation gap."

Why should there be such a thing: a chasm to separate loving family members? The Markham children were free to do their own thing, and she and Rand did their own thing, but there was much mutual ground on which to meet. She would have no part of a generation gap. She would will it not to happen to them.

Liz made The Pink Prune get out of the tub and made Jimmy get in.

She was back at her desk in the bedroom when Rand came in. She hadn't counted on this, and, expecting a confrontation, she feigned busyness, pretending to reread the letter she had been writing. He sat on the foot of the bed, then laid back with one hand over his face, the other hooked in his belt loop. Liz finished her letter, addressed the envelope, and stamped it. She felt trapped.

When she was sure he was asleep, she turned off her desk lamp and felt her way in the darkness toward the closed door, careful not to touch the bed where she knew he lay. Her hand brushed his knee; simultaneously, it seemed, his fingers gripped her wrist and he drew her gently but firmly to the bed beside him. Liz tensely lay in the circle of his arm with her head on his chest waiting for him to either speak or release her. She was soothed by the warmth of his body against her own and felt herself relaxing. But why must

Jimmy's Home

he always be so taciturn, so withdrawn? She thought he slept again when he spoke softly.

"I'm sorry."

An apology was not what she expected, and again she was tense, alert. "For what, specifically?" she asked quietly.

"Specifically," he answered, and she thought she detected an iceberg beneath the chilly water, "for not calling."

Oh. What about everything else? Aloud she said, "Not for leaving me alone all night?"

"You weren't alone."

"You know what I mean."

"I had to think."

"You could have thought here. I wouldn't have bothered you."

"I'm sure of that."

After a long silence, she asked, "And what did you come up with?"

"Not much."

"Don't ever do that to me again, Rand," she said softly, gently, lest she alter their course. "If you do, I'll call the police and report you as a missing person."

"And I'll tell them you're crazy and I want to be missing."

A giggle began in her throat before she had time to hold it in check, and he pulled her hard against him, kissing her forehead. Then his arms held her and he kissed her eyes, her lips, her neck.

"No, Randy. The children . . ."

"No, Randy. The children . . ." he mimicked. "The kids know what we do behind closed doors . . ."

Liz put her hand over his mouth. "Kids don't believe their parents do what other people and dogs do, no matter what they learn in health class. Besides, we've got some unsettled problems . . ."

"I can't think of a better way to solve problems."

"If only that were a magic solution."

"Sure would make living a lot more fun, huh?"

"Why don't you sleep for a while?" she suggested, pushing herself away from him. She needed to get away. She wasn't ready to let down her wall.

"Stay here with me."

"I've got to see to the children. Jimmy has probably turned into a purple prune by now."

"Who cares? Stay here."

"I can't."

He released her. "Call me in twenty minutes."

Charlotte and Jimmy, smelling of April Showers, chose a book from the previous day's library selection. The reading of a new book usually meant constant interruptions every ten words or so. No exception, this one. Liz tried patiently to answer each question, even if it was, "I don't know. Why don't we research that one?" They liked that phrase and frequently used it.

Jimmy sneezed. "Are you getting a cold?" Liz questioned.

"It's from my loose tooth," he explained, wide-eyed, impressed with his own knowledge. "It's a tooth cold. From a loose tooth," he reinforced his previous offering.

She knew a teething baby's nose usually ran as if from a cold, so she supposed a runny nose from a loose tooth was equally possible. She had much to learn.

Then, without moving his head from where it rested on her arm, he exclaimed, "It's out!" He held up the bloody tooth between two fingers. Sending him off to the bathroom to rinse his mouth, his fingers, and the tooth, she thought, *so much for the cold.*

When Liz sat down with her handwork later, Rand appeared refreshed from his nap. The children had already gathered to watch a favorite TV program. His head propped on his hand, Jeff was stretched out full-length on the floor, and Liz thought, as she had so many times lately, *How tall he's getting! Like his father! My son is almost a man! But he's becoming a stranger to us.* Charie was on her stomach in back of Jeff with her chin resting on his knees. Now and then he moved, deliberately it appeared, causing her head to drop. "Don't move, Jeff." She gripped a fistful of his jeans in an attempt to restrict his movement.

The sofa was Pam's special spot, and there she curled up in a fetal position with her bed pillow topping the pile of cushions under her head. Sneakers was asleep in the circle of her body with his head nestled in her neck. Her hand rested on Mini's head, and occasionally she scratched his neck.

Jimmy, flat on his back with his legs stretched out toward the TV, rested his head against Jeff's middle. His arm was across Mini's rump, and he scratched his back. Tedley and Bearsh, the quietest of spectators, sat side by side on the ottoman.

Not yet fully captivated by the story in progress, Rand read the newspaper. His interest in the show would be kindled soon and a recap of the first portion of the saga would be required. It happened every time.

Liz's heart warmed, then faltered as her glance lingered on the one tawny head among the four, and its contented face. Jimmy was such a confused mixture of love and hate, of willingness and stubbornness, of laughter and tears. He so needed the firm yet tender care they were giving him; and Liz grieved to think this circle might soon be broken. He was not their little boy. Two years ago he had walked into their lives and straight into her heart. Sight unseen, he had bounced into their living room and plopped himself, with his bubbly smile, into Rand's lap.

Charie and Jimmy had become instant friends and they spent many play hours together, on the swings, in the sandbox building elaborate sand villages, riding their trikes, learning to roller skate. Jimmy began to spend as much time at the Markhams' as he did at the Blairs'.

Then the accident: On their way home from a friend's anniversary party one night just five weeks ago—*had it been only five weeks?* Liz reflected—another car had skidded into the Blairs' and both Don and Jennie had been seriously injured. The next morning, as soon as Liz heard of it, she hurried over to their house to offer help. The three Blair children were being taken to the already overflowing home of an aunt, and no one seemed to know what to do about Jimmy.

"Let me take him home with me," Liz promptly offered, "at least until the dust settles and everyone is thinking coherently again."

Rand was openly irritated. "You shouldn't have. You knew I would object, Liz. And you are just letting yourself in for a lot of heartache." His brow creased into a frown. He had been consistently and adamantly negative about her pleadings to take in a foster child.

"But Randy," she had reasoned then, "think of all the unwanted children. Randy, there are so *many!*"

"No. Liz."

"So why can't we help one? And I can't imagine what it would be like to be a child that no one wanted."

"See what I mean about you biting off more than I can chew?"

"Then let me help you chew it."

"No."

"He has no one to really care. *No one!*" Tears were near the surface, and she bit her lip in an effort to retain control.

He shook his head. "You've got enough to do with three without taking on any more."

"I wouldn't mind. Honestly . . ."

"I would. You're so tired by bedtime now you can hardly roll over to kiss me goodnight."

She let it drop, but she knew eventually she'd win him over. She always managed it, and he was a pushover where kids were concerned. It might take awhile, but he would yield and agree to take Jimmy in, at least as a foster child. Eventually he would. She knew it.

But now he was annoyed. Randy loved children, and they responded spontaneously to him; but she had stepped on treacherously thin ice bringing Jimmy in to stay, however temporary the arrangement.

"Make sure whoever is in charge knows this is a temporary arrangement. A *brief* one."

But since the accident, since Jimmy had come to stay with them, Liz had been praying for a miracle. Jimmy belonged. He simply could not leave them. Somehow she had to make Rand understand how much she cared, how much he needed them, they needed him. Rand *must* understand.

If only they could adopt him. But the foster home issue came first. *For now,* she mused, *one step at a time.* Once Jimmy was "in," he might never have to leave. But why was Rand so stubborn? He, of all people, should know what it felt like to be excess baggage.

"It's gone!" Jimmy shrieked, bringing her out of her reverie. He was now on his feet. "My tooth is *gone! It's-gone-it's-gone-it's-gone-it's-gone!*" he wailed.

"Shut up, Jimmy," Jeff growled. The circumstance lent weight to his argument that he should have his own television in his bedroom. Even better, he had great dreams of an apartment-type arrangement for himself when their addition was complete. The new playroom and deck, and the apartment over the garage which would someday be for Liz's mother, held a big attraction for Jeff as well as for Pam. "But Gran won't want to give up her house for lots of years," he reasoned. "And I'll be out'a here by then." Work on the addition was to begin soon.

"That's true, honey. But we can put the extra space to good use until Gran needs it." *Well,* Liz continued silently, *it might not be a bad idea for you to move up there and Jimmy into your room. We'll see.* But she wasn't making any promises as far as bedrooms were concerned.

"It's gone! It's gone!"

Jeff groaned, then reached for the remote to turn up the volume on the television. Jimmy searched his pockets as he tried desperately to contain his tears.

"Come here, dear," Liz comforted. "Jeff, turn it down. And say, 'Be quiet, please,' not 'shut up!' Are you sure you put it in your pocket?" she asked, turning to Jimmy. He nodded angrily, wiping his cheeks with the back of his hand. "Let's look good for it."

After turning his pockets inside out and searching his area of the floor, they concluded that the tooth was indeed gone.

"I'm sure it will turn up, Jim," she consoled.

"The Tooth Fairy won't mind saving your nickel until another night," Rand added his condolence.

Miserable, he glared at Rand. "Charie got a quarter."

Rand guffawed. "Oh, a quarter then."

"Charlotte, Jimmy, time for bed," Liz announced. The program had ended, but Jimmy protested loudly. "No," she warned, "I'll do my best to find the tooth in the morning. You must go to bed now. Go brush your teeth."

"One less to brush tonight, Jimmy," Rand grinned wickedly. Before long Charie was back. She held up a finger as her mother started to reprimand her and said, "Just one minute, Mommy. I forgot to tell Pammy something."

Pam rolled over so her head hung off the edge of the sofa while Charie whispered her message. Then they swapped roles, and Charie became the listener and Pam the whisperer. Then off Charie trotted.

After endless delays, the two youngest snuggled down in the guest room, a special treat, where Jimmy usually slept alone in one of the twin beds. Tedley and Bearsh had been tucked in already.

"Tedley wants to ask you something," Charie prompted as Liz leaned over to kiss her. Giving Jimmy a sidelong look, Charie urged, "Go 'head, Tedley."

Jimmy held the bear in front of his face, wiggling the arms as he spoke. "Auntie Liz," he started, then paused to turn the thought around for a moment. Finally he blurted, "Can I—I mean, can Jimmy call you Mommy instead of Auntie Liz?"

Silent for a moment, Liz petitioned, not sure whose wisdom she sought. *Oh God, how I want this to be a reality!* She was still searching for an answer when the children's uplifted eyes indicated another presence in the room. She heard Rand's voice and her heart skipped a beat. What would he say?

"I'll tell you what, Jim—I mean Teddy."

"Tedley," Jimmy corrected.

"Oh, good grief. *Tedley*. It's okay if Jimmy calls Auntie Liz 'Mommy,' just as long as he knows she's really *not*. She can be his mom while he's here—she'll be a mom pro tem. That's Latin, and it means temporarily."

"A mom pro tem," Jimmy giggled.

"Literally it means for the time. But someday soon he'll be going back to the Blairs' house, and Mrs. Blair will be his mom again."

"But why can't I stay here?" Jimmy asked in surprise as Rand kissed Charie, then ruffled his hair and poked him in the belly. "I like it here best of any place, *ever!*"

"Well, don't forget," Rand reminded him in a big, important voice that assured him of his importance, too, "you're just here for a visit while the Blairs recuperate from their accident."

"'Sides, Mrs. Blair's not my mom. She's a crab."

"That's an opinion," Rand stated forcefully with suppressed humor and pretend annoyance. "Yours."

"And Mr. Blair's." Jimmy was determined to have the last word.

Liz reached for her husband's hand. He took hers and pressed her fingers. *Thanks, Randy. You're super. Sometimes. And,* she added wordlessly, *please let him stay in this place he likes best.* Rand abruptly released her hand, then turned to go.

"Goodnight, Dandy Randy," Charie giggled.

"Goodnight, Dandy Daddy," Jimmy echoed his own version. "Goodnight, Mommy," he uttered proudly. "I'm going to ask God to let you be my real mommy." His voice changed as he spoke softly to Charlotte. "I want to stay here. Let's ask God if I can."

Liz's mother, *Gran* to the children, made certain they attended Sunday School every week, and consequently the two children often talked of the Almighty, knowing Him to be a real entity in their lives.

"Liz Ann," her mother, Betty Cunningham said, using the pet name of Liz's childhood and running the two together so it sounded rather French, "you should be taking them yourself." Though Liz had attended church God-fearingly as a child, she had lost interest as an adult. Irrelevant, she had decided. Her church attendance was now sporadic, virtually nonexistent.

I wonder if it would help my cause if I went and learned some effective prayers, she mused. "'Night, loves," she extinguished the light as she spoke, knowing Charie and Jimmy would whisper for a long time.

Later, while Rand was showering and Liz was readying the kitchen for tomorrow's morning rush, Pam, yawning and squinting in the bright kitchen light, reappeared in her long flannel nightgown. "I forgot to tell you, Mom," she yawned again, too tired to conceal it with her hand, "remember that huge molar the dentist pulled a couple of months ago, and I saved it just for the heck of it? Remember, Charie called it a boulder? She just borrowed it for Jimmy to put under his pillow."

"Is *that* what you two were whispering about!" Liz exclaimed. "Glad you remembered to tell me, Pam. He would have been so disappointed if the nickel—I mean *quarter*—hadn't been under his pillow!" Liz kissed her older daughter and pressed her shoulder. "Goodnight. Sleep tight, honey."

But Pam poured herself a glass of milk and sat at the table with it. "Mom," she finally spoke after turning her glass several times, "you should hear Millicent yell at her mother." Liz, carrying three boxes of cereal between two open palms, waited for her to continue. "I'm glad you don't let me talk to you that way."

"You mean you would if I let you."

"Probably. Sometimes I feel like it, especially when you're unreasonable, which is quite often," she announced tongue-in-cheek. "It sure grates on me though, when I hear her."

Liz put the cereal on the table and sat opposite Pam. "Do you really feel like it sometimes?" She hadn't needed to be told. "That's what growing up is all about, Pam: not always doing things we feel like doing, and sometimes just the opposite: making ourselves do things we *don't* feel like doing."

"But I have no choice." Pam's eyes met her mother's and a frown wrinkled her nose. "At least in that I don't. Do you know what Millie said to me today?" Rand appeared in his bathrobe and slippers, and Pam redirected her question to include her father. "She said, 'Y'know, I've never heard your mother and father fight.' She was surprised. Her parents go at it all the time. In front of me, too." Liz knew Rand was looking at her, but she willfully refused visual confrontation with him. "I got to thinkin' about that," Pam went on. "Y'know," she lowered her lids as if shy about revealing so much of herself, "I never really thought much about it before . . . And I just want to tell you—well, I'm glad I fell into this family and not hers. Or worse."

The lump in Liz's throat kept her from speaking, so she pressed her big girl's hands in both her own. Pam looked at her with the hint of a sparkle in her eyes, kissed each of them, said goodnight, and was gone.

"Quite a speech," Rand remarked, clearing his throat. He put his arms around Liz's neck as she sat at the table and rested his chin on top of her head. "She's going to be okay. Don't you think so, Liz?"

"I can't help but wonder. But I hope so. They know we love them. Unconditionally."

It was quiet until finally he cleared his throat again and said, "What about us?"

"What about us?" she asked with a hint of sarcasm.

"We've got some problems." He drew her to her feet and toward the stairs. "We were talking about how to settle them," he said on the way.

"Rand, we need to *talk*."

Jimmy's Home

Liz lay close beside Rand in the circle of his arm, her mind too busy for sleep. Disagreements were a part of every marriage, and she and Rand were not too different in that. It took so much giving, she sometimes wondered if she had anything left to give. It was true, they made it a policy never to argue in front of the children, and though they came close to it on occasion, they usually retained control. She weighed the advantages and disadvantages of such tactics. Wouldn't a brief, loud explosion be healthier for them, yes, even in the presence of the kids, than allowing an unpleasant brew to simmer? Probably, except that when they did get around to airing problems after waiting until they were alone, usually the plot had lost its punch, the effervescence had dissipated, the soda pop had gone flat. More often than not, instead of being embroiled in a royal donnybrook, they were capable of handling matters in a sane, mature discussion.

Sometimes Rand did such sweet thoughtful things, she felt like a queen. She noticed the kaleidoscope had been removed from the trash can again and was nowhere in sight: probably in the basement on his workbench. But sometimes he was a bear. They had had problems, tough ones. Tough enough that they knew the dangers of taking each other for granted. But he was so darned independent. Sometimes his self-sufficiency caused her to wonder if he really needed her. *Really* needed her. Physically, yes, of course; he made that apparent. But emotionally? She couldn't help but question.

"I love you, Rand," she whispered, testing his level of consciousness.

"Hmmm," he muttered sleepily. "Same. I *like* you, too."

"Randy," she started lamely, swallowed hard, and started again. "Randy, the Blairs aren't going to be able to take Jimmy back with them."

"I wondered," he mumbled, trying to rouse himself from the edge of oblivion. As he eased over toward her he said, "They're going to be a long time recuperating, aren't they? What do you suppose will happen to him?"

It was quiet again, and Liz was uncomfortable. "Randy—"

"Honey," he interrupted gently, firmly, "haven't we discussed this enough? Can't you understand how I feel about it? Didn't I make it clear yesterday?"

"Can't *you* understand, Rand?" she asked softly, unaccusingly. "He's a *person*, a *boy*. Not a stray cat. He's a human being who needs love and attention."

"So am I."

". . . and someone," she continued without hesitation, "to *care* what happens to him." She choked, "How can you turn away from a child in need?" She tried so hard not to cry, but the tears filled her eyes, her voice.

"How can *you*? I'm a person with needs, too."

"Fulfilled ones . . ."

"Please don't try to make me look like some kind of a cad, Liz," he advised, fully awake now. His voice was softer, and controlled. "Our family is complete. I do not want to take on any more responsibilities, financial, physical, social, or emotional. Period. Don't keep harping on this. I can't take it. Honestly, Liz."

"I do not understand you, and I never will. Goodnight."

"Goodnight." He kissed her lightly and turned away, whispering as he did, "I love you."

"Oh, I love you too, Randy," she cried. "Oh, Rand, couldn't he stay here then until they find a permanent place for him?" She knew she was buying time, hoping Randy, too, would become so attached to Jimmy, a parting would be unthinkable.

"The longer he stays, the harder it will be, honey." There was a big, unspoken *NO* in the statement.

Pretending instead to have heard a yielding in his voice, she said, "I know that. But at least maybe he'll be able to get his feet on the ground by then. At least he'll know someone really cares."

"No. I know what it will do to you. I can't agree to it."

"And what do you think you're doing to me? To us? Just tell me why."

"How many times do I need to tell you why? One: You've got all you can handle without him. Two: Our family is complete. Three: I don't want any added responsibilities, financial, social, physical, or emotional, as I recently mentioned. Four: I need some attention. Five: You'll get too attached. In fact, you already are. I'm trying to do you a favor. Six—"

"Thanks for nothing."

"It's not nothing. You give me a headache."

"And I've had a pain in the neck for twenty years." She flopped over angrily. "I don't understand you," she reiterated, "and I never will! *Never!*"

From their battle stations, neither budged. Finally, Liz edged a foot over and touched his leg, then withdrew it quickly to make it appear accidental. After a moment, Rand did a half-turn toward her, and she moved an inch in his direction. After he touched her arm, she put a hand to his face. Then she was in his arms, clinging to him.

"I do love you, Liz," he whispered again, still nursing his wounds.

"And I love you. Nothing will ever change that." *But please understand how I feel!*

"I'd like to get back to normal living."

"And so would I," she stated, piqued.

Long after her husband had gone to sleep, Liz gazed into the darkness. The outline of the windows was blurred by tears she tried to blink away, then she blotted them on the edge of the sheet.

Please care, Randy. How can you not care when you know what it is to be a child in need?

The clock on the mantel struck three. She stared at flames licking greedily at the log she had placed on the still-glowing embers in the famiy room fireplace. Her eyes were heavy and her head hurt, but she couldn't sleep.

Oh, God! Please make him care.

CHAPTER SEVEN

Liz was fidgety. Several weeks had passed, and try as she might, she could not budge Rand from where he had planted himself. The discussions had been endless, the results always the same. The decision could not be postponed any longer. The state worker on Jimmy's case would be coming early next week. Liz would have to admit failure.

The evening in the City had been lovely. During dinner at the French restaurant, Rand had told the very French waiter, "Yes, I'll have pie à la mode. You know," he explained when the poor fellow failed to understand his French, "pie, with *ice cream*." Liz had laughed delightedly, and finally Rand had caught the humor. He had not complained when, at the concert (they had held hands through the entire program, even when his arm rested across her shoulders), he had to rescue her shoes from beneath the seat. Perhaps now, during this quiet ride home along the Parkway, she would bring it up and they could have a civilized talk. Their times together, especially for discussion, were negligible, and this might be their only opportunity to be alone for a while.

Jimmy's Home

"What's on your mind?" her husband asked, and she realized she had been stroking his hand nervously. He placed his hand at the back of her neck and pulled her toward him.

"Not much," she lied.

"The usual?" he spoke kindly, and she was encouraged.

"I lied," she said, giving him a glance from the corner of her eye. Even in the dark she knew he was not smiling. His silhouette was rigid, his lips taut, his eyes staring at the road. "How did you know where my mind had wandered?" she questioned. She glanced at him but couldn't read his expression in the flickering, passing lights.

"I recognize the mood. I wish you'd never gotten on this kick, honey." His words were softer than she'd expected. He seemed concerned, and she was hopeful.

"I can't help caring, you know. You can't turn love on and off like a water tap." She moved out of his reach. "I *care,* and I can't help it."

"I'm aware of that, and I do too, Liz. Jimmy's a great kid, and I'd like to see him situated in a good home."

"But not ours." Her voice was a whisper.

"Not ours."

It was quiet but for the hum of the tires on the pavement and an orchestra playing show tunes, this one "On the Street Where You Live," turned low on the car radio. "There's something I have to say. Would you hear me out before you make any comment?" Liz asked.

"Liz!" he rebutted. "Do I have a choice?" Then he spoke with resignation. "Go on."

She swallowed hard, pausing briefly to ensure her best articulation. "The caseworker from the agency is coming next Monday." She sensed an intake of breath as if he were about to speak, and she quickly continued. "She said they'd like to leave Jimmy with us—temporarily, you know. He's so content. And, you know, they don't like to keep shuffling kids around . . ." Again he started to speak. "I'm not done. Remember?" She smiled woodenly and hoped it was not evident in her voice. "We have to be approved as foster parents if he's to stay any longer, and there are certain formalities, papers to sign, et cetera." *Darn these tears!* she thought. *Why can't I talk without getting emotional?* Then she blurted, "Oh, Randy, please. Don't let them take him away! Please let him stay until they find a permanent home for him! *Just* until they find a home for him?" She sobbed into her open palms.

He was silent and rigid as they sped over the dark, almost deserted Parkway. She stared at the pavement ahead, the broken white lines separating the lanes, the grotesquely shaped trees against the night sky.

She tried not to sniffle. "I'm done," she finally offered meekly.

He drove on, reaching their exit and riding the two miles to their house without speaking. After he pulled into the garage and extinguished the car lights, she turned to him. "I'm done," she reiterated.

"I doubt it," he said blandly, casting a quick look in her direction as he got out of the car. His manner showed no upset, no animosity. Nothing. She wished he would say something. Anything. He was harder to take this way than when he exploded. He shut the car door without another word.

Liz prepared the morning coffee so it was ready to press the start button. She turned off the light her mother had left on in the kitchen and made the rounds of the bedrooms to check on the children. "We're home, Mom," she spoke softly through the guest room door and was glad that her mother, the evening's babysitter, didn't open the door.

"I hear you, Liz Ann. Have a good time?"

Liz answered affirmatively and said goodnight. Her mother would make sure Jimmy, her roomie for the night, was well covered. She was such a good mother, a good mother-in-law; ask Rand, who called her his grand-gran-in-law. As a gran, she couldn't be topped.

Charie had said hopefully, "Maybe Gran will play Flinch® with us," when she learned her grandmother was coming.

Jimmy answered, "I'd rather play Muggins®."

"You always say that, Jimmy. I get to pick because she's my gran, not yours."

"We share things with Jimmy while he's staying with us, Charlotte. That means sharing Gran, too. She's so special, we shouldn't mind sharing her."

"But she is *my* gran, isn't she, Mom? Not Jimmy's?"

"Let's pretend she's Jimmy's gran too, Char, okay? You're very good at pretending."

"Me too," Jimmy added.

Now Liz stepped over Mini, the protector, in the girls' doorway and kissed Pam and Charlotte lightly on their cheeks. Pam stirred and mumbled something like, "Hi, Mom." Sneakers was curled beside her to fit the contour of her body. Charie sighed and her lips curved into a slight smile. She clung to Bearsh. "Nite, Aunt Lottie," she murmured.

Liz paused at Jeff's door without opening it. All was quiet beyond. She wondered if her son had resigned himself to the tasks his father had laid out for him for the following day. The heated argument the two of them had had earlier that evening had not set a happy mood for this evening out.

"But Dad," Jeff, angry, had sputtered, "the other guys don't have to work so hard. Seems like I'm always having to turn something down they're suggesting 'cause I've got work to do."

"Plan your work right and you'll be surprised how much you can fit into a schedule. You've got to plan ahead," Rand emphasized. "And besides, we've never patterned our lives according to anyone else's habits," his father wound up the debate. "And from what I observe, in many cases it's a very good thing." Because of his early circumstances, Rand had learned to work hard, and he had no tolerance for slothfulness, no patience with laziness. "Anyway," he added, "we're not about to start now."

Jeff's frustration with his father, Liz thought, was a cover-up for a deeper bitterness.

But surprisingly enough, her husband had seemed to put the problem aside as soon as he and Liz had left the house. She wondered, as she now stood by his bedroom door, if Jeff had, too.

How easily they each drifted off to sleep, and how soundly they slept. She wished she could do the same.

The next day Liz drove home from her shopping trip reveling in the relaxed and unhurried feeling which she so seldom experienced. Her dinner was ready and in the oven on the timer, the table was set, and the earliest the girls would be home was five o'clock. Charie was at her little friend's birthday party, and no doubt would be full of cupcakes and ice cream. Pam was studying for tests with classmates at Millicent's. After mowing lawns, Jeff would be at home doing his Saturday job of cleaning the garage, hating every minute of it and resenting his father for making him do it.

"Jeff, you can get Jimmy from Morrisons' when you get home from your mowing jobs. Keep an eye on him while you're working," she had instructed him this morning. "I should be home before you're done."

"Does he have to be here?" he had complained. "He's a pain in the butt. You know, Mom," he moaned, "he bugs me. Let him stay at Morrisons'. I don't want him here!"

"He'll be good. Won't you, Jimmy?" And to Jeff she added, "You know you don't mind."

"Who says?"

"I'll help you clean the garage, Jeff," Jimmy offered, nodding assent to Liz's question on his behavior.

"Okay," Jeff grudgingly conceded, seeing the prospect of free help in the arrangement. "That is, if you do everything I tell you."

"How much do I get?"

Jeff pondered briefly. "A dollar."

"I'll do *any*thing!" Jimmy exclaimed happily.

"But then," Jeff added crossly, "I'll have to charge you a dollar and a half for fixing your bike next time, or whatever else might need fixing."

"I'll help you for nothing," Jimmy returned good-naturedly with a toothless grin.

Liz was glad her shopping had taken less time than she had allotted for it. On impulse, she detoured down a tree-shaded side street. After several turns, she reached Haven of Rest Memorial Park and drove in between two wrought iron pillars. She passed two flower-blanketed graves, then parked the car in the gravel roadway and walked almost silently across the thick grass. The flowering cherry trees were thick with blossoms, and fragrant.

The simple marker imbedded in the plush turf read, SAMUEL MARKHAM, INFANT, and then the date. Just one date. Her third baby and second son had seen birth and death the same day. Eight years ago. Where had those years gone? Many tears had been shed then as the tiny casket was set to rest at the foot of her grandfather's grave, Samuel's great-grandfather: Tears, certainly for the unknown, much-loved being who was now, she supposed, in heaven, for where else would innocent babies be sent? But also, and to a much greater extent, tears of grief for Rand and herself, the crushed parents whose time of joy had taken such an unexpected, heart-wrenching turn. Her empty arms. She was unable to control her grief when she saw young mothers with their infants and toddlers.

The song that came from the chapel, her mother had said when Liz asked her about the strangely familiar tune, was something about being safe in Jesus, the Saviour's arms. Had the Almighty Himself come and carried her little one away? She wished He hadn't. He was supposed to know what was best for everyone; then why did He give things and then take them back? Or had an angel come and taken him, to place him in Jesus' arms, her beautiful, internally deformed child? Religion did seem to help in difficult times. It was a comfort, a crutch, a support when you couldn't stand alone. And she was trying to stand alone.

The stinging pain had eased to a dull ache and then to a sad emptiness during those years; the void was filled, especially with the arrival of Charlotte five years later. But often Liz remembered so vividly the pain in her heart, the aching of her own empty arms. *Why* had God taken a baby they so desperately wanted when so many beautiful, healthy, *unwanted* children were granted life, or even aborted? There was no answer. It was so unfair. She only knew she must emerge a better, stronger person for it or the experience would be wasted.

The last time she had visited the cemetery, she had been accompanied by Charie, and had watched her kneel before the little grave, kiss her hand, then pat the kiss onto the flat marker set in the grass. Liz had been touched. She could scarcely talk beyond the lump in her throat.

Now, alone and overwhelmed with memories, Liz knelt before her father's grave and pressed back the grass so no part of the marker was obscured: Louis Edward Cunningham. She kissed her hand and touched it to the stone bearing his name. It was a private moment, one for Liz and her dad. The lump in her throat refused to budge.

Sitting down on the cool damp lawn, she allowed her thoughts to reach farther back, beyond those eight years, to the night her father died. "It is so unfair!" she spoke aloud. She had mentally shaken her fist at Deity. *My children will never know, never remember this wonderful man who was so much a part of our lives!* Jeff had just passed his second birthday and Liz was pregnant with Pam when that late-night call had come to jolt them out of a sound sleep. Randy had reached the phone first, for, as usual, his getting out of bed had awakened her rather than the ringing of the phone.

What can be more alarming than the sound of the telephone in the middle of the night? Liz's thoughts raced backward, and it was as if she were reliving that night again. The tone had seemed different, and she had known the news was bad. Maybe it was Randy's voice. She could hardly breathe, even after she heard the words.

"Your father is . . . gone." Rand's face was void of expression, for the fact had not yet seeped through his senses to trigger an emotion. Liz clutched her pillow as if trying to clutch him, to hold on to him, to bring him back. Her dad. She did not cry because she knew it was not true.

Not until later, while she was spending the remainder of the night with her mom, did she become sane enough to feel, to know, to remember. And even with the remembering, she was numbly aware of the present, of Mom in the next room with tearless, sleepless eyes, sitting at the window, too stunned to crawl into a cold bed. Liz would eventually fall into an exhausted sleep that night, but she knew her mother would not. Better not to have to face the morning shock, she thought. Mom had a strength to be admired, coveted, but what was ahead for her, for them? She was still a young woman . . .

At this point, Liz's remembering was secondary to her suffering, but nevertheless it was there, a shroud-like, bodiless finger, somewhere connected to an equally bodiless voice, "Heavy, heavy hangs over thy head . . ."

Was it just the night before that she and Dad had exchanged harsh words? What is time, anyway, but memory upon memory upon memory—one memory to disturb, another to delight, another to destroy? *And often in their making we are so blind as not to know the difference. Consequently,* she contemplated, *I will bear the full load of a burden I do not feel equipped to carry.*

The days before the funeral had been a painful blur. The tears Liz should have shed were stopped up somewhere around her heart. Rand, suffering too at the loss of a special person, his mentor, his friend, had tried to be Liz's strength, but no one could reach that very personal, private place she had closed to the world.

The evening before the funeral service, before the final closing of the casket, the family had been alone in the large flower-filled room when the pastor and his wife began singing softly: "Blest be the tie that binds our hearts in Christian love." Many of the family had joined in the singing through their tears. "The fellowship of kindred minds is like to that above." It wasn't until the last verse, when the pastor's beautiful tenor voice, also tearful, was left singing alone, "When we asunder part it gives us inward pain," that Liz had broken. Shaking with sobs as she had fallen across her father's chest. Rand had gently pulled her back and held her firmly against him, then circled his other arm around her mother. "But we shall still be joined in heart," the pastor continued, "and hope to meet again."

In their sorrow they knew they had the assurance of a heavenly reunion. But at the time not one eye remained dry.

Suddenly she jumped up, abruptly ending the tryst with her thoughts, and hurried to the car. She had to get home to tell Jeff something. He was so angry with his father so much of the time. Why hadn't she told him before? Because she was unable to face it herself.

Jeff was sitting at the kitchen table, sorting nuts and bolts, screws and miscellaneous items into plastic containers. Liz poured herself a cup of coffee and sat across from him.

"Where's Jimmy?"

"Somewhere. Playing."

She told him about the late-night call so long ago.

"You told me about the night Grandpa died." His voice exuded boredom. How could she be so stupid as not to remember that?

"I know, Jeff. But there's something I haven't told you. I've been carrying a weight in here," she paused to place a fist over her heart, "that's too heavy. I think it will help if I tell you about it. I've never told anyone. Will you listen?"

"I doubt if I have a choice."

She winced but went on. "My dad snapped at me for blocking the drive, the only access to his small business office at the rear of their house, as you know. I stormed out, fool that I was, slammed the door, and drove away. Jeff, I never saw him again until I saw him in the casket." She waited for that to sink in. "Jeff, my daddy died . . . He was *dead*, Jeff, with un-erased, unforgiven, harsh words between us."

The kitchen was silent except for the *plunk plunk* of hardware falling into containers. Finally Jeff mumbled, "It was probably just as much his fault as yours." He loved his grandpa and grieved his passing.

His coldness stunned her, and she hesitated to go on. Swallowing hard, she continued, "But I have to answer for me." There was a long silence before she spoke again. "For me." She softly echoed her own words. "Did you know I did dumb things when I was your age, Jeff?"

He looked at her, but his eyes revealed nothing of what he was thinking. "You still do," he chuckled sheepishly.

"But my dad was so patient with me," she continued, ignoring him, strangely pleased at his humor. "Kind of like somebody else I know. I loved him so much, Jeff. He was such an important person in my life."

"You weren't the only one, you know." His gaze held hers, and his eyes held a deliberate defiance.

"Do you know why I'm telling you all this?"

He looked at her again, shrugged his shoulders, and looked away.

"Now that my dad is gone, I have nothing left of him. Nothing that matters. Nothing but memories. They matter. Of course they do. What else, I wonder, can we keep of those we love? You know, most of my memories of my dad are happy ones. All but one. I wish I could say I'm sorry to my dad. Your grandpa. Maybe God will tell him for me."

She sensed a wrenching inside him, as if the sound of anything holy was offensive to him. She had done that to him. Her reaction was often the same. But there was that crutch again. She would use it, only as a crutch; Jeff would refuse it.

The quietness was not awkward this time. Liz sipped her coffee, and when she spoke again, her voice was husky. "When it comes to fathers, Jeff, yours compares to mine. Not perfect, mind you, but darn near it. That's why I married him. He's the best. You are so lucky . . ." *Even though I don't want to admit it myself right now!*

"Come off it, Mom . . ."

"You'd better take good care of him." She marveled at how easily the words had come even though, at the moment, she doubted their veracity. Right now she wasn't sure if she loved or hated her husband.

Jeff placed the covers on the plastic boxes. "Can I go now, Mom? I've got to finish and get cleaned up before supper." He stood. "Don't forget, I have to eat early. Shep and I are going to a game. Actually, I can get a hot dog there."

"Your supper is ready."

Hurt and angry, Liz became increasingly agitated as the evening wore on. Hadn't Jeff heard a word she'd said? Didn't he have any feelings?

From the kitchen window she watched Charlotte and Jimmy playing on the grass with their bunnies as the late-evening sun cast long shadows across the yard. Plants hanging from the tall tree stump that earlier in the day had basked in full sunshine now hung in shadows that occasionally let in slits of light as gentle breezes stirred the foliage. It was a perfect evening. The sky was the loveliest shade of blue, more vivid because of the white puffy clouds dotting its surface. Mini observed the rabbits indifferently, and Charie held Potter to the dog's nose for a kiss. Jimmy followed her leading with Peter, then put him on Mini's back.

She brought herself up short. Of course Jeff had heard her! He wouldn't reveal his feelings to her any more than she was letting on how crushed she was! By him. By Rand. By so many people and things she cared about.

Yes, Jeff had heard every word she'd uttered. Every word.

Liz groaned. Charlotte was hugging her so tight she had to tickle her to free herself. "Are you going to let Pammy get her hair cut?" Charie asked. Liz knew the sudden interest: monkey see, monkey do.

"Maybe," she replied, still tickling her youngest, "maybe not. But yours is going to stay the way it is."

"I don't even want mine cut," Charie covered herself, faking a pout and recognizing a losing battle before she entered the fray. "Someday I will. Anyway, Pammy's goosky."

"What does goosky mean, Charie?" Liz asked.

"Well, like a goose, but also like a duck," she explained, spreading her palms upward to demonstrate the obvious.

"Now tell me: First, why is Pam like a goose?"

"Well, a goose is pretty, but also pretty silly."

"And a duck?"

"A duck is dumb and, well, clumsy. Not pretty at all."

"If ducks are dumb, then so are you, Charie. Because some ducks are pretty," Jimmy interrupted and defended the webbed creatures. "The boy ducks are. Mallard ducks are *beautiful*. They have pretty blue and green on them. Didn't you ever see one?" he questioned patronizingly.

"Not the girl ducks, you dumbbell."

"Well, a girl goose isn't pretty either."

Liz could foresee a dead-end street on this one, so she called a halt and kissed them goodnight.

"Did you feed your rabbits?" she asked. Liz hoped that, gender-wise, they had been named correctly so their count would remain at two. They both grunted affirmatively. "And lock the hutch door?" She knew Mini, though fine with the rabbits when the children were around, might not be so gentle when left alone with them.

Jimmy's Home

They repeated their unintelligible utterances. As Liz turned to leave, Charie said from beneath her covers, "Anyway, Pam is goosky."
 Closing the door, she heard, "So are you."

CHAPTER EIGHT

A late-afternoon sunbeam ricocheted off the beveled edge of the huge mirror over her dresser and splashed a tiny rainbow on her white Martha Washington bedspread; it extended to the floor to leave a bright spot on the dark tea-rose carpeting. Liz let her robe drop to the floor and quickly donned her underwear, letting her beige camisole fall gracefully into place, then hung her robe on a hook in the closet.

She had mentally organized and then reorganized her schedule while driving Charie and Jimmy to her mother's house: Stop at the store for milk and bread, return the children's books to the library and grab some more, pick up Rand's suit and shirts from the cleaners', then hurry home to finish packing and get showered and dressed.

Mom would take the two younger children out for supper, to the playground, and then for ice cream before returning them home. She had readily agreed to keep house for the four children to enable Rand and Liz to accept a weekend invitation from Nick's folks in Boston where they had moved. Jeff and Pam had full weekend schedules, so Mom would be chauffeur, cook, babysitter, and referee.

"Be sure to put Mini in the basement when no one's home, or he'll drive the neighbors nuts with his barking. And don't forget to feed the rabbits," Liz had reminded them on the way to Gran's. She would leave a list of general reminders for all of them and underline the instructions referring to the dog. He was a perpetual problem if left loose in the house when the family was away. The dog warden had already been there for numerous visits.

"We won't forget to feed the rabbits, Mom. Besides, Gran will do it for us if we forget. Maybe she'll play Flinch with us."

"I'd rather play Muggins," Jimmy's inevitable reply had come. Sometimes he was so predictable.

"Play one of each," Liz intervened before the argument started. "Or two of each. Or however many you can get Gran to play. You can have a weekend tournament."

"Mommy, I wish we didn't have to share our gran with all the others," Charie revealed her secret thoughts, referring to her many cousins, Gran's other grandchildren.

"Well, *your* children will probably have to share *me* someday. Jeff will maybe have a family, and Pammy—"

"Jeffy be a *father?*" she squeaked, then giggled. "No," she continued seriously, "he's too crabby. But Mommy," she went on before Liz could explain that he might grow up; he just might. "We'll all be living with you when we get married. We won't move out, we'll all move in!"

"Oh. I see." Liz smiled and pinched her arm playfully. "Well, would you like for all of *us*—Uncle Robert, Uncle Steve, Uncle Andrew, Aunt Cassie and their families, and *us*—all to move in with Gran?"

"If she had a gi'antic house."

"And Gran could do all the cooking," Jimmy offered.

Scowling at him, Charie exclaimed, "That wouldn't be fair! But we'd help her make cookies, like we always do."

"And for that many people you'd get sick of making cookies."

"Never!" exclaimed Charlotte.

"And you two could do all the dishes," Liz declared.

They laughed at the absurdity of it. "We'd never *ever* get to play Flinch," Charie responded sadly. "Or Muggins," she added with an eye toward Jimmy.

"I think it's nicer for everyone to have their own house and get to visit each other."

Liz quickly dropped the children off at her mother's and soon became lost in thought. She was absorbed in the weekend ahead, thinking that what she and Rand needed was a weekend by themselves. Though she was looking forward to the trip—it would be stimulating—she knew, with their increasingly strained relationship, they needed time alone to work out the tangle. Their time away from home could have been a boon, and yet she really didn't want to be alone with him. The end result was inevitable calamity.

The weekend schedule would include sightseeing, dining out, and long, late-night conversations. They always returned stimulated and animated, but exhausted, especially Rand, since she usually crashed on the return trip and slept the three-plus hours away.

During the past few weeks she and Rand had acted more like business acquaintances than husband and wife. Where were they headed? Their hurts never had time to heal before they were reopened by fresh assaults.

She heard the clunk of the faucet as Rand turned the shower off, and she quickly brushed her damp hair.

Why do I always hurt so? she silently questioned the stranger in the mirror. *I must try to put on a good act this weekend or we'll* become outcasts from our own circle. In an offhand manner, she wondered if she really cared about that. *Why was everything going stale? We need an extended vacation,* she thought; *maybe a trip to the Caribbean. Somewhere delightful, exciting, and romantic. Oh, maybe a cruise to Alaska!*

That wasn't the answer. Her soul had been restored so many times, only to shrivel up again five minutes after they returned home. One aggravation after another.

Take Nina Schmidt, for example. They used to be good friends, but no more. A one-woman show, Liz decided, who didn't know the meaning of teamwork. Liz wished Rand wasn't such good friends with Norm.

And then there was Mitzy, with her ritzy house, her hair in that perfect French braid, and her fancy airs. Ritzy Mitzy, that's it. *Those two have nothing in common with each other except for their vexation of me.* They were the most *un*matched friends Liz could think of. *They bug me!*

She didn't know why Nina and Mitzy were shutting her out, but there was a widening gap between them. Nina obviously liked to surround herself with those she considered key people, those who met her requirements and made her look good. Liz had this fantasy: One day she would become famous. Then Nina would see who got snubbed. She didn't like herself when she had thoughts like that. Liz gave herself a mental shake. I mustn't get myself into a stew. *Forget what's past*, she admonished herself, *and go on from here.* But Liz had protected herself, erected a wall around herself that allowed her to get out at will and no one to get in unless she permitted them to. With every hurt the wall became higher and thicker and tougher.

Liz's biggest exasperations, though, were here at home: the widening rift with Jeff, his occasional brush with the law, the strain between Rand and herself, Pam's adolescent changes, Charie's sauciness, and of course, Jimmy.

Always Jimmy.

Liz ran her hands over her neck and shoulders to remove the excess bath powder, and suddenly stopped in mid-motion as she became aware of Rand, his freshly showered body draped in a towel, watching her. Their glances met in the mirror, and she was unable to look away. Finally Liz deliberately broke the spell and began dabbing cream onto her cheeks. Rand took his shorts and socks from the drawer and put them on the bed.

The last of the sun's rays were filtering into the room. Then he was standing behind her. Their eyes met again in the mirror. This time she was powerless to break the spell. *He's hurting too,* she thought, and it was a new thought.

She stiffened as he took her shoulders and gently turned her to face him, his towel falling to the floor.

As his arms encircled her, she took in a breath that resembled a sob, and he drew her close in a strong embrace. Holding her silently until she was quiet again, he kissed her with a tender urgency. She began to push him away, then clung to him and responded eagerly.

"Rand, we'll be late," she mumbled into his neck.

"Sometimes I like to be late." He drew her to the bed.

Oh, God, how I love him! her heart pulsated.

As she relaxed quietly in his arms, she reiterated, *Oh, how I love him!* She wanted this to last, this comfortable closeness. If only a union could take place, an emotional conception that would cause Jimmy to become theirs. *Please, God, if You're there, make it happen. Make it happen soon!*

As they sped along the interstate toward Boston, Rand held her hand and occasionally pressured it, sometimes reaching a hand to caress her shoulder. *Everything's okay,* she thought—*for the moment.*

The weekend was a nonstop whirl of events: seafood dinner late Friday evening at a coastal inn; a late, lingering Saturday breakfast; candlepin bowling Saturday afternoon; dinner theater that evening; and long late-night chats, including disagreements on politics, world affairs, medical advances, home improvements, and kids. Provocative to the point of aggravation, it was stimulating.

The best part, she concluded, was being comfortable again with Rand.

Feeling better about herself than she had in a long time, Liz's main anxiety as she stretched out between the sheets of her own bed on Sunday night was the visit from Jimmy's caseworker the next day.

Monday afternoon came, despite Liz's desire to stop the clock, and with it Sylvia Bradshaw from the agency. She and Jimmy enjoyed a tea party while they visited, then she sent him off to play with Charlotte.

"I've never seen that boy so happy, Mrs. Markham."

"I know. We have our moments though . . ."

"And who doesn't? Your home has been good for him."

"You're not ready to take him away, Mrs. Bradshaw . . . ?" Yet Liz knew the answer.

"Are you ready to sign the papers?" Sylvia asked.

"Yes." Liz swallowed hard, but the lump in her throat stayed. "But Rand isn't."

"We may be able to postpone it another month, but I'm in a spot, you know. Children this age are not so easy to place for adoption, so we simply cannot continue to delay. There's a double catch since you are not official foster parents."

"I know that. I'm working on that, too."

"You *should* be, you know."

"Should be working on it? I am . . ."

"Foster parents, I mean. You're naturals. Potential adoptive parents, once they've made a choice and the paperwork is completed, won't adhere to unexplained delays. So even if you were to keep him as a foster child—"

"I appreciate any postponement you can give us. Jimmy belongs here. I just need a little more time to convince Rand."

"Adoption of Jimmy by you two—by this family—would be the most favorable route."

"You know that's my sincerest wish. I want it with all that's in me."

Sylvia Bradshaw rose to go. "Get to work on it, lady. I'll see you in a month."

Liz breathed in deeply and exhaled with an audible puff. What a relief! A month's reprieve! That meant Jimmy would be with them for a very minimum of two months. She couldn't have hoped for such a miracle. Maybe that was all the time she'd need.

Rand's office was undergoing renovations. He sighed as the hammers and power saws continued irregularly and relentlessly, blotting out any coherency to his thoughts. He was situated in a temporary office next to his own, but it afforded little relief from the chaos.

Jimmy's Home

Maybe he'd go home. No, that was just as bad. And what would it be like when they began the construction project there? Wasn't there *any* place he could find peace and quiet? He once found it at home, but that appeared to be a thing of the past. If only Liz would ease up. He could take the *routine* jungle life, but not this domestic zoo home had become. He longed for normalcy.

Rand rang for his secretary and when she came in, he said, "I'm going to lunch. Join me and we'll try to find a quiet spot to go over the Sherman account." He tapped the papers he was about to put into his attaché case.

Bebe nodded, looking at her watch. Two o'clock. "I ate, but I'll have coffee. A bit hard to concentrate here," she agreed. "Give me five, okay?"

As they exited the elevator, Rand took her arm and steered her toward his car. He knew just the place where the back room for overflow crowds would be almost empty at this hour, and reasonably quiet. He had nothing but business on his mind, and visibly, so did she; but he couldn't help sensing her pleasure, it was almost tangible. They were seated in the almost empty room. He ordered a Reuben sandwich and a salad, and they both ordered coffee.

At four o'clock, after two coffee refills, Rand collected the papers before them, put them back into the attaché case Liz had given him for his birthday, a Moroccan leather one with polished brass initial plates just beneath the handle, and stood. "The carpenters should be leaving about the time we get back to the office. If you're not in too big a hurry, I'd like to stay and put the finishing touches on this."

"Just one phone call, and it's arranged," she responded with lowered lids, then raised her huge dark eyes to his before rising from her chair. Without a doubt, she was pleased. He wondered what she was about to cancel or postpone.

Nancy J. Sell

By six o'clock the office was empty except for Rand and his secretary. The silence was delightful; even the piped-in music had been turned off. He had called Liz and told her not to wait for dinner, that he'd eat when he got home, no matter what time. Bebe pulled her chair close to his, and he spread the lists, contracts, and riders in front of them, subconsciously and unobtrusively leaning leftward away from her. It didn't seem to matter; her arm was always touching his, sometimes pressing against him as she busied herself with the papers. When she left to make fresh coffee, Rand stood and gazed out the window.

This temporary office afforded a grand view of the Hudson River, and he followed its line from the Tappan Zee Bridge in Tarrytown all the way down to New York City. The river wasn't always visible past Yonkers where he had grown up. It went on to the George Washington Bridge that spanned the Hudson from Manhattan to Fort Lee, New Jersey. It was a lovely evening: The river water sparkled with drifting diamonds in the lateness of the afternoon sun, and the Empire State Building was clearly visible. Planes taking off from LaGuardia Airport shimmered briefly as they banked away from the City and circled out toward the Atlantic Ocean. An occasional plane took off from White Plains, another from Newark.

"Beautiful, isn't it?" Bebe stood beside him, too close. Her arm had contacted his before she spoke, and Rand looked down at her without answering. She put her arms around him, nestling her face into his neck, and, taking hold of her arms to free himself from her embrace, Rand instead found himself holding her to him. She responded by pressing herself against him and reaching for his lips with her own, her warm breath and delicate perfume intoxicating him.

Rand, hungry for such attention, knowing it was inappropriate, responded to her touch, to her kiss. Suddenly he removed her arms and shoved her away, paling when he did as intense pain tore through his chest. He dropped into his leather chair, put his head down on his desk, and closed his eyes, taking no notice of Bebe's panicked expression. Before he realized what she was doing, she had dialed 911. "No!" His voice was strained but commanding, and he put his finger on the phone button.

"Yes!" she countermanded. "You need help!" In his distressed state he wondered if it was a guilt response. Did she believe she had caused his pain, that he was having a heart attack because of her? Whatever the onset of her reaction, he had no doubt she was genuinely concerned. He wished he was alone.

"I just need to rest. I'll be all right." His voice was weak. "Why don't you go home."

"And leave you here like this? Not a chance."

"I'll be fine," he snapped, with a lame attempt at forcefulness. "I'm going too, after I lie down for a few minutes."

"Then I'll wait." Bebe busied herself for longer than necessary, straightening his desk, then her own, while Rand stretched out on the sofa in his office. A sharp knock on the door startled both of them.

"Police," came an official-sounding voice through the door. "Oh, God," Rand whispered, groaning the intense, sincere prayer. He knew that dialing 911 automatically locked your location into the switchboard at the police station. Bebe's call must have connected. "Wait," he motioned to Bebe while he headed for the men's room, then she opened the locked office door.

"We did have a problem . . . Someone was sick and we thought he'd need an ambulance, but he's fine now. Left for home right after we started to call you." Rand heard her through the door. She lied so expertly.

"Are you alone?" the policeman inquired. She nodded. *Are you okay?* he mouthed the words. Again she nodded, and seeing the twinkle in her eyes, he was assured. "I'll see you to your car," he offered, more as an order, as Bebe picked up her purse.

"I'll be fine," she assured him, then, to defer suspicion, she conceded. "Why, is something wrong?"

He spoke to his partner on his portable radio, then escorted her to her car and waited until she drove away.

Reentering the lobby, the two officers noticed the elevator had climbed back to the floor they had just left. As they watched, it began its descent back to the lobby. Rand exited, looking startled as he caught sight of the policemen, regained his composure, and continued toward the glass doors of the lobby. They blocked his way, their manner friendly but firm.

"Excuse me," he said determinedly, as if they would of course oblige. "I'd like to go to my car . . ."

"Just a few questions."

They released him after Rand convinced them that he *had* been ill, that his secretary hadn't been aware of his problem and consequently had been alarmed, dialing 911.

"And that's why you have lipstick on your neck . . ."

Rand made another stop in the men's room before continuing on his way. Taking the long way home and driving through town, he drove into Parkland Park, pulled his car into a spot overlooking the beach, got as comfortable as he could, and closed his eyes. He knew he looked terrible. He really should see a doctor, but the pain was not constant, and so consequently it was easy to forget when it wasn't there. He would have had it checked before this, but until now it never became severe, never became unbearable. That was a good sign, wasn't it? If the problem were serious, he'd be dead by now, wouldn't he? This had been the most unpleasant bout, and it hadn't been intolerable, just frightening. He'd have to lay off all that caffeine, of course; that's what had caused the attack.

If it gets any worse, he promised himself, *I'll go have it checked out. No,* he resolved, *I won't wait. I won't put it off any longer.*

"You look awful, Rand," were Liz's first words when he entered the kitchen from the garage. "Are you sick?"

"I'll be fine."

"I'd better call Dr. Rinaldi."

"Just let me take a shower and go to bed. No, no supper. Maybe a cup of bouillon, a couple of crackers . . ."

It seemed like hours later when Rand awakened to feel Liz gently crawling into bed beside him. He was still. He didn't want to talk, and he was certain she thought he was asleep.

"Musk," she whispered almost inaudibly.

"Hmm?" he responded unintentionally.

"Musk. That's what you smelled like when you came home."

"Bebe."

"I know."

"She gets too close. I keep trying to move away—"

"Oh. Really. Do you like her?"

"Sure."

"Oh."

"She's a nice person."

"Oh."

"Let me go to sleep."

"Sure." She moved to a comfortable position.

"She has a magnetism—"

"That's obvious. She has a real pull on you."

"Go to sleep."

"You're not denying it."

"No, I'm not denying it," he spoke softly, but there was an edge to his voice. "I like the girl. The woman. How can I work with a secretary I don't like?"

"Just remember to whom you belong."

"How can I forget?" Rand spoke tartly. "Just remember, I love you." Then he softly mumbled, *"But I can't remember why."*

"Just remember, you're mine," Liz spoke. "I hurt more than you can imagine, but I do love you too."

"Yeah. Right."

Rand remained in bed the next day, and then, feeling better than he had in a long time, he promptly forgot his resolve to see his doctor.

CHAPTER NINE

Exposing raw nerves and touching off flares of heated emotions, torrid temperatures had been plaguing New England residents for over a month before the official commencement of summer. Liz was tense, and appearing calm and controlled to her world required a genius of acting ability.

Her relationship with her husband was neither hot nor cold, neither peaceful nor tumultuous, with only now and then a rare period of closeness. The beginning of summer, however unbearably unpleasant the heat and humidity were, marked the beginning of a new armistice, and Liz would take heart.

The arrival of this unstructured season with its long, busy unscheduled days, seemingly without a genuine spring, was simultaneous with the last day of school, its conclusion having been delayed by too many snow cancellations during the winter. Charie was ecstatic: Her playtime with Jimmy would be virtually endless, and now she would answer questions regarding her school status by saying, "Yes, I go to school. Well, I do in September. *And* I get to ride on the school bus! And I'm going to learn to read, then I get to write on the big white board!"

"Oh Mommy," she exclaimed on the final day when Jimmy arrived home at noon, "Bearsh and Tedley want to celebrate with a party!"

So Liz fixed peanut butter and jelly sandwiches, cookies, and a teapot full of juice for them to have at the little red and yellow picnic table in the yard under the linden tree. "Don't let Tedley and Bearsh eat too much," she warned. "It's very hard to cure a teddy bear tummy ache!"

"Don't worry," Jimmy allayed her fears, "I'll help Tedley eat his, and Charie can help Bearsh."

Liz tried to ignore them as they gargled with red punch. She almost intervened when Charie began to choke on hers, but she recovered nicely.

"You don't know how to gargle, Charie," Jimmy boasted.

"He'll eat his own," Charie retorted saucily, ignoring his remark and returning to the previous one. To Liz she said, "They're all excited about going on vacation with us, Mom. They like the beach, and they promised they'd behave if we let them come."

"They won't want to be left behind, I know, but there's lots to think about before vacation." Liz knew how the children felt about vacation; she too was anticipating their camping trip to the North Carolina shore in July. *We need a change of direction, some different scenery, some new people in our lives.* "The Neighborly Picnic is coming up in two weeks . . ."

"I know!" Charie shrieked. "I been telling Jimmy all 'bout that too! It's so fun. 'Course I was pretty little last time, but I 'member it. 'Member when Daddy hit that home run and forgot to touch first base?"

"That's because Mr. Schmidt moved the base from under his foot just before Daddy's foot touched it."

Charie squealed at the recollection.

The Neighborly Picnic was *the* big event of the year, barring none but Christmas. Their short right-of-way with six houses ended in a cul-de-sac, and all six families participated, plus three families who had moved away but made a point of returning each summer whenever possible. They claimed nothing short of disaster would keep them from attending the annual picnic. Usually they stayed as guests in the homes where they had once lived.

The entire afternoon of the last day of school turned into a celebration. Liz filled the small plastic frog pool for the children, and they splashed and carried on for hours. She waded in it herself after they solemnly promised *no splashing*. Several times they had to chase Mini who wanted to sit in the middle, which left no room for anyone else.

"We need one of those big round pools, Mom," Charie advised. "One that comes up to here." She put her hand on top of her head.

While Liz prepared dinner she tried to anticipate Rand's temperamental climate. His emotional barometer was so affected by his meetings with J. Randolph Markham Sr., and today there was a scheduled meeting. She wondered why a father who had deserted his children deserved any acknowledgment.

"We're told to honor our parents," her mom had admonished her. "The Bible doesn't say *if they deserve honor.*"

"No more pencils, no more books," Rand sang later as he took his seat at the dinner table. His mood was light and playful, not withdrawn, gruff as it usually was when he had met with his father. Liz, perplexed, questioned him with a look. "He didn't show up," Rand shrugged.

Charie laughed. "Oh, Daddy, you're so funny!"

"Hilarious," Jeff drawled.

"Yes, and hats off, boys. Don't make me tell you at every meal," Rand reminded them. "Well, what I want this minute is to see some report cards. And that may not be so funny. Right now! Or will they spoil my appetite?" He paused. "Well, no one's hurrying to get them, so maybe we'd better wait." His eyes twinkled. They decided it would be best for all if they waited until after the meal.

"Daddy," Charlotte offered, disappointed that she didn't have a report card to display, "I know how to spell Mom."

"Really?"

"W-O-W."

"Bring me a paper and pencil," Rand ordered amid chuckles from the crew. "Now write it for me." Charie laboriously wrote the letters with a red crayon she had found on the floor. "Now turn the paper over. What does it say now?"

"I don't know."

"Make the M sound: Mmmm."

"M-O-M. Mom," she giggled.

"W-O-W spells *wow.*"

Turning the paper up and down, she chanted, "Mom! Wow! You're an upside down wow, Mom!"

All but Jeff enjoyed the joke.

"Now, time for report cards," Rand stated.

"Not bad," he said, laying two report cards out on the table. "In fact, excellent. We're proud of you, making honors again, Pam. You did fine too, Jim. Where's yours, Jeff?"

"I don't know."

"Why?"

"Why what?"

"Why don't you know where it is?"

"It's in my room. I'll look for it later."

Liz, Rand, and Jeff were still at the table. Pam was talking on the phone; Charie and Jimmy were hard at work cleaning up the mess they had made in the yard before the promised rainstorm started.

Liz was anxious to get supper cleared away before Mr. Paris, the architect, arrived to go over plans for the addition. The delays for the start of the work were endless, and the original plan was to have it finished by fall. If it wasn't a delay by the architect, it was the contractor, or a lack of unity between herself and Rand. Sometimes she felt like they would never get started.

"Now, if you don't mind," Rand contended, looking directly at Jeff. "The architect will be here any minute and I'll be busy until bedtime. I'd like to see it now."

"It doesn't matter anyway."

"Why would you think something as important as a report card doesn't matter? It always matters to me, and ideally it would matter to you also."

"Because I'm not going back."

"Not going back? Where?"

"Stop playing games, Dad."

"Games, Jeff?"

"You know what I mean. To school. I'm quitting."

"Sure. After you finish high school, and hopefully four years of college."

"I'm quitting, Dad. I've decided. I don't need to waste all those years in high school and college when I could be out making some bucks instead of spending them."

"There's not a thing to discuss . . ."

"I know," he returned defensively. "End of discussion."

"Says who?"

"I've decided. It's my life. I'm quitting."

"You don't belong to a breed of quitters—" Rand went on without skipping a beat. He was making every effort not to blow a fuse. "Jeff," he began again calmly, "we can't let you do something you'll always regret. It's your life, I agree—"

"Then let me run it."

"—but you're not in it alone. You have no choice about this."

"I've *made* my choice! Why shouldn't I decide for myself?" he snarled angrily. "I'm an adult, so stop treating me like a kid."

"You are a kid."

"I do a man's work, and you know it!"

Rand nodded. "Yes, you do. You're a good worker, Jeff, and you make me proud."

"Then don't try to run my life."

Rand took a piece of paper from his pocket and began jotting notes. "Okay, let's say you do decide for yourself. You'd need this much—I mean a *minimum* of this much—to rent an apartment. They aren't cheap around here." He wrote down a figure. "How much for food, Liz? Twenty-five a week? Let's say a hundred a month, and that's a modest amount unless you're going to live on canned spaghetti and hot dogs. Now, how about electricity . . ."

Angry, Jeff shoved his chair back and stood. His face was red and his neck veins stood out. His eyes flashed.

"Sit down." Rand spoke with a quiet firmness that left no room for debate. Liz's heart warmed to him for his patience, though she feared for Jeff. Rand never flinched, not outwardly, under Jeff's intimidation. "Or better still, go get your report card. *Now*," he added determinedly when Jeff did not move. "We'll wait right here."

Jeff rose slowly, each movement deliberate. When he returned, he defiantly flipped the card in question onto the table in front of Rand and turned to go.

His father addressed his back. "Now sit down. *Sit down*," he repeated to Jeff's back where he had stopped, motionless.

Jeff plopped in his chair and slouched. Liz moved to her husband's side and scanned the report card. "I'd say that's not too bad,"

Rand commented. "Not your best, but certainly not disgraceful. Don't you agree, Liz?"

"Why didn't you want to show us, Jeff?" his mother asked.

He didn't answer, and Rand spoke again, tapping the card on the table and finally breaking the long silence. "Answer your mother."

"Because it doesn't matter. I'm quitting."

"Negative." Rand paused; the silence was awkward. Then Rand spoke again. "Your mother's car has a tire that's going flat. How about taking care of it right now." It was a statement rather than a question.

Jeff inhaled as if preparing to explode, looked daggers at his father, then left the room.

"Mom, Dad!" Pam entered, almost colliding with her brother. "Wow! What's eating him?" She continued without a breath. *"Please* let me get my hair cut! Persie does a wonderful job, and it would be so much cooler for the summer."

Persie Smyth, fresh from Great Britain, was a new friend of Pam's, and she was creating discord between Pam and Millicent.

"Honey, your hair's so pretty we hate to see it cut." Liz and Rand had privately discussed Pam's plea. "But if it's what you really want—"

"Oh, it is!" she interrupted. "It is, Mom. Thank you, thank you, thank you!"

"Hold on a minute! If it's what you really want, I was about to say, I'll make an appointment for you at Antoine's."

"Oh, Mom," Pam sighed disappointedly. "Forget it. I'll keep it long and suffer."

Rand cut in. "What's the big deal with having Persie do it? Has she been to some highfalutin' hairdressing school?"

"No, Daddy, but she knows a lot about hair, and she has a fantastic way of doing it. Forget it," she reiterated.

"Okay. Forget it," he agreed. "Suffer."

The next day everything seemed to go wrong. Liz had a headache, and that compounded the negatives. She thought she might suggest, if she knew to whom to address it, making June 23 National Murphy's Law Day.

Charie and Jimmy had selected, one by one, an assortment of doughnuts at the bakery. Jimmy said, "Jeff likes blueberry with white sugar on top."

"No, he doesn't, Jimmy. He likes white custard ones with chocolate icing."

Jimmy spoke authoritatively. "No, he doesn't, Charie. He likes—"

"He likes both," Liz stated emphatically. "Get him one of each. *Two* of each."

"He likes white custard ones with chocolate icing the best," Charie reiterated, unruffled, determined to have the final say. "Pammy likes chocolate cream with white icing. Daddy likes plain coffee cake ones. I like cinnamon apple . . ."

Finally they had a dozen in the box, and the three customers behind them sighed with relief.

"I'll keep them on the front seat," Liz told them when they returned to the car.

"We won't open them, Mom. Let us keep them back here so we can take care of them."

Liz gave in. They were almost home when she realized the box was open. "You are very disobedient children!"

"We're just smelling them."

Nancy J. Sell

As Liz was getting the bundles from the back of the car, Charie shrieked, "Jimmy, stop pushing!" With that, she fell backward in an awkward sprawl on top of the doughnuts.

"Good job, kids," Liz uttered in disgust. "Now who do you think will want to eat them?"

Charie was in tears. "Me and Jimmy'll eat them," she sobbed.

"Not me," he pronounced firmly. "Not after your behind was on them."

"It's just my jeans, Jimmy," she yelled. "Not my behind!"

Liz's headache was worsening by the minute. "Forget it. For*get* it!" she snapped.

After taking two aspirin and putting the purchases away, she called up the stairs for Pam. "Time to set the table, Pam." Silence. "Pam?" She had almost reached Pam's door when she heard . . . was it crying? "Pam?" she repeated through the door. The noise stopped. Liz opened the door a crack and peeked in. Her daughter's body was stretched full length on the bed, her head buried beneath the pillow.

She questioned again, "Pam?" as she tried to take the pillow, but two hands gripped it and held it firmly in place. Suddenly the sobbing started again, and a red-faced, swollen-eyed Pam—at least Liz thought it was Pam—the clothes looked like Pam's—emerged from under the pillow. Liz stared in horror.

"*Pam!*" Where her daughter once had soft smooth sleek hair, she now had what looked like short sticks protruding from her head.

"Oh, Mommy, what am I going to do?" she cried. "I should have listened to you! I *should* have! Oh, Mommy . . ." her voice trailed off in a wail.

Liz let her cry while she tried to sort out her thoughts. Finally she said, "What *are* you going to do? I can hardly have any sympathy for you, Pam. You deliberately disobeyed. Now you're going to have to suffer for it. You said you would suffer. Now you will. And I think we will, too. We're going to have to look at you."

"O-o-oh," she moaned, putting her head back under the pillow. "Don't say that!" From her tunnel, she said, "Mommy, you have to bring my supper up here. *Please!*"

Again Liz was silent, weighing the situation. "Sorry, honey," she spoke softly, firmly. "You're going to have to face the family sooner or later. Might as well get it over with."

"I can't! I can't!"

"Pam, what do you think you're going to do all summer? What about all the special events coming up? The Neighborly Picnic next week, vacation . . ."

"I've already thought of that. I don't know," she wailed. "At least on vacation no one will know me. Only Ellie . . ." Pam referred to a girlfriend she had met at the beach two years before.

Liz left her to her misery and tried to deal with her own. What next? Were Charlotte and Jimmy going to have these almost-daily crises in their lives when they became teenagers? She wasn't sure she could survive.

Pam arrived at the dinner table a half hour later with a scarf on her head. As she sat down, Jeff yanked it off questioning, "What's this?"

Pam grabbed it and replaced it. There was a stunned silence. Liz wished she had warned them.

Finally Jeff spoke. "Holy Cow!" He then lapsed into peals of laughter. Rand was silent, and when Liz looked at him, he sat, elbow on the table, his face in his hand. He was angry, but was he laughing? *No, Rand, don't laugh. I will fall apart.*

"Persie cut your hair funny," Charie said.

"I don't like it either," Jimmy added.

Pam shrieked, "Who asked you?"

Charie continued, "I'll never let her cut mine. I'll have Antione do mine."

Pam spouted, "Shut up! *Shut! Up!* Everybody, shut *up!*" Liz tried not to look at her, for she didn't know whether to laugh or cry. Periodically Jeff burst out in a fresh gale of laughter, and when Liz gave him a wilting look, he held his sides, then pointed at Pam, as if the cause of his mirth required an explanation. Pam refused to look at anyone, and fresh tears erupted at regular intervals.

"Cool it, Jeff," Rand managed to speak, his voice painfully controlled.

The meal continued in a subdued manner with an undercurrent of expectancy and an occasional snicker. Now and then, when Liz stole a look at Jeff, she saw his shoulders shake, his head bowed as he chewed. Jimmy and Charie followed her glance, and Jimmy said, "Mommy, Jeffy's still laughing."

Liz almost excused Pam from the table but remembered her earlier statement, *You're going to have to face the family sooner or later.* Pam was paying a high price for her disobedience, and this no doubt would be the easy part. Liz had no intention of letting her stay in her room all summer.

"You may leave the table now, Pam," she finally conceded. Pam took her untouched plate of food and left.

"Heavens to Betsy," Jeff chirped when Liz brought dessert, "who sat on the doughnuts?"

"Just eat them, Jeff." *I can't take any more,* Liz thought. *In a few minutes we'll all be laughing hysterically, and Pam will never forgive us.*

"Charie sat on them in the car."

"I did not, Jimmy! Well, if I did, you pushed me!" Charie was appalled to think she might take full blame.

"Yuk! I'm not eating any. They probably got 'doo' on 'em." Jeff elaborately dropped his on his plate, shook his fingers in his water glass, and wiped them on his napkin.

"We will either eat the doughnuts," Liz stated firmly, "or we will not eat the doughnuts. But we will not discuss their condition any further." She hoped that was the end of it.

Pam spent the evening in her room, to her mother's relief. Liz would deal with that situation later, she decided as she pushed the remaining eight doughnuts one by one into the garbage disposal, though she saw no solution in sight.

The two youngest were in constant disagreement, and Liz was getting sick of trying to settle their disputes. She went into the family room where Rand was working at his desk, turned his swivel chair to face her, and sat on his lap. He tossed his pen onto the checkbook and pulled her close.

"She did it on her own, huh?" He referred to Pam's awful haircut as he welcomed his intruder. "She'll never forget this day, will she?"

"This *summer!* It's going to take a long time for her to look presentable again. There's not even enough left in some spots for Antoine to give her a pixie cut."

"You're not going to make her go public!"

"She has to, Randy! We can't let her stay in the house all summer."

"Maybe I should take her to Tony, the barber."

"There they go again," Liz said, referring to Charlotte and Jimmy and getting up from his lap. "They're like Kilkenny cats."

"Come back and talk to me. Shut the door so you can't hear them."

She did and returned to his lap. "She won't go to your barber! What do you want to talk about? We don't always want to discuss the same subjects."

"There's nothing left to discuss on one of them."

"Yes, there is."

"No, there's not. And you know it."

"There is."

"If we have to, we have to. But you must realize I have nothing further to add." His mouth was set in a firm, disapproving line. She started to get up, but he pulled her down.

"We have to. I don't want to talk about it, Randy, but Mrs. Bradshaw is coming on Monday . . ."

"I'd like to know just what else needs to be discussed." He sighed in frustration. "Liz, I don't know where this is going to end."

"Rand, I beg of you. Don't do this to me, to us."

"I'm not doing *any*thing to *us*," he reasoned. "And you're doing it to you."

She refused to acknowledge what might be his indisputable observation. "You know as well as I do that this is Jimmy's home. He is a part of this family, and we cannot send him away."

He gently pushed her from his lap and sat her down in his chair. She sensed his silent mood. He stood before her with his feet planted firmly, his arms crossed, his eyes unblinking. He unfolded his arms, placed his hands on the arms of the chair, and leaned into her face. "Liz, Jimmy is a visitor here, and I will repeat it if you don't understand." He enunciated each word clearly. *"Liz, Jimmy is a visitor here,"* he repeated, *"and I will repeat it if you don't understand. Liz, Jimmy is a visitor here* . . . He is not part of this family now, nor will he ever be. We are doing a terrific thing for him, giving him these months to get straightened out. But understand this: When Mrs. Bradshaw finds a home for him to be adopted into, or another foster home, or if his mother reclaims him, he will leave here. If he is not very far away, I will have no objections to you—to any of us—seeing him, or to him coming to visit. For a day. A week. A month. I will enjoy that, too. But he is not going to be a permanent member of this family. *Ever!*"

Liz shrank into the chair to avoid his face so close to hers. She said meekly, "We have to sign papers . . ."

Frustrated, he spoke in a falsetto, "What for, if she's trying to place him? *What—ever—for?*"

"To keep him until . . . His mother hasn't signed his release yet . . . So he can't be adopted . . ."

"GOOD!" He was beginning to shout in his frustration. "Maybe she'll come to her senses soon and learn how to be a real mother to him."

"Oh, Randy—"

"You're always biting off more than I can chew, Liz." His voice shook and his face reddened. His gaze, locked with hers, was unflinching, unblinking.

She matched him for volume, and returned his look boldly. "Randy, he's like an orphan." Then she thought of something she had heard her mother say. "And you know what the Good Book says about orphans . . ."

"Keep it up," he spoke softly, gritting his teeth, "and you're going to have a whole houseful!" Shutting the door firmly behind him, he left the house.

Stunned, she sat motionless until she realized the house was getting dark, and she had not checked on the children for a long time.

Jimmy and Charlotte were still arguing. "Mommy, Jimmy says the doughnuts bein' sat on was my fault 'cause I opened the box to smell them."

"Forget the doughnuts," she almost shouted. "Please! I do not want them mentioned again!"

"You always try to get me in trouble, Charie!"

"You liar!"

Aghast, he shouted, "Charie! *God won't love you anymore if you say that!*" His eyes were large round circles, his mouth agape.

With that pronouncement of Heavenly Judgment, Charie erupted into tears, into heartbroken, convulsive sobs. Liz picked her up and sat in the chair where she had been sitting when Rand left. There was no consolation she could offer to stem the tide. Jimmy's declaration of divine wrath had left Charie undone.

Holding her daughter close in an attempt to protect her, Liz spoke in a controlled voice, sternly and firmly. "Jimmy, get your jammies on and get into bed."

"You didn't read to us."

"And I'm not going to. I want you in bed with the lights out in five minutes."

His eyes narrowed, and he met her gaze defiantly. "You don't love me."

Perforce. She remained calm. "I don't know how to make you understand this, Jimmy, but I have had a headache all day. I'm not about to discuss whether or not I love you. I am not about to discuss *anything*, for that matter. GO—TO—BED!"

He ran from the room. Liz could hear him splashing in the bathroom sink and playing with toys in the bedroom for a long time, but she didn't care. Thunder began to roll in the distance, and still Charie sobbed.

"'Jesus loves me this I know,'" Liz tried to sing the old Sunday School song which seemed appropriate for this moment, but she couldn't recall the words, so she found herself extemporizing. "'When I do the things I should.'" Her mother sang it often with the children, and although Liz wasn't sure about the theology of it, she saw it as a harmless gimmick. That crutch again. If it calmed Charie, it had some use. Charie put a hand to her mother's cheek and sobbed, but she showed evidence of relaxing and going to sleep. Liz continued to hum the old tune, thankful for God's unconditional love. *Yes, Jesus does love me,* she thought.

The storm broke furiously, the lightning illuminating the room for a few seconds before each unearthly crash of thunder. Where was Rand? Didn't he know she needed him? He was always letting her down lately. Where *was* he?

"Mom?" Pam's voice caused Liz to jump. "Don't you want Jimmy in bed?"

"Immediately. I sent him what seems like hours ago. Before you go, Pam, turn on a little light."

"The power's off."

"Then light a candle, please. You'll find one under the kitchen sink. There's a flashlight there, too."

Charie breathed deeply, trembling involuntarily as she did. Even in her sleep she shuddered.

"Mom, I came to tell you I'm sorry."

"I know you are, Pam. I hope you are."

"I am. For real."

"You should be. You have every reason to be. I'd prefer not to discuss it now. I've a bad headache."

"Still? I'll get some aspirin."

Liz swallowed them with the water Pam brought and hoped they would not make her vomit.

"Where's Dad?"

"He—had to go out."

"Do you want me to put Charie in her bed?"

"No. Thank you." Liz was curt.

"Goodnight, Mom. And I really am sorry."

"Goodnight, Pam."

She disappeared.

"Pam?"

She returned to the doorway, and in the flickering candlelight she looked grotesque.

"Would you be sorry if your haircut had turned out beautiful?"

Liz thought she heard a groan of agony and a muffled sob as her elder daughter went down the dark hall to the stairs.

"Me and Charie forgot to feed the rabbits." Jimmy, still clothed, stood before her.

"They'll be fine."

"I'm going to feed them."

"You're not."

"Yes, I am."

Liz knew he would brave the storm, if only to challenge her. "Go to bed," she stated slowly. "Go directly to bed. Do not stop to go. Do not even open your mouth to utter another sound. *GO—TO—BED!*" She wanted to scream to enforce her words but knew the ineffectiveness of that method and thought better of it when Charie stirred. Jimmy disappeared into the hall. "And if you so much as set a little toe outside the house, I might lock the door and leave you on the other side of it for the rest of the night!" she called after him.

The kitchen door slammed, and Liz groaned. He was calling her bluff; all was quiet. She decided he had really gone to bed.

Liz avoided staring at the candle for she feared being hypnotized by it. How long had she been sitting here? Had she slept? She looked at the digital clock on Rand's desk just before the candle flickered out: one forty-eight. Almost two o'clock. Where was Rand? *Oh, God, where is he?*

The storm had passed, and moonlight was creating unfamiliar scary shadows in the room when she heard the overhead door of the garage. She listened to Rand wander in each area of the house where he thought she might be. The bedroom first, the living room. Finally he was in the doorway of the family room, and he stood silhouetted against a dim light that had come on with the return of power.

Kneeling on the floor, Rand rested his head against the numbing arm that held Charie. Liz, resisting an impulse to push him away, permitted his touch. Neither spoke. Charie gave another deep sob, and Rand stood, lifted her gently, silently. Charie whimpered. "It's okay, baby. Daddy's got you." She tightened her arms around his neck as he carried her to her bed. Liz hadn't moved, and when he returned, he took her hands and drew her to her feet; he held her firmly against him, then steered her in the direction of their bedroom. She followed him slowly as he drew her by the hand, turning off all the lights that had been left on when the power failed, turning on ones they needed to see the way.

Liz lay close to her husband, wide-eyed and sleepless. How she trembled at these silent times when she could not read his thoughts and he would not reveal them. He seemed gentle, loving, unaccusing; she knew it was not that he wouldn't talk, he just didn't. If she made advances toward him, he would respond eagerly—without a word. But she did not. She lay voiceless and motionless.

"Randy," she had informed him once when they had been married just a short time, "you're so quiet. I don't like it. Sometimes I think you're mad at me."

"Sometimes I am," he had replied with a grin.

"Hey, that works both ways! But I don't clam up!"

"I just need to think, and I can't do it with a lot of people yammering. I get quiet, you get noisy. I guess we kind of balance each other out."

That was true. She had learned to wait it out patiently, without pressuring him.

When it was time to speak again, what would they say?

"Rand?" He did not answer, and she knew he was asleep.

CHAPTER TEN

Liz finally drifted off into a light sleep and was awake again at first light of dawn. Careful not to disturb her husband, she got up and slipped into jeans and sweatshirt. She sat in the same rocker where she had spent last evening, and when the coffee was ready, she poured herself a cup and took it to the deck. She watched a robin pulling a fat worm from the dewy turf and hoped her early birds, Charie and Jimmy, would not follow their early bird patterns this morning. Not only did she want to be alone, she couldn't face a continuation of last night's fracas. She swallowed two more aspirin, then nibbled on crackers to settle her stomach.

So cool and still, she thought. What a beautiful morning. Moisture hung tangibly in the air, and she wiped a path along the metal rail with her finger.

I'm so tired. How can I get through this day?

But though she was tired, there was something special about these early morning hours; what was it? She breathed deeply of the freshness and caught a whiff of salt air coming off Long Island Sound four miles to the east. She watched a hummingbird drink at the feeder before a woodpecker chased him away.

Jimmy's Home

Finishing her coffee, she decided she wasn't ready to meet the troops. She'd let them manage for themselves. Getting her purse from the quiet bedroom where Rand was still asleep with his head under the pillow, Liz shut the door soundlessly behind her, then backed the car out of the driveway and took off, secretly, almost as if she had to hurry before anyone discovered she was gone and foiled her plan. She had safely escaped.

Liz wished she *had* a plan. She would drive on the Parkway for several miles—that was always pretty, and also relaxing at this hour. But before she turned onto the entrance ramp, she smelled the salt water again and continued driving to the beach. She knew her way: She had spent her childhood here. She stayed in the car, windows open, so she could enjoy the wonderfully familiar smell.

She moved to a bench and sat for a while, then removed her shoes and walked along the sand at the water's edge. It was damp and cold and delicious. The beach was deserted. A few cars were parked here and there that no doubt belonged to the fishermen she could see out on the jetty.

She picked up some pretty shells as she walked, then watched a pair of horseshoe crabs in the water. It was mating season. When she was small she thought one was a mommy carrying her baby on her back as she coasted along the rough bottom. But her dad had said, no, it was a mommy and daddy. Later she had figured the rest out for herself.

A slow-moving motorboat entered the channel and continued to the open water of the Sound. Liz clamored over the rough rocks of the breakwater until she reached the far end where she could look straight down into the gently lapping water, then sat. The breeze stirred her hair and she shivered, although she was not cold. There was something special about this time of day. Liz knew what it was, and she wished she could be a child again.

Nancy J. Sell

She and her dear dad had tiptoed through the darkness that would soon know the glow of a warm, early-summer sun. What on earth was better than going fishing with Dad? The chilly stillness, the first smell of salty sea air and mud flats, the early-morning haze that chased away the last regret at having to leave a warm, comfortable bed, that's what made it special. The silent expanse was theirs. Watching for telltale squirt holes at low tide, they had dug soft-shelled clams for bait, saving the best ones for a supper of steamers at home. Mom would have broth and drawn butter ready for rinsing and dipping. And of course they had to get some hard-shells, or quahogs, for Mom to make chowder. If they found enough cherrystones and littlenecks, they would enjoy them on the half-shell, or Mom might even thrill them with an ever-favorite clambake!

Hands already sore from the morning's work would begin to blister under the pull of the oars. Then would come the thrill of that first healthy tug on the line. Though they had joked about who was the best fisherman, she knew Dad was hoping she would catch the first flounder. And then there would be an occasional eel that struck without a nibble, and could hopelessly tangle the line if it wasn't kept taut. That prize would be skinned and cleaned, then rolled in flour and fried in Mom's special way, as the choicest delicacy.

They always picked the right day, Liz reflected, for even on those rare occasions when the catch was slim, the day was full: The idleness was brimming with unspoken thoughts, the mind a blotter to soak up cherished moments for another day.

Memory is tricky, she thought, and events often hold a fonder place there than in reality, but she knew in this, memory was playing no trick.

"Daddy's pet," that's what she was called, but she didn't care. She liked to be with him, to do the things he did. Besides, it was quite an honor being the special one of so many. Seven was not a large number, considering that her parents had fallen five short of their desired goal. Consequently she never felt like an unwanted child. She wasn't really his pet anyway; she simply enjoyed the simple things of life he enjoyed.

Her dad had a marvelous strength, was never afraid of anything that she could recall. Not even death. His only fear in that, he always affirmed, was that Mom would go first, and he claimed he could not live without her.

I can't live without Rand, Liz sighed. *But living with him isn't so great either. Why is he so pigheaded? Whatever is the matter with him? Surely he could see the value, both to them and to Jimmy, of making him a permanent part of their lives.*

Liz wished she had brought some coffee along as she let her mind drift off into comforting once-upon-a-times. They were so much easier to face than present realities. Her existence was polluted, just as some rivers and beaches. The best was still there for the taking, but alas, out of reach by virtue of local restrictions. The best of her life seemed to be slipping out of her reach also. When had she given up on God? Where was He in her life? She knew He was there, that she had just moved away from Him.

Her thoughts drifted first to her husband, then to each of the children as she thought about each one's big problems of the moment. Rand was stubborn and impossible. Jeff was obnoxious. Charie was precocious. Jimmy was, well . . . a challenge. And Pam was . . . "God, please help me," she prayed.

Liz allowed herself to go back to last evening, to Pam's debacle. She wanted to be close to her children without smothering them, to be able to laugh with them, with their friends, and to remain a safety zone for them. How was she to handle this one?

With a start, she realized she did have a plan, one that had formed instantly. She arose, reluctant to leave the tranquility of her hideaway, but promised herself a return visit. Carefully, she climbed back over the breakwater and perceived that the beach was beginning to hum with activity. Glancing at her watch, she decided that, by the time she reached the Connecticut Region Mall, the stores would be open. She wasn't dressed for shopping, but she was passable, and hopefully she'd meet no one she knew. Especially Nina . . .

Liz detected an obvious feeling of relief when she reached home. Charie and Jimmy were at the table eating cold cereal; Pam sat, not eating. She sulked. Jeff was out already, taking care of his Saturday yard jobs.

"Mommy," Jimmy cooed, "we were so worried about you!"

"Jimmy and I fixed breakfast for Pammy and Daddy!" Charie exclaimed. Apparently their spat of the night before had been forgotten. Bearsh and Tedley sat at the table with bowls of dry cereal before them. Sneakers sat under the table awaiting anything that dropped from the table to the floor. Charie was her usual bubbly self; Pam was unusually quiet; she wore a scarf around her head, washer-woman style. Rand said nothing. He didn't raise his eyes from the newspaper he was reading except for a brief glance at his wife.

Liz stood behind Pam and lifted her headpiece. Pam grabbed for it, but Liz opened her bag from the mall, took out the item she had purchased, and plopped it, helter-skelter, on Pam's head.

Pam looked at her in disbelief. "Mommy!" she exclaimed, running to the mirror in the front hall to adjust and inspect it.

"Oh, Mommy! You saved my life! Oh, Mom!" she squealed with sparkles in her eyes and a flush of color rising to her cheeks, "I love you so much!" she gasped. "You're so—so *wonderful!*"

"Pammy, you look like you again," Charie spoke admiringly.

Jimmy added, "You're not goosky anymore!"

"Mom, you're a *wow!* You really, really are!" exclaimed Pam.

Charie shrieked delightedly, "I knew she was!"

"You are *the* best, *the* most beautiful, *the* most special mom in Glendale! In Connecticut! In the USA! In the *world! Ever!*"

"She's magic," Jimmy chimed in.

"Oh, right, Jim. A magician if I ever saw one!" Pam continued her song of praise.

Liz poured herself a fresh cup of coffee. As she sat down with it, Rand stood, picked up his dirty dishes, put them in the dishwasher, and proceeded to the basement.

"Sit," she told Jimmy as he rose to follow Rand. "Finish your cereal first. And take your hat off." He obeyed, but picked up his bowl and drank what was left.

"Is your headache better, Mom?"

"Better," Liz replied. "Not all better. You look lovely, Pam. The style and color are perfect."

"I don't know how to thank you." *Was that a tear in her eye?* "I'll never forget this."

"I do hope not, honey. I surely do hope not."

"Wow, Mom!" Pam rested her head on her mother's shoulder. She was exuberant and was soon off to change her plans for the day.

As Liz put the milk and juice in the fridge, she heard Jimmy stomping up the cellar stairs. "Mommy, Daddy wants you down in the basement. He says if you're not busy." Jimmy held up a coin. "He gave me a quarter to sweep the deck. He said it would take at least a half hour to do a good job. *And* if I do a good job, I get another quarter!"

Unhurried, Liz finished filling the dishwasher, started it, put the food away, and washed the counters and table. Then she went to the basement to find Rand, all alone and doing nothing, sitting on his workbench. Unblinking, his eyes had followed her down the stairs and to where she stopped, out of his reach. He was holding her broken kaleidoscope. Putting it down, he opened his arms to her. She moved toward him, then hesitantly entered their circle. He pulled her close to him.

"We can't go on this way, Liz." His voice was soft and brought a lump to her throat.

"I know," she stated positively, wanting to move from his embrace. She gave no indication of compromise.

"I made a decision last night, and if you agree to it, I'm hoping we can get on with our lives."

She tried to still the pounding in her chest.

"I'll make a deal with you." He moved her away from him so they were facing each other, his hands on her arms. "This is the deal: I'll sign those confounded papers and Jimmy can stay here until he's adopted. I know your ultimate plan was for him to stay forever, but that's *not* part of the deal. It's this: that you will agree to let go at the end of that time with no more hassles, no more schemes, no more scenes, and that it will never be necessary to discuss this again." Her eyes were moist as their glances held, and she blinked several times to check tears. "This is against my better judgment, but to keep peace and try to make you happy—though I doubt it will in the long run—I'm offering what I feel is a compromise."

Liz was *not* happy. This was not what she wanted. She didn't want to bargain over the welfare of a child. She wanted Rand to want him, too, but she had no other immediate option than to agree to his offer. At least it was one step her way. Maybe Mrs. Bradshaw would postpone Jimmy's adoption forever. And Liz would be safe as long as his mother didn't sign his release. Then he'd be off to college, maybe get married. But he'd still be theirs.

"I'm not sure I can meet all the qualifications." Her hurt and resentment weren't well disguised, she knew, but she didn't much care.

"Try?"

She nodded. She was still hurting, still resentful, and as he drew her close and kissed her, she made it obvious.

He pretended not to notice the pressure of her hands against his chest. "I like what you did for Pam. I like you," Rand continued. Holding her face in his hands, he looked into her eyes and kissed her firmly on the lips.

She turned abruptly, leaving him on the workbench, and headed for the stairs.

CHAPTER ELEVEN

The morning of the Neighborly Picnic dawned clear and beautiful. The lingering pink glow of a lovely sunrise sprinkled the surroundings with a star-spangled wrapper. Liz was up early to frost her cake and finish making potato salad. There was much to do in the yard, but she wouldn't awaken anyone else yet as last night's heavy downpour had left everything soaked. So much rain lately! But today was wonderful. A day for new hope. New thoughts. New perspectives. But maybe it was a cover-up kind of day, a day to ignore troubles.

Given a few hours, most everything would be dry and ready for the eleven o'clock starting time. The out-of-towners were to arrive by then, sharp. "Don't be late," they had been warned repeatedly. "We won't," they had just as frequently responded. And barring any unexpected trauma, they wouldn't be. This was the day they had awaited, since last year's celebration.

Liz and Wendy Morrison were in charge of food; they had planned the menu and made assignments carefully. Nina and Norman Schmidt, along with Bud and Ceil Trent, were taking care of games. Liz was glad she hadn't been stuck with that this year.

Planning the food was her thing, not organizing and supervising games. She loved the challenge of planning a tasty, tempting menu, or preparing exotic mouth-watering dishes.

"*Wonderful* meal," Norman told her as he helped himself to another piece of her special carrot cake. "The best food we've had yet at one of these shindigs." He caught the withering look his wife sent his way: She had planned last year's menu. "You gourmet gals sure do try to improve on perfection every year," he added lamely.

"Okay, everybody," Rand yelled, "let's get the cleanup crew in operation. It's time to get over to the Dudleys' pool!" Liz helped store leftovers for later consumption, then drifted away from the food tables.

Many of the planned games took place in and around the pool. Excitement remained at a high level until the last event was over. Then at five o'clock they convened at the vacant lot for the scheduled softball game. This year the Markhams and Dudleys were playing against the Schmidts and Morrisons, vacant positions being filled by anyone who wanted to play.

"Oh, the field is still wet!" Liz cried in dismay over the two puddles, one in right field and the other behind the pitcher's mound.

"More's the fun," Rand told her, pinching her chin and shaking it. "Don't be a fussmusser."

At the end of the fifth, the Markhams and Dudleys were leading by two runs. Rand and Jeff were at their best, and Liz cheered the loudest when Rand cleared the puddle in right field to catch Norman's fly ball.

When they took the field at the bottom of the seventh, the Markhams and Dudleys were exuberant. "C'mon," Rand shouted, "we've just about got this thing wrapped up!" They had scored two more runs to their opponent's one. "Liz, you cover second. I'll stay at first. Jimmy and Charie work together pretty good in right field, so we'll switch Pam to shortstop." Jimmy and Charie counted as one player. They spent more time chasing each other and looking for crawling critters in the grass than they did playing right field, but Rand did an adequate job of backing them up.

Jimmy was making like a robot with his high pinging voice, and Charie stood, hands on hips, scolding. "Jimmy, you're not going to be able to chase the ball if you don't turn around and watch!" Both of them had their backs to the action. A fly ball was headed Jimmy's way while Jimmy gazed in wonder at the surroundings, and no matter the frantic warnings, he was oblivious. "Heads up, Jimmy!" Rand shouted. Rand was after the ball with all the speed he could muster and caught it three feet from Jimmy's head, doing a pirouette around the boy to avoid falling on top of him. He was rewarded with whistles and cheers.

Jeff was the new pitcher, and he was good. And he knew it. "C'mon, you guys! Just two more outs, that's all we need!" Occasionally, when Pam wasn't looking, he stomped in the mud puddle to spray her with muddy water.

"Jeff," Pam strained through clenched teeth, "you're getting my hair wet!"

"Behave, Jeff," his mother admonished, concerned for Pam and her wig.

"Jeff," Pam declared again, a few minutes later, and somewhat louder, "you're getting my hair wet!" The third time she told the world, "*Jeff!*" Shaking her head and stomping her feet, she shouted, "*You're getting my hair wet!*"

"Jeffrey Randolph Markham the Third," his mother chided again, more forcefully, "*Behave!*"

Bill Morrison popped a low fly ball just over Jeff's head. Jeff jumped for it but missed, and Pam almost had it in her glove when she tripped: Down she went with a thud. As if precisely planned, off flew the hairpiece, which fell, dead center, in the middle of the puddle.

Liz was momentarily speechless. The crowd went wild with laughter. Liz looked at Rand helplessly, and he was on his knees, painfully and hysterically doubled over. She looked to Jeff for help, but he was rolling on the ground, and he was not the only one.

But Pam sat with her head between her knees, both arms covering her head, trying desperately to get out of sight. Liz knew she was crying.

She started toward her daughter and caught a flash of movement out of the corner of her eye. Jimmy beat her to Pam's side and cradled her in his little arms. The laughter continued as the spectators fought to control themselves, and in the attempt were racked with fresh spasms. Liz felt a secondary impulse to laugh, too. She could barely control herself—but she was torn apart with feeling for Pam. Taking the wig out of the puddle, she shook it out. It dripped with mud and water. Liz squeezed it out, then shook it again.

"It's okay, Pam," Jimmy consoled. "Don't cry, Pammy. Please, don't cry!" Charie was on her other side, holding and patting Pam's arm.

Liz knelt before her daughter and shook her gently. "Pam. Pammy, are you listening to me? Pam," she said again, "laugh at yourself. You've got to laugh at yourself, honey. It's the easiest way out." Pam did not move. "Here, honey, put it back on, mud and all. And laugh. Laugh. *Laugh, honey!*"

By the time they got the wig back in place, Pam's tears were beginning to mix with embarrassed laughter, and Liz joined in. Jimmy jumped up and down as if he had created a miracle. Rand, still out of control, pulled his daughter to her feet, and put his arms around her. He gave her a bear hug, then kissed her soundly on both cheeks. Pressing his nose to hers, he puckered big and kissed the top of her head. He lifted the wig, turned it slightly, and replaced it on her head.

The remainder of the game was chaos as fresh bouts of hysteria continued to erupt. Norm, playing first base, picked up the base just as Pam, who had singled to center, attempted to put her foot on it. She chased him until he allowed her to catch him, then ceremoniously handed her the base.

The Markhams and Dudleys won, sixteen to twelve.

After a supper of leftovers and a new supply of food that seemed to magically appear, they lingered around the pool for hours, chatting while the younger ones fell asleep in their parents' arms. Torches burned brightly, drawing moths while chasing away mosquitoes, and creating a restful quieting effect. Most of the young people had drifted off, some to watch television or play games, some to talk in their own little groups. Occasionally the pool was occupied by a swimmer or two, and Pam, wigless now, was never dry. The steady hum of chatter from the small groups around the pool was laced with an occasional outburst of merriment or friendly disagreement.

Mitzy and Nina pulled deck chairs to where Liz sat with Jimmy asleep on her lap. Her mother held Charlotte. "*I* want to sit with *my* Gran," Charie had stated sleepily, with the right emphasis for Jimmy's benefit.

Rand and Norman, engaged in an animated discussion regarding foreign policy or lack of it, and the upcoming election, were one by one joined by the other men in the party. "Change the subject, you guys," Liz called. Truth was, she wanted in on the discussion, but she hoped the talk didn't develop into an argument. It would spoil the day.

Suddenly all attention was focused on a figure in the doorway, and not until he spoke did Liz realize it was Jeff. He was clad in swim trunks, a scarf for a bra, and Pam's wig. Half of his feet were stuffed into women's sandals. He promenaded around the pool, beauty contest fashion, reveling in the laughter and attention it brought him. *He's such a ham,* his mother mused. *He loves the spotlight!*

Jeff stopped near the group of men and spoke in a high voice, "Randolph, may I speak with you for a moment?" His father, at the time the willing stooge, moved to his side in an exaggerated response, and Jeff continued, "Privately, please." Rand's arm was around Jeff's shoulders and their heads were close together in conference as they moved away. Liz was thankful they were having fun together.

In an apparent unexpected move, Rand butted his son with his hip and sent Jeff sprawling into the pool. Floundering and sputtering as he surfaced, he shouted in his high voice, "Help! Help! Help me *please*. You're getting my hair wet!" Jeff's anticipated response from the onlookers was forthcoming. They howled with laughter.

"I'll help!" shouted Pam, landing next to him and pushing him under. "You rat!"

Jeff surfaced with much sputtering and spitting. They both choked with laughter. "Race you," he challenged his sister.

When it was quiet again, Liz watched the water continue to hump and recede long after the occasional swimmers had left. Occasionally her eyes met Rand's, and in the dim light of the gas torches, her cheeks flushed as her heart stirred in her breast. Being with him was almost pleasant again.

Let's go home, she tried to communicate to him. *It's been a great day, but let's not beat it to death.*

Finally she saw him ease away from the group, disappear into the house, and come out with Jeff.

"I think it's time to get these two in bed," Rand said. He took Charlotte from his mother-in-law, and Jeff lifted Jimmy from his mother's lap, then hauled him over his shoulder, in a fireman's carry.

"Liz, I'll stay with the children if you want to visit for a while," her mother offered.

"We're about ready to pack it in," Nina spoke through a yawn, stretching her arms and flexing her ankles gracefully. "What a super day it's been."

"I haven't laughed so hard since I don't know when," Mitzy yawned, too. "It's been fun. Pam's a good sport."

Rand helped Liz and her mother get the children to bed, then headed back to his poolside discussion with the men.

The next Monday Liz took Pam to Antoine's. "What am I to do with this?" he asked incredulously in his Italian accent. "You think I am a magician, Liz'bet? A boy cut. That is the only solution. *Then* cover it with the wig. Next time," he turned to Pam as he spoke, "next time you come to Antoine for a new hairstyle."

She nodded submissively.

CHAPTER TWELVE

Rand set his newspaper aside as Charie and Jimmy climbed onto his lap with a book. The privilege of reading to them tonight was his. His enthusiasm was forced, though; Liz was altering his new trousers for him to wear the next day.

Pam sat cross-legged on the floor, giving herself a manicure. Liz had made her get a tray for her equipment. "I won't spill anything," she grumbled, but she had complied.

Jeff, who had reverted to his miserable self, was at his friend Shep's, where the two of them were working on the minibike.

"Daddy, Mini took Potter out of his cage today!"

"What! No way, Charie."

"But he *did*, Daddy. Right, Mommy?"

"Well, in all fairness to Mini, we *think* he did. But who left the hutch door open?" All eyes turned to Charie. "Mini just wanted to play," Liz continued. "Poor Potter was so scared, he almost had a coronary."

"What does he need a crown for?"

"What? Oh, you mean coronation. No. A coronary is a heart attack."

"One of these days you're going to lose them for good," Rand warned, picking up the book to read about snakes, lizards, and dinosaurs. "Hey, this one looks like a polliwog, doesn't it?" He tried to sound enthusiastic, but Liz knew he'd rather be reading the newspaper, or watching a ball game.

"What's a polliwog?" Jimmy asked, laughing. "There's a Polly Widdle in my class."

"It's a baby frog, dummy," Charie responded, exasperated. "Polly Widdle is a *girl*. She goes to Gran's church."

"I know her too, Charie. You're the dummy."

Rand ignored them. "Someday I'll take you to a pond to find some. They're tiny creatures that look like this," he indicated the picture to Jimmy. "When they hatch out of the eggs, they're very tiny—"

"How tiny?" Jimmy interrupted.

"Oh, probably smaller than a pin head."

Liz held up a straight pin for him to see.

"Then they grow and grow until they're about this size," he held up his thumb and forefinger in demonstration. "Pretty soon they start to grow legs. As their legs get bigger, their tails get shorter. Before you know it, they're able to hop. They've become frogs!"

"Oh," Jimmy drawled disgustedly, "you mean tadpoles!"

"Daddy," Pam giggled, "*no* one knows what polliwogs are!"

"Well, Pam, I like that!" he exclaimed. "*I* do, and I'm someone. At least I used to be!"

Liz ignored his subtle jab, then winked at her daughter. "They do now, Pam!"

"Someday we'll go find some, or even some eggs so you can watch them hatch and grow," Rand said softly.

"Tomorrow?" Jimmy asked excitedly.

"Too late. They're all half-frogs by now. Maybe next spring," he started and caught himself, glancing at Liz and turning quickly back to the book. Next spring might not be an option. He knew it, but she didn't seem to. Bad slip. "Let's read about newts."

Spring will be fine, Rand. Jimmy will still be here if I have anything to do with it. We can wait until next spring to go polliwogging. Or frog-egging. And the spring after that. And the spring after that . . .

The phone rang and no one stirred. Pam was waving pink-tipped fingers in the air, and Rand had turned up the volume of the lizard saga. Liz bundled up her sewing, dumped it into her chair, and answered the phone.

"Shall we meet you at the hospital?" she spoke to the unfamiliar voice at the other end. Her voice was steady but her heart was racing. After placing the receiver back in its cradle, she gave a brief explanation to Rand who had abruptly halted in mid-sentence, to Pam who sat motionless, her fingers still pointing to the ceiling, and to Charlotte and Jimmy. "That was Shep's father. Jeff had an accident with his minibike and is on his way to the emergency room in the ambulance."

"Pam, finish reading to Charie and Jimmy."

"Can't we all go, Mom?" Pam pleaded.

"No, honey. I don't know how long we'll be. Fix them a treat, and get them tucked in. Brush your teeth good," she turned to them. They were staring at her, wide-eyed. "Don't worry, okay?"

But Liz was worried.

Rand had already backed the car out of the garage as Liz reached the front door.

"Mom, call. *Please* call soon," Pam cried. "And tell Jeff I love him—even if he *is* a jerk."

Each was mentally preoccupied with possibilities of what might be awaiting them at the hospital. "I wonder if the thing is worth selling now," Liz said, making an effort to ease her own tension; she had to say something.

"I wonder what condition *Jeff* is in. What—? What was he doing with it on the other side of town?"

"His friend, Shep, was helping him."

"Sounds like a dog."

"Shepherd. Bartholomew Shepherd, Jr. You know, those Shepherds—"

"Oh, that Shep." Rand was anxious.

"They got someone to truck it over to Shep's, got it running, and took it for a test drive."

"But they know they can't drive it on the road. I know that. They know that. But you know Jeff." Rand was angry at his son's irresponsible behavior.

They sped over the Parkway, then took the back roads to the hospital.

A pleasant dark-haired nurse with an unpronounceable name told them that Jeff was in an examining room, and that the doctor would fill them in on their son's condition. Meanwhile, would one of them sign forms permitting necessary medical procedures, please? Rand signed.

"Dr. Rinaldi is in the house," they were informed by the efficient, attractive nurse. "Just call me Mo," she told them, covering her name tag on her white lapel with her hand. "You can't pronounce it. Everyone calls me Mo," she smiled.

"Thanks, Mo. Where's Jeff? How is he?"

"The doctor will be with you shortly. But I hear he'll be okay. Try to relax and not worry, okay? And please have a seat in the waiting room until Dr. Rinaldi is ready to talk to you. Meanwhile," she continued, indicating a man in uniform who had just appeared from another area, "this gentleman would like a word with you."

The policeman was one whose name and face were familiar to the Markhams. Glendale was not a large town. He often visited the elementary school classrooms to talk with kids about drugs and safety.

He led them to a lounge. "I know how anxious you are about your son, so I'll be brief. He is in trouble, and as you know, this is not the first time. The bike, of course, is an unregistered vehicle and not allowed on the street. Also, he's unlicensed. Not only that, but in his effort to evade me, he collided with a woman pulling away from the curb on the wrong side of the street."

"Doesn't that make her at fault?" Liz questioned.

"Certainly. But that doesn't make Jeff innocent. Frankly," he turned to Rand as if he would be more likely to understand, "I'd keep anything with wheels away from that boy. Maybe even ground him and take away some significant privileges."

"Maybe we won't have to," Liz murmured.

Don't. Rand spoke with his eyes.

"I hear your boy Jeff," he said as he looked at papers he held, "will be okay. I'll stop at your house later to discuss this further and fill out my report, if you don't mind."

After he left, neither Liz nor Rand was able to sit still. Finally, Dr. Rinaldi appeared, shook hands with Rand, and greeted Liz with a nod and a squeeze of the shoulder.

"Let's have it all at once," Rand urged in his blunt way.

"Lacerations of the face above the right eye, right arm and right leg requiring about ten staples total. Fractured right arm. Contusions. Concussion. Extensive bruises. Possible cracked vertebrae, which cannot be fully evaluated until we see the X-rays in a few minutes. He's lucky."

"Yeah, right," mumbled Rand.

"Is he in pain? When can we see him?"

He answered the second question first. "Right away. Then he'll be moved to the floor as soon as his room assignment is completed. Yes," he met their questioning looks, "he'll be admitted, of course."

"Of course. We know that. He'll be in a cast . . . ?"

The doctor nodded. "But we can't cast until some of the swelling goes down. We've immobilized his arm for the present." They walked in the direction of the examining room, and the doctor continued, "He *is* in pain, of course, but I've ordered medication. He should be feeling a little more comfortable about now."

Jeff lay on an examining table with X-ray equipment pushed to one side. He raised his left arm slightly to greet them, but otherwise remained motionless.

"We're here, Jeff," his father assured. *We're here for you,* his words meant.

"Hi, honey." Liz took his uninjured hand, thinking of the many times she had held his hand to cross the street, to help him up after a fall, or just to squeeze. It had been a long time since she had held his hand, and he let her.

He closed his eyes and his face twisted in pain. They sensed that it was not wholly from his injuries: Jeff would give anything to have them not know about his foolish and illegal activities, but he wanted and needed their support. The confirmation of that was a tear that slid down his face toward his ear. Was his pain purely physical? Emotional? Liz had only to lean forward slightly to see a matching tear from his other eye. While her son was being admitted to the orthopedic unit, Elizabeth Markham went to a small private waiting room, dialed 9 for an outside line as directed, and called their home number.

"Oh, Mom, I'm glad to hear your voice!" was Pam's response.

"How's everything there?"

"How's *Jeff?* I—we were so nervous."

"He's being admitted..."

"Jimmy and Charie haven't been able to go to sleep, even though I let them have a campout in Jimmy's room."

"They're still awake?"

"Awake! You gotta be kiddin'! They think Jeff's dead and you're not telling us." Pam paused and took a deep breath.

"He's very much alive."

Pam exhaled audibly. "Whew! I'm relieved! You don't know what it was like waiting, Mom!"

"Yes, I do, honey. I've had some anxious waits in my lifetime, so I know how you've been feeling. I called as soon as I could." Liz explained Jeff's injuries briefly but thoroughly. "He has a broken arm, many bumps and bruises... Tell Jimmy and Charie that Jeff is sleeping now, so they can go to sleep, too. Yes, sure," she answered Pam's next inquiry, "he was in a lot of pain, but the doctor ordered medication for him. Right now he's not feeling much of anything. As soon as we're not needed here, we'll be home."

"Oh, good! I was afraid you'd be staying all night."

"That's not necessary. Oh, Pam," she caught her daughter before the connection was broken, "please call Gran and tell her. No, don't. She might be too anxious. Maybe you'd better wait until morning."

"I already did."

"Did you? That's fine then. But call her back, honey. Just try to sound matter-of-fact and don't alarm her. I'm sure she is praying."

"Mom, she's here. She's hemming Dad's pants. She's praying too."

"Oh, bless her. And I should've known she'd come."

"And you should've known she'd finish Dad's pants." Pam grinned at her grandmother and blew her a kiss. Gran patted her cheek where the kiss landed.

"Jeff *will* be okay, so there's no cause for distress."

"Mom, did you tell him what I said? If not, leave out the last part, okay? I mean, he really is a jerk, but this isn't the time to tell him."

"Too late, Pam."

"You didn't!"

"But I don't think he heard the whole thing. He was fading fast from the pain meds the nurse gave him."

"You're kidding, Mom . . ."

"I'm kidding, Pam. Actually, I forgot to give him your message. You can tell him yourself. Bye, sweetie."

Jeff spent two days in the hospital and they were difficult ones for all concerned. Much of the time he was irritable or quiet, sometimes both. After his discharge and follow-up visits to Dr. Rinaldi and the orthopedist, Jeff was cleared for physical therapy twice a week. His discomfort eased, and with each treatment, his flexibility returned. He cursed the cast on his right arm.

Liz and Rand considered canceling their vacation plans and communicated that possibility to the children. Their disappointment was apparent, their acceptance nonexistent.

"We couldn't *stand* not to go to the beach, Daddy!"

"Mommy, let's just leave Jeffy home. He *wants* to stay home anyway!"

"We *have* to go!"

"Ellie will be a wreck if I don't get there." Pam referred to a girlfriend from Syracuse she had met there two years before. They had carried on as online pals, and they had been able to spend a few days together the summer before.

The week before their scheduled departure, Rand said he was glad they hadn't canceled their reservations. Going to the shore wasn't out of the question after all, he decided, since Jeff was showing so much continued improvement. The doctor confirmed his ability to travel, his court date wasn't for another month, and so Liz picked up where she had left off in packing the camper.

They were looking forward to this trip. All but Jeff. He had decided months before that he would stay home to work, but his accident changed those plans: He could not do adequate yard work with his arm immobilized. He promptly subcontracted his jobs and became the supervisor, using his old bike for transportation.

Daily physical therapy sessions were now reduced to two per week. All were thankful when Dr. Rinaldi had informed them that Jeff's X-rays revealed no cracked vertebrae. He was bruised and sore, but had no breaks. "But be sure to keep up with your exercises. Do them at home. Keep mobile. The rest of your body took a beating, too, you know," the doctor had said.

Jeff was soon back on his skateboard, with Jimmy the avid admirer and student.

"You're not as bright as I thought you were, Jeff." Rand, clearly irritated, had arrived home from work in time to witness the demonstration. "Put that thing away."

"Doc told me to stay flexible. Besides, I'm just showing Jimmy how to pop a wheelie."

"And how to break your other arm, right? And your can besides."

"Wouldn't think of it, Dad. I'm planning on keeping this with me wherever my fate leads me." He hesitated to say what he meant: on the North Carolina vacation, if he couldn't get out of going.

"Cool it, Jeff. Stop. Now. Put that thing away!"

Rand addressed Liz as she turned on the gas grill for steaks. "Do you know what your son's doing out in the driveway?"

She turned to greet him with a peck on the lips. "He's your son, too, and whatever it is, I hope you told him to stop."

"Skateboarding. That's what. He's out of his mind," Rand stated as he disappeared into the house. "Crazy. Cracked. Loony. Of course I told him to stop."

"Sounds like something you would have done at his age," she called after him.

"Thanks for your support," he returned as he headed for the newspaper. *Yes, you're right, Liz,* he thought. *Exactly what I would have done.*

So Jeff was unable to continue his summer jobs, and Rand insisted he accompany them to the North Carolina shore with no skateboard. "We'll find a therapist for you down there."

"Just let me stay home," he argued. "Shep is helping me with my jobs, and he can take me for therapy. I'm getting to know the people there, and they know what I'm supposed to do. Besides, *I* know the exercises I'm supposed to do. I don't need them any more anyway. *I don't want to go.*"

"Shep is one of the reasons we plan for you to go. You've turned into a stranger since you started running with him." Rand was the picture of patience, which indicated the outcome was set.

"Don't talk about my friends that way."

"Even if it's the truth?"

"Why don't you say it? You just don't like him."

"Because I'd be telling a lie, Jeff. I like him. He's fun. Intelligent. Friendly. A real wit. I just don't trust him with someone I care about, namely my son. What I don't like, Jeff, is the effect he's having on you."

"I don't want to go." His teeth were clenched and he glared through narrowed eyelids.

"Humor us. We may not have our complete family with us for many more summer vacations. And we're just sentimental enough to think it's something special."

"Then let Shep come with us. He can sleep with me in the pup tent."

"There's no room in the car."

"Then let me stay home."

"Only if we take your skateboard with us."

"Take it."

"No. We'll take you. You know I was kidding."

And round and round it went. But Jeff knew he was doomed to spending two weeks at the North Carolina shore. *Someday*, he thought, *I'll do as I please.*

CHAPTER THIRTEEN

The storm had raged for three days. A sou'wester, it was called, and it was about to expire. The oceanside camping complex was almost deserted, for one by one the weary, water-logged campers had pulled out. Tenters, the most vulnerable of all, had been the first to go; some of them had gone home, some of them to motels, but everyone's camping equipment was in shambles. Long-awaited summer vacations had now become disasters.

"Three days," the old-timer had told Rand when they heard the first storm warnings, "then it will stop. Not 'fore then."

The longest three days of our lives, Liz thought wearily. *Three days out of our first week! How many more games of Flinch and Muggins can I stand? Of Tic-Tac-Toe?* She had even agreed to play several other board games. *I wish Mom was here.* She was thankful Uncle Robert had not taught the children how to play 150 Pick-Up!

"I wish Gran was here," Charlotte sighed as she slowly, painstakingly dealt the cards, all 150 of them.

"C'mon, Charie," Jimmy chided. "You're taking too long."

"So what's your hurry? There's no place to go anyway, Jimmy," she whined. "I'm takin' my time and doin' it right."

"But I don't like just sittin' here watchin' *you.*"

"Then close your eyes."

"You mean take a nap. Good." He put his head down on his folded arms.

Liz again wished Gran were here, too. She'd had about all the games, and all of these two little ones, she could tolerate. "Come on, Rand. You too, Pam. Play a game with us." Pam joined them out of sheer boredom, but Rand shook his head. He was sitting on a bunk perusing some business papers, desperately trying to ignore the bickering over the game and his own discomfort.

Liz had the lowest card, so she started the game, ever conscious of the incessant rain on the hard plastic roof of the camper. They had listened to it night and day for almost three days. The tall trees that lined the rows of campsites offered little protection from the deluge. Now its intensity had spent itself to a light pattering, and the wind had diminished to a gusty whine. The tension inside the camper was at the snapping point. Liz did her best to keep her mouth shut.

Dampness had crept into every corner of their existence and permeated their clothing, bedding, and food. Even the game cards felt moist. Liz's hair, usually softly curling around her face, wilted, then frizzed, from the humidity; she had convinced herself she didn't care. Someday it would matter again, but not now.

"We could pretend we're in Noah Zark," Jimmy had offered at one point; no one had laughed.

Jeff came in after hanging his slicker on a hook under the tarp. *What a long face,* Liz thought. *I almost wish he had stayed out.* She quickly chided herself. *No, I don't. Of course I don't.*

"Want to play?" Jimmy asked.

"Get serious!" he snarled, turning on the radio.

"Turn it down, Jeff," his father said. Jeff pretended he did not hear by putting his ear to the speaker. Liz tapped him on the knee, and when he looked at her, she pointed to Rand. Jeff turned down the volume and looked at his father with feigned innocence. "I said, 'Turn it down,'" Rand repeated.

Jeff turned it off.

"Turn it back on and see if you can get a weather report."

"Make up your mind. Anyway, I don't need to. I can give you one. Tomorrow sunny, hot and humid. A real scorcher. Continued brutal weather through next weekend. Sunny and pleasant in New York. Wouldn't you like to be home?" *Oh, to be home . . . I wish.*

"Jimmy, you did not play your card in time. I yelled, 'Muggins,' and then you played it. That's not fair! You're a cheater, Jimmy!"

"I did too play it in time, Charlotte! You yelled, 'Muggins' too quick—"

"Let's play something else," Liz sighed, leaning back against the hard canvas cushion. She lifted Jimmy's hands, which were protectively spread over his cards, then swept the cards into a pile and returned them to their box.

Suddenly she looked at Rand with what she knew was, for the children, an impossible-to-read look. *Rand, so many sirens . . .*

"There goes another police car," he intruded on his wife's thoughts before she had finished forming them. No one stirred.

Suddenly they were on their feet. Ennui, inertia, inactivity, the utter frustration of the past three days found them scrambling for windbreakers, slickers, and sandals. The wail of a siren came closer. Liz felt her skin prickle,

"Hurry!" she shouted. "Maybe we can help!"

The two little ones were into their slickers before she was. She and Pam grasped Jimmy's and Charlotte's hands as they ran down the muddy, gutted dirt road. She sensed their reluctance, their apprehension. Or was it her own? Yet they would not stay behind. Jeff had dashed on ahead with Rand not far behind.

The ambulance passed them, its siren muted but not silent, and then they passed it where it was parked near the end of the long wooden foot bridge that crossed the swash to the beach beyond. The water, dark and turbulent beneath the bridge, and the beach, deserted and desolate, held little semblance to the usually busy, tranquil mid-summer scene.

They reached the end of the bridge and stepped into the fine white sand of the beach. Wordlessly they stopped, kicked off their flip-flops, and ran over the dunes. As they reached the summit, the wind caught at them, forcing them to bend their heads against its fierceness.

The clammy cold sand gave way beneath their feet and clung. A few days ago it had been so hot that their feet would literally have been blistered had they dared to walk in it barefoot. Sea oats, their fronds usually wafting gracefully in the gentle ocean breezes, slouched miserably from their weather-beating.

They ran past the lifeguard's chair, and Liz fleetingly recalled the incident just after their arrival when she and Rand had strolled past the area where Jeff was lingering with some of his peers, both fellows and girls. His arm was draped across the shoulders of a petite shapely blonde female in the skimpiest of bikinis. The words he had used had jolted them to the core, but they had willed themselves to show no sign. When he turned to see them passing and unflinchingly met their gaze, Liz wondered, and she was sure Rand did, too, what he was thinking. He revealed nothing in his expression. His look was arrogant, defiant.

A crowd had gathered near the mouth of the swash. The Markhams recognized the boy on the stretcher as one with whom

Jeff had been friendly. Liz looked at her son to catch his reaction and saw Rand doing the same thing. This young man had played catch with one-armed Jeff the day before the storm broke, and they had watched him surfing a number of times. Whenever a group had gathered to play volleyball, he had been involved, enthusiastically, in the game. And they had seen him on his minibike, kicking up a dirt storm as he rode up and down the lanes past their camper.

"Foolish boy," Liz said, not unkindly.

But the crowd at the water's edge had not dispersed, and they became a part of it just in time to see a man plunge into the treacherous gray surf. Here where the tidewater ran into the swash, the current was sucking, swelling, rolling, and the undertow was deadly.

"There!" someone shouted, then shook his head in disappointment. But the man in the water had seen something too, for he was fighting his way in that direction.

"Jake! Come back!" Liz heard someone else scream nearby. The ashen-faced woman, her fists clenched and pressed to her temples, opened her mouth again, but her voice was lost in the roar of the ocean and the noise of the crowd. She sank to her knees in the wet sand, and several women moved close to her, knelt beside her, embraced her, but kept their eyes on the churning water.

"It's his son," a man explained, helplessness in his voice, to no one in particular. "His son's out there . . ."

Jake's son was out there at the mercy of the sea, and Jake had gone to save him, and now neither one of them could be seen. A hush fell over the spectators. The only sound came from the emergency crew working over the boy on the stretcher, and the surf, mocking, warning, breaking on the shore.

The silence, the anticipation, the tension suddenly exploded as the young man in the water came briefly into view. Was it really him, or were they hoping too hard? There! Again! Indeed, he was much closer now, as if some supernatural strength had brought him nearer shore, then lifted him slightly for the benefit of the rescuers.

Two big muscular fellows, newly arrived and clad only in swim trunks, immediately plunged into the surging brine, leaving their scuba gear on the beach. Before Liz and the children could grasp what was happening, Rand and some other men were helping them drag the man-size youth, Greg, whose name she had heard from someone, onto the soggy sand.

Liz watched Jeff wipe his cheeks with the back of his hand and poke at a sand dollar with his big toe. He seemed not unconscious of its worth but uncaring, and he broke it. Pam was crying too, and Liz drew her close. Jimmy and Charlotte clung to her.

The emergency medical technicians from the ambulance took over, and putting an Ambu bag to the young man's face, they forced air into his lungs. He began vomiting salt water, and between his bouts of retching, they continued working on him. The two rescuers were back in the water, knee-deep, watching for any sign of Jake.

Liz saw Rand put a comforting hand on Jeff's shoulder and waited for the inevitable wrenching away. It was delayed, but it was there, and Jeff, stricken, moved to another vantage point. Liz couldn't watch any more, nor did she want to. She couldn't bear the pain; and Jeff's coldness to his father at such a traumatic moment was salt in a wound.

He resented Rand so. Why? Just last night he had gone out in the storm, as if staying in the camper with his family was the most demeaning thing he could think of. When he had come in, quietly so as not to awaken them, Rand said nothing, had only turned his flashlight on his watch to check the time, then turned it off again. She knew that would enrage Jeff. He was already miffed that his father wouldn't let him sleep in the pup tent until the storm ended. They had dismantled it and stored it in the trunk of the car. She knew how frustrating Rand's silences were to her, too. What were they to Jeff? He had taken a pillow and slept in the car.

She wondered so many things as she walked back to the camper with Jimmy and Charlotte: She wondered if they'd ever get to sleep that night; she wondered if the sun would ever shine again; she wondered if Jake's son, Greg, would ever forget what his father had done for him that day. The depths of it all were yet to be fathomed. Two hours later Jake's body was carried up onto the beach.

"The greatest love in the world . . ." Rand, overcome with emotion and unable to finish, spoke in a soft husky voice when he told them. He empathized painfully and realistically with Jake's heroism.

Liz fixed the evening meal, but no one ate. She wanted to say, *Hey guys, you need to eat or you'll pass out before breakfast*, but she couldn't eat either. She wrapped the hot dogs in foil, bagged the chips, rolls, and cookies.

"I'm so sad, Daddy," Charlotte murmured with her arms around Rand's neck. She was kneeling on the bench where Rand was sitting at the table in the camper, and began stroking his hair.

"Me, too," Jimmy echoed, resting his head against Rand's other arm.

"I'm so glad Jeffy wasn't swimming with those boys. You would've had to go save him."

Jeff arose with such a vengeance that the folding stool on which he was sitting collapsed and crashed to the floor. "Don't you two ever *shut up?*" he exploded. Not bothering to pick up the chair, he shoved the door open, slamming it forcefully behind him, and left.

Petulantly, Charlotte questioned her mother, "Do we have to shut up, Mommy?"

"Yes," Pam answered quickly and quietly.

An hour later, the rain had stopped completely. It was almost dark in the camper and no one bothered to turn on a lamp. The two youngest were falling asleep, so Liz fixed their beds and made them get in. They didn't resist. As Rand pulled a sweatshirt out of the closet and put it on, his eyes met his wife's. No need to explain: He was going out to look for Jeff.

Later Liz looked at her watch in the light of the gas lantern she and Pam had turned on. Rand had been gone for almost two hours. Pam had fallen into an exhausted sleep while reading a novel. Liz had tried to read, too, but she was restless, agitated. She extinguished the lantern, donned a jacket, told her neighbors she had left three sleepers in the camper, and headed for the beach.

She crossed the bridge over the swash, and as she climbed the dunes that separated the campsites from the beach, she gasped at the loveliness of the scene before her. There was not a cloud in the sky, and the moonlight on the surf was breathtaking. Several groups of people walked or stood on the beach, apparently working out their cabin fever.

Which direction to go? One way led to the inlet that created the swash, and she didn't relish crossing that, even at low tide, without Rand to cling to; she wouldn't consider it alone at night. When they had crossed it several days ago, Rand had first carried Charie over, then Jimmy, and had returned to help Pam and herself. They had been careful to return long before high tide.

She walked the other way. The cool breeze on her cheeks and the beauty of the night were refreshing, and she felt her spirits rise. Life would go on in spite of the Gregs, the Jakes, and the Jeffs. Life would go on, but not untouched.

As she rounded a curve of beach that formed a bight, even from a distance she recognized Rand, sitting on a driftwood log, silhouetted in the moonlight. As she drew closer she saw Jeff too, sitting on the ground with his back against another log. The black, wet ashes of someone else's campfire lay between them.

Rand's head was down, his elbows on his knees, his head resting on his clasped fingers. He moved only slightly when she sat next to him and slipped her arm under his, her hand into his hand. *Where did I come in?* she wondered and kept silent.

Rand had looked a long time before finding Jeff slumped against the log. He sat for another long time trying to decide the right thing to say to his son, then said nothing.

The sound of the rolling surf against the shore was constant, with only the hum of an occasional jet high in the sky to break the irregular pattern. After a lengthy wait, Jeff spoke in a stifled, almost unrecognizable voice. "I wanted to go swimming with them."

He was quiet again, and his parents heard him snuffle. Jeff swore, asking God to damn something, and Rand pressured Liz's hand when he felt her tense, as if to say, "Let it go."

Jeff went on. "I would have gone with them if it hadn't been for my stupid accident. This rotten, *stupid cast,*" he strained through clenched teeth.

Rand waited, reluctant to disrupt the mood. Finally he said, "Jeff, you *didn't* go." He cleared his throat. "We're thankful you didn't. If it took an accident—"

Jeff sat up straight, suddenly lucid. "Don't you understand, Dad? You don't see it, do you?" he declared. His voice grew loud as if he had moved away and they couldn't hear.

"Of course I see it, Jeff. But I want to know what you see—"

"You would have been there with Greg's father . . . Just like Charie said . . ." Jeff's voice broke and he seemed to be wrestling with an elusive emotion.

Liz wanted to give Rand a nudge when he didn't move, but she didn't move either. After a long quiet wait, Rand stood and moved to where Jeff was seated. Cautiously, ever so cautiously, he put his hand on Jeff's head. Then he sat beside him and let his hand slip down to his son's neck. Finally, when Rand knew it was accepted, he slid his arm across Jeff's shoulders where he let it rest.

"I'm sorry." Jeff spoke so softly they were not certain he had spoken at all. Again that quietness. Rand's arm tightened on Jeff's shoulder, and he gently pulled him closer. Jeff shook with sobs. So many hurts, so many heartaches, such a long way back . . .

At last, after a long, silent wait, Rand stood and gazed down at his son in the moonlight.

"Jeff." Rand waited.

"Let's go," he finally spoke softly. Reaching a hand down to Jeff, he pulled him to his feet. They stood, without a word, facing each other.

When Jeff spoke again, his voice was shaky and he struggled to steady it. "I'm sorry, Dad. So sorry . . ." Sobbing, he again allowed his father to hold him in a close embrace. Soon Rand reached out to Liz and drew her into the circle. She put her arm around Jeff and he responded with an arm at her waist. "Mom, I'm sorry . . ." They didn't move until Jeff was quiet again.

Then, with one arm around her and the other around his son, Rand slowly led them back to the bridge. Liz kept her hand on Jeff's arm as they walked. She had had difficulty suppressing the sobs that repeatedly caught in her throat during the walk back.

Jeff stopped before they crossed the bridge. He seemed drained, subdued, lifeless.

"I'm going to stay on the beach for a while," he told them. "To think."

"Would you like us to stay?"

"No. By myself, okay?"

Rand nodded. Liz pressed Jeff's arm, then kissed his cheek and held him in a close embrace before she and Rand walked slowly back to their camper. Many campsites still hummed with activity: computers, portable TVs, and radios, muted so as not to disturb neighbors, groups playing games at outdoor tables after repairing tarps and mosquito nettings, some reading by lantern light or toasting marshmallows. There was a hush, a quiet mourning. No one openly shared their agony or their joy.

Neither Rand nor Liz spoke until they were in the darkness of their own place. Then Liz turned to her husband. Putting her arms around his neck and pulling his face close to hers, she choked, "Rand . . ."

His cheek was moist as he pressed it to hers. He held her tight against him as if he were afraid he might lose something special if he let go.

CHAPTER FOURTEEN

The next morning Liz was up before the sun; she dressed quickly and quietly so as not to disturb the motionless humps in the beds and headed for the beach. She liked the solitude at sunrise, the gentle roar of the ocean, which often had a cleansing, calming effect on her and that she needed right now. She gave a friendly, noncommittal nod to the fellow early risers she happened to pass. As the sun came full circle over the horizon, a gull, searching for his breakfast, strutted ten feet ahead of her with his head angled to watch her with one eye, making sure she got no closer. Finally, he gave up and flew away.

There were four kinds of people who traveled the beaches, she had long ago decided: the joggers, the walkers, the amblers, and the combers. When she was with the kids she was a comber, ever hunting for black ebony-like sharks' teeth, which they frequently found near the water's edge. With each receding tide, there was the possibility of a new sparse supply. When Rand combed with them, he picked up pretty, clear colored stones that he planned to use someday in a project at home. He had collected so many that Liz often walked ahead of him, sometimes standing on ones she knew he would pick up, or picking them up and releasing them in the water under the pretext of rinsing the sand off her hands, thinking of the piles of agate, pyrite, fossils, and petrified wood at home which he had collected over the years.

Liz was an ambler this morning, but she occasionally picked up a shark's tooth and slipped it into the pocket of her Bermuda shorts as she pattered along at the waterline. More often, however, her eyes were off to the unreachable horizon, which seemed to conform to her untamable thoughts.

Life was so good for some, but when sudden death upset the routine, it was devastating. What if that *had* been Rand last night instead of Jake? Rand, like Jake, would not have hesitated for one second to be in that surf looking for his son.

And life was so terrible for others who suffered such physical or emotional pain that it seemed death must be a relief. Or was it? Were they ready to meet their Maker? How would she know? They would have to answer for themselves. Was she ready? Was Rand?

Liz was already covered with salt air and spray, so she didn't bother to wipe the tears from her cheeks. Could she ever pick up and go on as before? Could Jake's family?

"My grace is sufficient for thee." Gran would have quoted Jesus' words in II Corinthians 12:9. Was it sufficient for Jake's family? Would it have been for her? Is the grace only there when you need it?

She and Rand had stopped at Jake's camper after dinner the night before to offer assistance and condolence, but so many people bustled about, they had not stayed. The family would pack up with the help of neighboring campers, and return to their home in Virginia later this morning.

Liz heard a jogger coming up behind her and turned to see Rand approaching. She turned again and resumed her slow pace. Without breaking stride, he smacked her seat and called, "Meet you at the Spinnaker for coffee!" She was glad he didn't stop. There was no one in the world she'd rather spend this lovely time with, but this morning she preferred aloneness.

After a while, Rand jogged back to her, and they walked the remaining short distance to the Spinnaker together, hand in hand. Neither spoke until Rand ordered coffee.

"Let's have breakfast," he suggested. "Don't worry about the kids. They can eat cold cereal," he reasoned, knowing what she was about to say. "I'll have pancakes," he told the young girl who waited on them, "with sausage. My wife wants an English muffin with cream cheese and strawberry jelly." He grinned at Liz as if to say, *You're so predictable.*

She sipped her coffee while awaiting their order.

"Tough time?" he asked her before putting a bite of sausage into his mouth. Her muffin sat untouched. Tears filled her eyes before she could answer, and he grasped her wrists and pressured them. "Try to let go, Liz." He felt the tragedy deeply, yet he willed himself to think about other things, and tried to understand his wife's emotions. "We have to move on."

"And forget last night?" she almost snapped.

He spoke patiently. "Of course not. But when we get knocked down, we have to get up again. And again. And again."

She tried to speak but shook her head slowly when words wouldn't come, bowing it to hide new tears, which came in a stream this time.

"Let go, baby."

After he consumed her muffin, they left the coffee shop and walked along the beach, silent, arms encircling each other. Suddenly Rand picked her up and headed for the surf.

"No, Rand! No! I won't speak to you for the rest of the day . . . for a week . . . forever! If I go, you're going with me!" she screamed, locking her hands around his neck. She was fully inundated and came up fighting, splashing her husband until the top half of him was as soaked as the bottom.

Charie and Jimmy ran toward them, squealing delightedly. "Mom, I thought you didn't like to go swimming so early in the morning!" shouted Charie.

"I don't," Liz replied crossly. Rand splashed her again. "You're going to get yours," she warned.

"My what?"

"Your punishment for bad behavior. Just you wait and see."

Charlotte continued almost in the same breath, "Pammy fixed us sausage and pancakes, but she burned the sausage and then cooked the pancakes in the same pan, so they didn't taste good. We gave them to the seagulls."

"Were they he-gulls or she-gulls?" Jimmy asked.

"*She*-gulls," Charie giggled.

"He-gulls are prettier. Can't you tell, Charie? Just like the ducks."

Pam arrived in time to hear the tale of the pancakes. "They were *not* burned, but they refused to eat them."

"Mommy," Charie continued, "Jeffy told us that when we go swimming, all the sharks were going to come after us to get their teeth back. So Jimmy threw all his into the water!"

Liz was dismayed. "Oh, Jimmy! Why didn't you ask Daddy or me first?"

"I told him just that, Mom," Pam offered, "but he wouldn't listen. He was really *scared!* Jeff is a turd."

"You can find more, Jimmy. And Jeff can help you," Rand promised. Jimmy wanted Charlotte to share hers with him.

"No sir," she hastily replied.

"No, *sir*, Jimmy," Rand intervened. "You threw yours away. That's the end of that." And the boy knew that was the end of that.

That evening, Liz and Rand walked along the beach while the two little ones looked for sharks' teeth. Jeff had helped Jimmy hunt for them for over an hour during the afternoon, but his parents suspected that Jimmy had found the few they had displayed when they returned. "Now *these* sharks are going to bite his butt, too," Jeff had warned, tongue-in-cheek, before heading out on his own.

Rand pretended to pick up an object. "Look at this, Jimmy!" He held a large black tooth in the palm of his hand.

Liz knew it was the gift shop's two-dollar size. "You must have spent all your 'lowance on that one," she mumbled under her breath.

Rand grinned at her. "I did."

"Can I have it, Daddy?" Jimmy questioned excitedly.

"I kind of like it myself," mused Rand, holding it up between two fingers to assure good visibility. "And I wouldn't want anyone to give *this* boulder back to the sharks!"

"You know I wouldn't!" Jimmy admired the tooth where Rand held it out of reach. "That's a beaut. I sure would like to have it."

". . . or lose it," continued Rand.

"I'd be real careful. I wouldn't lose it . . ."

"It's yours, Jim. Take care of it."

"Thank you, Daddy!"

"I hope you have another one," Liz whispered, "or someone's nose is going to be in trouble." Grinning, Rand winked at her.

Well, Liz thought, *everything is back to normal. Whatever normal is.*

CHAPTER FIFTEEN

Betty Ann Cunningham had an infection on her lower leg just above the ankle, and the doctor had prescribed oral antibiotics for her. He had given her instructions to soak the leg twice a day in a solution for which he had also prescribed medication.

"Nothing to worry about," he assured Liz's mother. "Just take these until they're gone," he tapped his prescription pad, tore off the page, and handed it to her. Betty relayed it to Liz, who would pick up the medication for her. "Do the soaks as instructed, and I think we'll see the end of this nuisance," the doctor concluded in his matter-of-fact way.

Her mother said to Liz as they pulled into her drive, "I need a new bucket anyway, so get me a good sturdy one. And big. One I won't have to fold my toes over to get my big foot into."

That was how Liz happened to be in The Market Square a half-hour later, in the housewares department between linens and hardware, with her foot in a pail, when Nina and Mitzy rounded the corner by dish towels and pot holders. Liz had examined every size and shape of bucket and couldn't be sure which one would accommodate a foot. Then after glancing self-consciously about her, she had slipped off her sandal and tried the square orange one on for size, turning her foot kitty-corner to make it fit comfortably. Her mother's slender size 6 narrow would fit better than Liz's 7½ medium.

She looked up to see Nina and Mitzy staring at her, eyebrows lifted and lips pursed. Liz detected slight quiverings at the corners of their mouths, mentally pulled herself up straight and sucked in her breath, then turned a color that almost matched her footwear.

"Frankly, I think you look better in blue," Nina offered.

Mitzy quickly picked up on it. "I never thought you'd go in for the wet look, Liz," she clucked, "but you look great in it."

Liz made an effort to smile and join the fun until Nina burst into raucous laughter at her companion's humor and then added, "I always thought pumps were more your style."

Liz started, "Well, you see—"

"We see, Liz. You know we're kidding," Nina said, lamely attempting to make peace.

"You're a thousand laughs, both of you."

Rand joined them just then, carrying the small bag of medicine from the pharmacy. Glad for a diversion, Liz removed her foot from the pail and slipped it into her shoe. "How's it fit?" he inquired with a wink and a grin.

"Super," she replied, latching on to his cue to aid her recovery.

Rand chatted briefly with the two women while Liz feigned interest. She grasped the pail handle in one hand, the small shopping basket that held her other purchases for Pam's birthday party in the other, and when a comfortable break occurred, she bid a hasty farewell to Nina and Mitzy. "See you around. Sometime."

"Oh, Rand," she moaned as they got into the car, "I'm mortified."

"Why?" he scolded mildly. "They're just people."

"No, they're not just people. Nina used to be a people. In the pre-Mitzy days she was a people, but not anymore. Miss Right and Miss Righteous, that's what they are now. They're both cats. Of all the people to have walk in just when I was doing such a dumb thing . . . And we didn't even explain . . ."

"Good. Let them wonder."

"You can say that. You weren't the one with your foot in the pail."

"Well, it was funny. It's a good thing I didn't say what I was really thinking." She looked at him quizzically. "Something about you kicking the—"

"You wouldn't have! Yes, you would have if you had thought of it before this very minute! Thanks for nothing."

"Look," he brought her up short. "Laugh, Liz. Laugh at yourself. Seems to me I heard you advising someone else to do that recently." They stopped for a traffic light, and putting his finger under her chin, he turned her head so she had to look at him. He took her hand again and said, "It really does make it easier."

"Thanks," she said, and meant it. "I was trying to."

"Doesn't Nina ever call you anymore?"

"No."

They dropped the purchases at her mother's, and after a good laugh with her over Liz's predicament, they went on to Tailor Made to pick up the suit Rand had purchased and left for alterations. Liz browsed while he went to the men's department. She bought birthday gifts of a denim purse, purple sweat suit and knee socks in several colors for Pam. After finishing their shopping they drove north on Middle Ridge to the Parkway.

"How will I ever face them?"

"What? Oh, forget it, Liz. You're too hard on yourself. You make yourself miserable for nothing. You're also missing the fall foliage. You know what they say about taking time to smell the roses."

"I know. The foliage *is* lovely." Rand was right. Autumn's dress was far more beautiful than she had ever seen it in her lifetime. "Of course I say that every year," she told him as they drove toward home.

The children were at home this Saturday afternoon. "We can't birthday shop with you guys along," she had told them when they had begged to go. She appreciated these infrequent times when she was able to shop without them, and also to have Rand along to help make decisions and carry the packages. It was the second week of October; the kids had been back in school for over a month.

Jeff, too. He had gone back without a mention of his money-making plans, which had eliminated a continuing education. His current mind-set was to get more involved in sports.

"What would we experience mentally, or even emotionally, if we were seeing all this magnificent color for the very first time?" The reds of the maples and the deep rusts of oaks, the yellow aspens, the deep greens of the pine trees, and the blueness of the spruce were typical fare and drew the tourists to New England each year at this time. Complement that with a sunny blue-sky day and a few hours to dream.

Rand responded, "You say that every year, too."

"But I'm always so overwhelmed, and I'm sure each year it's more spectacular than the last."

"That's because our puny little minds can't retain such splendor," Rand reasoned. "Fortunately we're able to forget not-so-pleasant things, too." Liz wanted to comment on that but let it pass. He was in a good spirit, and she decided it best to keep the conversation light.

"Don't ever ask me to leave New England. Each season has its own surprises and secrets."

"I was thinking of retiring to Florida," Rand joked, giving her a sidelong glance and a wink. "Tell me," he continued, "what kinds of secrets and surprises do the seasons hold? Summer, for example."

"The summer just past was far from routine, you must admit."

"Then how would you define *routine?* For us it doesn't seem to be related to mechanical performance or habit. Nor is it related to the seasons, per se."

"It is, in that our activities per season vary. We don't break our necks sledding in July."

"And heroes don't rescue drowning swimmers in December. You're right. I also think that awesome episode at the shore has had an everlasting effect on us."

"It cost so dearly. We can't help but relate to it in a personal way, by superimposing ourselves into the lead roles."

Rand nodded. "It was tough on Jeff. Me, too, when you consider where *I* would have been." Liz began to relax in their closeness. "You would have been in the water, with not a moment to spare. Oh, Rand . . ."

They rode on in a comfortable silence, both of them thinking back to the events of their summer as well as today's events.

The day after their nocturnal beach encounter, Jeff and Rand had gone to town to get a part for the SUV, and while sitting over lunch, they had aired some grievances.

"Tell me honestly, Jeff," Rand had encouraged as they sat down with hamburgers and drinks. "What have I done? What am I *doing* that bugs you so?"

Jeff remained subdued, but there was a dawning, an openness with his father, however fragile it was. But the door was ajar, and Rand in a quiet way was nudging it wider.

"You really want me to tell you?" Jeff looked at his father in surprise. "Honestly?"

"Really. Honestly."

"Even if you disagree?"

Rand nodded. "How can we correct something we can't see?"

"You don't always take disagreements too easy—especially from me."

"I'll take it, I promise."

"You sure you want . . ."

Rand nodded affirmatively.

"You won't get mad?"

Rand shook his head negatively. "I won't."

Jeff was quiet for several minutes, and Rand could see his struggle, could sense his change of direction. Then Jeff began hesitantly. "Sometimes I can't breathe." Then he blurted, "You smother me! Dad, you do!"

"Do I, Jeff?"

"And—and—you're always so—so—*right*, Dad."

Yes, I can see why he feels that way. "Go on, son."

Jeff paused before continuing. "And—you'd never know anyone else was qualified to have an opinion."

"Yes," Rand encouraged quietly. He could understand Jeff on that matter, too.

Jeff looked at his father and back at the half-eaten hamburger in his hand. "You won't even listen when I want to discuss something you disagree with . . ." Jeff's voice trailed off uncertainly.

Rand nodded in agreement. "And?"

"Well," he hesitated again, "sometimes I like to make decisions on my own, and you treat me like I'm Charlotte's age. Then other times I *want* you to decide something for me, and you won't."

Rand stated carefully, somberly, sincerely, "I see."

"I'm not sure you do, Dad. So many little things . . ."

Rand nodded affirmatively.

"Dad!" Jeff exclaimed. "I thought we were going to *talk!* That's another thing. Sometimes you don't *say* anything, and that *really* bugs me!"

Rand guffawed loudly.

Jeff's hurt was apparent. "What's so funny?"

"I'm sorry, Jeff," Rand apologized, still laughing. "That seems to bother some other people, too, so you must be right."

"Like Mom?"

"Like Mom." He continued earnestly, "You're right, Jeff. About everything. So I guess I'd better try to do something about it." Rand paused thoughtfully. "I'll really try to do better. Will you give me another chance?"

Jeff turned the drink glass and wiped at the condensation with his finger. Finally Rand spoke again. "Jeff?" he prodded.

"There's something wrong with this conversation, Dad. I can't figure it out yet, but I will. Give me time. Something wrong—I know." He stopped fiddling with his glass and looked directly into his father's eyes for the first time in many months. "You're so clever, Dad. You got me to talk about *my* gripes. How about *yours?*"

"What makes you think I've got gripes, Jeff?"

"Come off it, Dad. You obviously frown on me a *lot* . . . Sometimes I think you even *hate* me. Yet you keep all your thoughts to yourself."

"You're wrong on that, son. I don't hate you one bit, and I don't know where you ever got that impression. I care very much. I love you, Jeff, more than you'll ever know."

"Sometimes it's hard to tell."

"Don't forget, I've never had a sixteen-year-old son before." Rand was thoughtful. "I guess I'm afraid for you. I was sixteen once, you know. And I know that many of your problems—hang-ups, whatever you call them—you will outgrow, so I'm trying not to let them bug me."

"But don't you see, that doesn't help things right *now?* Maybe it helps *you* to put them on the shelf, but it's doing nil for me. And maybe they're not hang-ups. Maybe they're changes in the times that you can't face up to. Did you ever consider that?"

"Yes, I have, son. It's not easy, but I always try to keep that in focus."

They had talked for two hours, and the events of those two days were instrumental in clearing the air. Communications with their son had definitely improved, but they were by no means free from the tangle.

Jeff had fully recovered from the physical injuries he had suffered in his minibike accident and was back in full swing with school sports and yard jobs. Jeff worked well, and his customers were pleased with his thoroughness. And he was dependable. He worked slowly but steadily. A sore spot in the situation was the fact that he was still paying the town for his foolishness. His fines were heavy. His parents gave him full responsibility for his debt.

His interchange with non-family was, his parents suspected, far superior to his interchange with those at home.

Liz thought about how she tried not to interfere when Rand was reprimanding one of the children, but often she was ready to intervene, to say things he was so obviously omitting. This was often true when he was dealing with Jeff. Especially Jeff. But the wisdom in holding her tongue, when she did, always seemed apparent afterward. She had learned this early in their parenting days, and it had helped to eliminate much confusion. That night on the beach in North Carolina she had been ready to confront Jeff regarding his foul mouth, his attitudes, his friends. But she had restrained herself, had left it in Rand's hands, and the end result, surprisingly, was far superior to what it would have been had she offered her two cents. She had never seen anyone so eloquent in his silence as that husband of hers, and so capable of reading the unuttered thoughts of others; Rand knew every hurt that Jeff's brief apology had covered. She was certain of that now.

With the children back in school, the quiet mornings were enjoyable for Liz, though by the time Charlotte returned from a half day at kindergarten, her mother was ready to share her domain with her second daughter. She was a dear, and Liz's heart warmed to her. But when Charlotte returned that first day, she had dissolved into tears; school was a failure. She had gone to school with high hopes. A dismal failure—she had not learned to read.

While the first part of the summer had been abuzz with activities, the weeks after vacation had been, conversely, as Pam put it, "dull." A routine had set in, to Liz's relief, allowing her more freedom each day. She had packed picnics for the beach, had taken the two youngest to amusement parks and the Bronx Zoo, and she had been reluctant to have summer end and autumn begin. Her feelings were ambivalent: The quietness was a treat, but she was lonely.

But Jimmy's status seemed to be on "hold," and she was grateful for that.

Except for the encounter in The Market Square, she had seen little of Nina and Mitzy since the Neighborly Picnic, and she missed her good friend. Through the years, through thick and thin, she and Nina had dropped in on each other to chat, to encourage each other, to laugh, to cry over coffee, and Liz missed her. She had other friends with whom she shopped, lunched, gabbed, but none took the place of her old friend, Nina.

"Well, if that's the way she feels, who cares?"

Liz had learned through painful experiences to adopt an uncaring attitude; it protected her against hurt, much as the wall she maintained for ready use—both assisted in the concealing of her bleeding wounds. They made it easier after episodes like today's. Sometimes she wished Mitzy would move away, but if her presence was serving to reveal the true Nina, what good would that do? She longed for a good friend.

As Liz and Rand turned into the drive Liz exclaimed, "Look, Charie and Jimmy are helping Pam rake leaves! Leave it to Pam, she's made a game out of it. They have a way of looking busy, though, without getting much done."

"That's okay. When it carries over into adulthood, however, it becomes intolerable. Anyway, they're getting the message they can't sit on their duffs all their lives and have the world wait on them." Rand continued, "And they are being creative, aren't they?"

Pam came to help with packages. "What did you buy us?"

"Oh, furniture polish. Charcoal. Bug spray. A new tablecloth that was on sale. Groceries. A bucket for Gran." Liz smiled weakly at Rand.

"Terrific," Pam grinned.

"Pam, you're getting cuter every day," her mother teased, smacking her lightly on her bottom.

"Ouch. It's just my beautiful hairdo," she retorted, assuming several poses to show it off. Though she went wigless most of the time at home, Pam knew her hair looked ridiculous even though it had grown an inch or so over the summer. By Christmas they might be able to style it again. The Markhams joked about it now, and Pam joined in like the good sport she was. She had a cheerful spirit most of the time, and her parents made every effort to nurture that valuable asset.

Liz shoved a bag into her daughter's waiting arms. "Here. Be good for something more than a wig rack!"

"Look, Mommy! Daddy!" Charie exclaimed. "Pammy showed us how to make a house!"

There on the big lawn outlined in leaves, much like an architect's drawing on paper, was the floor plan of a house.

"I hope the wind doesn't blow. They've been playing house for hours," Pam explained.

Charie and Jimmy took them on a walking tour of the house. "It certainly is big. I'm glad I don't have to clean it," Liz commented.

"Daddy!" Jimmy scolded, "You're standing in the bathtub!"

Rand looked startled and, lifting his feet one at a time and shaking off the imaginary drips, carefully stepped out. The children laughed gleefully.

After their tour and enthusiastic compliments, Rand led the way through the rubble of the old patio and they carried their packages into the house. Mr. Stuart's backhoe was just as he had left it at quitting time yesterday and would stay that way until he returned early Monday morning. He would arrive, weather permitting, before they were out of bed. The children had been given strict orders to stay away from it after being disciplined several times for trespassing.

Progression on the new addition was in its earliest stages, but started at last. Never mind now that it was being started when it was supposed to be being *finished;* at least they could *see* something developing. The expansion would take in a new deck where the patio had been and would be over a large playroom. The boys might move into the rooms that would someday be Gran's apartment. There would also be additional garage space.

"For my new motorcycle," Jeff explained, tongue-in-cheek, "when I get it."

Liz was caught up in the excitement of planning the decor for the new rooms. "The playroom has to be big enough for a pool table," Rand had insisted. And they needed a ping-pong table.

Jimmy followed them in, proud as could be, carrying the heaviest grocery bag. Liz commended him for his strong arms and willing heart. He was scarcely recognizable as the same boy who had come to them eight months previous. Tantrums were milder and less frequent, laughter was spontaneous, and smiles were almost instantaneous.

"Can we have an ice cream sandwich, Mom?" he asked after spotting them in the bag he carried.

"Not now."

"Oooh! Lucky us!" Charie exclaimed a few minutes later. "Can we have some ice cream?"

"No," Jimmy answered. "We can't—"

"You're not the boss!" Charie interrupted.

"Mommy said, 'after now' we can have one," Jimmy concluded patiently.

The promise Liz halfheartedly made to Rand had been simple to keep thus far, but she wasn't sure she could keep her word if push came to shove. As long as Jimmy's mother refused to sign his release for adoption, there was no need for aggravation, and Jimmy's removal was not a threat. On Mrs. Bradshaw's last visit, she had commented that Jimmy's mother was about to marry her latest live-in. That could put a new kink in the chain. If Jimmy's mother signed his release too soon, before Rand gave in, disaster was imminent.

Such a dear boy. How could anyone *not* want him? But Rand didn't, at least not on a permanent basis. Too much of a commitment, he said. Well, it would be a commitment for her, too. If only she had a guarantee that Jimmy would be with them for an extended period of time, but guarantees were not available for foster parents.

Next to Jeff, Jimmy had been most affected by the beach tragedy. Often when Liz was alone with him, sometimes putting him to bed at night, he would mention it. "Greg doesn't have a daddy anymore. He must be sad." One night he commented, "I didn't have a daddy either until I came to live here." Liz choked up and gave him a hug to cover her emotions.

"*Jimmy's home,* Rand," she contended. "This is Jimmy's *home.*" He had moved in bag and baggage, right into her heart and life. He was as warm and real as those who were conceived in her womb and born to her.

Another time he demurred, "I hope I don't lose my daddy."

That new suspicion niggling in her mind, the one she never allowed to the surface where it could be faced and dealt with, the one that caused her to awaken in the night in a cold sweat: Jimmy's mother might want him back. *And I will be helpless. Completely helpless.* If only they could have adopted him long ago, but Jimmy's mother also held the key to that: the unsigned release. This marriage could spur the very thing Liz dreaded most—losing Jimmy. A new husband in the picture to offer security and who wanted a ready-made family was not a factor she had bargained for.

And suppose he *didn't* want a ready-made family? In fact, suppose they wanted to close the book on the past? If she were to sign those papers and Rand still refused to give up his bullheadedness . . .

It must not happen.

CHAPTER SIXTEEN

Mr. Stuart's backhoe was noisy, and Liz wished he would finish. Judging by his persistent plugging away at the job, he wished the same.

"Whatever you do, Mrs. Markham," he warned, "don't use the downstairs bathroom. The sink and tub and washer are okay because they drain into a drywell, your husband tells me, but don't use the john. Just close the door and lock it." Liz could see the six-inch pipe protruding from the end of the house, shoulder height to Mr. Stuart as he sat on his orange monster.

"Liz," Rand had cautioned too, after standing in the excavation conferring with Stuart Construction on the project before leaving for work, "don't, whatever you do, flush *any* toilets."

A short time later Charie shouted, panic-stricken, as she ran through the kitchen, "Mommy! I flushed the toilet! I forgot! I forgot!"

Liz, Charie, and Jimmy arrived at the window in time to see Mr. Stuart catch a plume of *eau de toilet* on the side of his left leg. It generously sprayed him from the hip down.

With reddened face, he shouted angrily, "Do you want this job done, or don't you? It's up to you, but I'm not putting up with this kind of nonsense!"

Liz ran out the back door. "Oh, we're so sorry, Mr. Stuart. The children—"

"Are old enough to understand and cooperate!" he bellowed.

"We're sorry," Liz repeated weakly. She turned to Jimmy and Charie after Mr. Stuart and his machine returned to work with a fury. "Let's not use the downstairs one at all, okay? Just so we don't forget and flush it again."

Liz, chuckling in spite of herself, returned to her cabinet cleaning. Charie, loudly singing a ditty she made up as she went along—"Bliggle, bluggle, blingle, Mr. Stuart got all wet"—busied herself with a sticker book.

"It's supposed to rhyme, Charie," Jimmy announced with superiority.

"Who cares? Go do something else."

"I care. Songs are always supposed to rhyme, dummy."

"Then tell me a word that rhymes with wet," she stated annoyedly.

"Get, let, set, met, toy . . . *let*. Ha ha!"

She started singing again, "Bliggle, bluggle, blingle, bet, Mr. Stuart got all wet. Get, let, set, met. With water from the toy-let. Like that, Mom?"

Jimmy, with a felt-tipped marker he had obtained from his personal supplies, worked on what appeared to be a sign. "Mom," he asked, "how do you spell *flush?*" He held it up for her to see. "'DO NOT FLUSH,' I'm writing. Then I'll need a string to tie it on."

Liz spelled it for him, then watched as he headed for the bathroom. "Be careful, Jim," she warned. "On second thought, maybe you'd better stay out of the bathroom . . ." His sturdy little body strutted with importance.

"I flushed it!" he screamed, running toward the window again. "I was tying the sign on the handle, and I flushed it!" He was frantic.

Liz and Charie dashed after him and reached the window at the same time. As Mr. Stuart caught this one in his lap, Jimmy prostrated himself on the floor, screaming hysterically.

Mr. Stuart, in a *rage royale*, looked up at the window, the wrong one, with fist shaking. He turned his backhoe around, drove it onto the trailer, and left. He didn't hear Liz calling loudly, "Oh, Mr. Stuart! Please! We're sorry! Please! It was an accident, Mr. Stuart . . ."

She turned to look at the children in exasperation. Then she collapsed on the floor in a fit of uncontrollable laughter. She held her sides and rocked back and forth as tears ran down her cheeks. Charie, swift to pick up on her mother's reaction, sat on the floor facing Liz, and laughed loudly and gleefully. Jimmy was still crying; he sat up and looked at them, his eyes wide in bewilderment.

Liz was still howling when she reached an arm around him and pulled him close to her. Though he was baffled, he soon began to join them, hesitatingly at first, then loudly and wholeheartedly.

"Oh, Jimmy, you're such a fussmusser!" Charie strained through giggles.

Liz poked an index finger toward her daughter, indicating that she was, too. She was unable to speak.

"So is Mr. Stuart," Jimmy bubbled.

As soon as they began to quiet down, Liz became convulsed again, and the children joined in unreservedly. Finally she got to her feet, then flopped down on the sofa as hysteria returned.

"Oh, Mommy, this is so funny!" Jimmy jumped up and down, suddenly realizing he was the instigator of such mirth, and miraculously, he didn't seem to be in trouble for it.

Jimmy and Charie began chasing each other. Then Liz joined them, making them laugh more as she tried to catch them. They were carrying on thus when Pam came in. Through fresh spasms, they explained the cause of their merriment.

"You've got to be kidding!" She wholeheartedly joined in.

The lighthearted mood carried through the evening meal and long after, spontaneous laughter springing up from all areas of the house.

"You can laugh all you want to," Rand spoke, smirking as he picked up the phone, "but I'm the one who has to talk to Mr. Stuart. Hey, Jimmy," he added as an afterthought, "how about *you* explain to him what happened and try to get him back to finish the job, since you're the one who chased him away?"

Jimmy's eyes grew round as he exclaimed, "Not *me!*"

"Did you, or did you not?"

"I didn't. I didn't mean to, but I'm not calling him."

Rand made every effort to be serious as he talked, but Liz and the children were not easing matters for him. "He'll come back on Monday," he informed them after hanging up, "but I'd suggest that all you troublemakers stay away from the house for the whole day. Go shopping. Go to your mother's. Go anywhere. Go *some*where."

"At least it was clean the second time."

When Rand and Liz were preparing for bed, Rand said, "You know, I've heard Mr. Stuart laughs harder than anyone when that happens to someone else."

"You mean this is a common occurrence?"

"It happens quite frequently, I'm told."

"Cut that out!" he scolded as he tried to kiss her. "How can I kiss you when you're shaking so much?"

"I just can't stop, Randy. I've been laughing for hours, and it just won't go away."

"Good ol' Jimmy."

"What do you mean by that?"

"Well, he's not the most coordinated kid, you know."

"He's no different from any other almost-six-year-old. Oh, Rand, if only you could have seen him! He went into one of his tantrums. I guess he thought he was going to catch it . . ."

"He would have if I had been here."

"Oh, you lie. Then when Charie and I were cracking up, he looked at us so puzzled. It took awhile before it hit him that we were *laughing*."

"What's the latest with him, honey? I don't mean to put a wet blanket on your fun, but didn't you meet with Mrs. Bradshaw yesterday?"

Liz's spirits sagged, but she refused to succumb. *How good laughter is*, she thought. *It kind of frees you up for a while.* "Jimmy's mother may get married."

"Not a bad idea, since she's living with all the privileges. Is she going to become a mother simultaneously with becoming a wife?"

"I haven't the foggiest."

"You realize it's a possibility."

"I'm hoping not. She doesn't deserve him."

"So is there *any*thing new about him being placed?"

"Not until she decides. Mrs. Bradshaw thinks her spouse-to-be won't want him. So she'll probably sign his release." She lay quietly against him, feeling his heart beat against her cheek. Softly she said, "Rand, don't let him go. I can't bear it," she choked. She felt tension in the stillness that followed.

"What happened to our agreement?" he asked after a numbing silence.

"I said I'd try."

"And you didn't."

"I did. I did try. But I can't give him up, Randy. I can't."

"I haven't changed my mind, Liz."

Quietness engulfed them again. Liz put her arm around him and kissed him warmly, caressing his face. "I'm not laughing now," she mumbled against his lips.

The light spirit in the Markham household was short-lived. When Liz walked into the bedroom after breakfast the next morning, Rand was sewing a button on his black pinstripe suit coat.

"I'll do that," she told him.

He continued to struggle with it. "I asked you to three weeks ago."

"Why didn't you remind me?" she said, defensively.

"I left it on the chair so you'd see it. You put it back in the closet so you wouldn't see it." His annoyance was obvious.

"You know how I hate things left on chairs. You should have said something . . ."

"You didn't used to need reminding of things like that."

"I've got a lot on my mind right now."

"But not me."

"What?"

"You don't have me on your mind."

She held out her hand for the coat, but he ignored her.

"So have I. Got a lot of things on my mind," he added in answer to her questioning look.

She whirled around and sat on the bed. "I'm not like one of your Miss Efficient Effervescent Secretaries . . ."

"Maybe you could take a lesson from them."

". . . who has nothing to think about at work but work. And you. Like sweet sickening Miss Bebe Buchar—whatever her name is."

"Miss Effervescent Efficiency," he countered angrily.

"Well, just let me trade places with her and we'll see . . ."

"Is that what you want?" Rand stood and touched her arm as Liz snatched the jacket from him. He glared in her face. They both lingered on her unsaid, unintended meaning.

She threw the jacket on the bed and went to the bathroom to blot her eyes and blow her nose. When she returned, Rand was putting on his suit coat. "Hold still," she snapped, cutting the thread with the needle dangling from it with her manicure scissors. He turned abruptly and left without another word.

"Mommy," Charlotte informed Liz the next afternoon, "I been thinkin' 'bout Gran all day long. How is her sore foot?"

"I haven't talked to her today, honey. Why don't you call and ask her?"

Charlotte was carefully dialing the phone when Jimmy announced, "I want to talk to Gran, too."

"Wait until Charie's done, Jim, and then you can have a turn."

"Hello, my sweet Gran," Charie purred. "I've been so worried about you. Is your boo-boo getting better now?" Liz had to imagine the other half of the conversation.

"Did you take your medicine like Dr. Rinaldi told you, and do you soak your foot twice a day?" Charie put her hand over the phone and turned to Liz, "She says it's much improved today."

"Gran," she spoke into the mouthpiece again, "why don't you come have supper with us tonight? We're having hamburgers and 'tata chips. You can bring some good pickles you made." Charie listened for a full minute, then said, "The rabbits got out again, but Mini took care of them. Oh, Gran, we didn't tell you about Mr. Stuart, and how we flushed the toilet *twice* right on top of him! Well, I did it once, and Jimmy did it once." Charie laughed melodiously, and it was apparent she was getting a reaction from the other end. She gave her grandmother a detailed account, suspecting that her mother had already done so. "Okay. Bye."

After replacing the receiver she said to her mother, "She can't come for supper 'cause hers is all ready, and then she's going to her next neighbor's for a 'zert party. They're moving, y'know."

"I wanted to talk!" roared Jimmy. "Charie, you hung up on purpose so I couldn't talk!" His voice, Liz thought, would shatter the crystal.

"Hold on, Jim," Liz said, grasping him by the shoulders and holding him almost nose to nose. "Charlotte forgot you wanted to talk."

"No, I di'nt."

"You can pick up the phone, James, and call Gran back, but I will not have such a fuss over nothing."

"Let me go!" he bellowed. "I don't want to talk to her anyway! *I don't want to!*"

"Go sit in the rocker," Liz ordered firmly. "You can talk to Gran when you're ready to be nice."

"I told you I don't want to talk!" he cried. "Charlotte told her everything!" He plopped in the rocker and folded his arms, hugging himself, his face twisted in anger.

"Now, young lady," Liz stated, facing Charlotte and taking her by the arms as she spoke, "why did you hang up the phone when you knew Jimmy wanted to talk to Gran?"

"Because I told her everything," she stated saucily, spreading her palms upward, a picture of feigned innocence as she gazed, undaunted and unblinking, into her mother's eyes.

"Jimmy might have had something to say that you didn't know about. Did you ever think of that?"

"Gran said her supper was ready," Charie said, ignoring her mother's comment.

"Apologize to Jimmy."

"You said not to lie, and I'm not sorry."

"Go to your room."

Charlotte took Tedley under one arm and Bearsh under the other as she strolled casually toward the door, her very manner exuding defiance.

"Give Tedley to Jimmy," her mother ordered as again she feared for her good crystal.

Without missing a pace, Charie lifted an elbow and let the bear drop.

"I didn't say drop Tedley on the floor," Liz said with ill-concealed exasperation, "I said give him to Jimmy."

With feigned sweetness, Charlotte turned and returned to where the bear had landed, picked him up, and walked to where Jimmy sat, shoving it brusquely into his face. "I'm sorry I hung up . . ."

Putting his hands over his ears Jimmy shouted, "I'm not listening to you!"

Again, Liz sent Charie to her room where she was to remain until she was called to supper. Liz looked up to see Jimmy heading out the door.

"Where are you going, young man?"

"To my room. If Charie can go to her room, so can I."

"Sorry. Back to the chair. You don't make the rules around here . . ."

"*That's not fair!*"

"Who said life was fair? Anyway, when it comes to this house, I'll decide what's fair. Back to the chair."

He obeyed under protest, mumbling. His body language was eloquent. "Anyway, Daddy's the boss around here."

"What makes you think that?"

"'Cause you always ask his 'pinion about everything."

"Not quite everything."

I must be crazy, she thought, *to want to adopt.*

That evening Charie came to her mother to report another infraction. "Mommy, Jimmy used a bad word."

"Did he really?" Liz asked noncommittally, exuding indifference.

"It was really bad. Don't you want to know what he said?"

"No. Not really."

"He called me a fart."

Absolutely crazy, Liz decided.

An exuberant Rand came home from work that evening: He had been given two tickets to a World Series playoff game. The Mets and Yankees were anticipating a much-publicized Subway Series at Citi Field, the first in many years. Liz wanted to go with him, but Rand had already called Jeff and invited him to go. Liz was disappointed but happy for them to share this special time together.

CHAPTER SEVENTEEN

It was an unseasonably warm Saturday late in October, and Liz had planned to go to her mother's for the day. She would take Charlotte and Jimmy with her. She had promised to help Betty finish her fall cleaning before the Thanksgiving holiday.

"We're going to Gran's on Sat-ah-dee," Jimmy sang happily.

"Jimmy, you're stupid. It's Sat-ur-day."

"That's what Gran says. 'Sat-ah-dee.'"

"You must think Gran's stupid then."

"No. I don't!"

Liz chose to ignore them.

The days were growing shorter, especially with the upcoming reversal of Daylight Saving Time, and the area was experiencing weather typical for New England: bright warm days, clear crisp nights. The aroma of burning wood, either from fireplaces or from basement stoves, was delightful. Liz missed the nostalgic smell of burning leaves in the fall; however, the restrictions and fines for not only pollution but also for accidental wildfires were imposing in this heavily populated area. Much of the foliage was still on

Jimmy's Home

the trees, though, and she savored the last remnant of the quickly passing beauty.

This sunny, sparkly weather seemed to be ideal for the day's project, for when the children tired of helping, they would play outdoors. It was usually difficult to coax them in, even if their noses turned red and their fingers numb.

Hurrying to finish laundry so she could be on her way to her mother's, Liz removed jeans from the washer and decided to take a few extra minutes to hang them outside. She loved the outdoorsy smell of clothes dried on the line. She lifted them from the dryer door to a basket, then paused at the stove to turn off the kettle.

"Hey, Mom, I need my jeans quick."

"Then put them in the dryer, Jeff." She sighed and put the basket down again. "I'm in a hurry to get to Gran's." Jeff, rummaging through the wet laundry, recognized faded patches, tears, and spots.

After hanging the remaining clothes on the wheel in the backyard, Liz began putting breakfast on the table. She heard Sneakers at the door. *He usually just scoots in when the door's open*, Liz thought. But Sneakers wasn't at the door.

She returned to her work.

"Mrowrr," she heard again. Liz yanked the cabinets open, one by one. The basement door. The broom closet. The utility room. No cat dashed out.

Rand was in the shower when she entered their room to make the bed and tidy up. Returning to the kitchen, she heard, "Mrowrr," and again, "Mrowrr." *Where is that cat?* She went to the laundry and turned off the dryer so she could better locate the sound.

The dryer! Liz yanked the door open and pulled out a very hot, dry unhappy cat. His legs sprawled in four different directions and his nose hit the floor when she put him down. Slowly he staggered to his feet and waddled to the door. Liz lifted him to the ground and put him in the shade of a yew bush. He panted, dry-eyed and unblinking, then duck-like, he doused his head repeatedly in the bowl of water she brought, shaking off the excess. Finally Sneakers began to drink. Liz refilled the bowl. The cat panted for long periods between drinks.

As Liz and the children got ready to leave for Gran's, she tried to coax the dehydrated feline into the cool comfort of the basement, but he would not be moved, so they replenished the pail of rain water, providing ample reserve.

"Oh, my poor baby," Charie crooned. "You don't belong in the dryer. That's for clothes!"

"He won't do it again, I bet!" Jimmy offered.

"He won't go *near* it again," Rand submitted as they got into the car and he bid them goodbye.

"Don't forget to check the water dish, Daddy," Charie reminded him.

They filled Gran in on every detail. "Poor Sneakers!" she commiserated. "Why didn't you bring him so we could keep him comfortable?"

Liz assured her he was recuperating exactly where he wanted to be.

"You have enough to do without taking on my work," Betty protested as she pulled out paper towels and cleaning supplies. "I'll be over to help *you* next week."

Before long the little ones meandered outside, soon to be engaged in one of their inevitable arguments: Jimmy, with a bat, wanted Charie to pitch balls to him; Charie wanted to have a catch. Didn't Jimmy know she didn't *like* to pitch balls? "If you *hit* them Jimmy, then I have to chase them, too!"

"So what, Charie. I do things for you sometimes. You don't pitch them so I can hit them anyway."

"Then let's play catch. 'Sides, you wouldn't get my pencil I dropped yesterday, about ten times."

"That's 'cause you were closer."

"So *what?* I do things for you sometimes, too. But not chase balls."

Liz summoned them for a conference. They stood at attention shoulder to shoulder. "Must you always argue?"

Charie responded with a shrug, "I guess so."

"You have to alternate choices. First one, then the other."

"First me," offered the little girl willingly.

"Why you first?" Jimmy quipped. "Mrs. Johnstone said in Sunday School we should always put others first."

"Then you should let me go first. Ladies 'fore gen'lemen."

Grasping each by a hand, Liz stationed them on opposite sides of the sliding door. She then gave each a spray bottle of water and paper towels and set them to work.

Almost immediately their scowls and growls turned to titillated laughter as they aimed their liquid ammo at each other with the sliding glass door between, ducking and giggling at the same time: swipe and aim, over and over. Liz and her mother decided it was well worth the extra cleanup to keep them entertained.

"It's cheaper than the amusement park!"

"Seems like the same trick I used on *you*," Betty chuckled. "You and Cassie were always having a spat about something."

"After we clean the windows some more, can we go watch the new neighbors move in?" Charie questioned after lunch.

Liz replied, "If you can watch without going into their yard. And without arguing about it."

"We'll stand in Gran's driveway, by the garage," Jimmy offered. "We won't fight."

"We'll try not to," added Charie.

Nancy J. Sell

The spot in Gran's driveway was the only place that afforded a view, where the hedge had been trampled into a path. They had stood there a few weeks before, to watch the old neighbors move out.

"Mommy!" Charie yelled a half hour later. Liz poked her head out of a closet to face her daughter. Charie giggled. "Your face is dirty. Anyway, there's a man over there," she exclaimed aghast, pointing in the direction of the new neighbors' backyard, "and—and—he sits in his space seat. He says he'll be stuck on earth forever if he can't get his spaceship fixed!"

Jimmy reinforced her concern. "And when he goes back to Wiggawabba Land, he'll make honey bees out of children!" Jimmy's brown eyes widened into quarter-size discs. "He's a *busy man in his space chair!*"

Liz was angry. "What kind of nonsense . . ." Putting her cleaning cloth and Gran's former foot-soaking bucket aside, she stormed toward the door.

"Don't be hasty, Liz Ann," her mother warned.

The children were close on Liz's heels, their fears allayed in her protective company. Betty followed.

Liz stopped short when she saw the ruggedly handsome man: large, muscular, masculine. He was Gran's new neighbor. He was in a wheelchair.

"Hello there, neighbor," he boomed in a friendly voice. The depth and volume of his voice were remarkable, Liz thought. "Do come over. I'm Bill Sutton, but everyone calls me The Spaceman."

"Well, hello," Liz stammered, slowly closing the distance to his back door where he sat. She was immediately attracted by his warm, friendly manner, his big smile.

"These two ran off before I found out what kind of honey bees they'd like to be."

Liz laughed, liking the man but not sure she liked his game. She was, for once, at a loss for words. "Say hello to Mr. Sutton, kids," she offered meekly.

"We already did."

"Oh, and here's my wife, my HoneyBea. And my daughter, Betsy, and my son, Bobby. There's about two more. Last time I counted there were four, right, Bea? They're Sutton's honey 'B's.' Now tell me what kind of honey bees you'd like to be. Oh," he interrupted himself, "here's Bonnie, and Billy."

Liz shook hands with each of them. "I'm Liz Markham. This is Charie, and this is Jimmy. You've met my mother, I believe."

"Charie. Is that your name? I'm glad you came to visit."

"I'm really Charlotte and I don't want to be a bee, they sting," Charie stated stubbornly. "And 'sides, you're telling a lie." Liz started to correct her daughter when the man raised his hand to stop her.

"My apologies," he repeated, "but you don't have to be a honey bee, you know. Not if you behave." With an aside, and a hand to block his words, he told her, "I don't really make bees. It's for fun. It's our game. But who is this young man?"

"He's Jimmy. He's a boy."

"Of course he's a boy. What kind of honey bee shall I make of him?"

"I don't want to be a bee either," Jimmy interposed. "I'm just going to be me."

But Charie spoke up, refusing to move closer to this odd man. He wiggled a "come-on" finger to Charie and Jimmy, "I have a secret." They shuffled their feet but didn't move an inch. "I don't make honey bees. You're safe. It's just a game—for fun," he explained.

The children were soon occupied, trying to help Betsy and Bonnie set up a badminton net. The two girls were too polite to say they would do better alone. "Just hold these poles," the taller one advised.

Liz found Bill Sutton to be fascinating. She longed to ask the reason for his confinement to the wheelchair but was so absorbed in the man himself, his physical handicap grew less and less important. Mrs. Sutton was quiet, charming, a good balance to his exuberance. They seemed so relaxed, so content with life, so accepting of their lot. Liz wondered how much of what she was seeing was genuine.

But as Bill Sutton talked with her mother, his children soon captivated Liz's attention. Lovely Betsy with smooth brown complexion: *maybe Jamaican*, Liz thought; she was a beauty. Bobby: clearly oriental. And Bonnie was dark, Spanish, maybe Puerto Rican, a shy petite teenager. Another beauty. And Billy, obviously the youngest, no more than six or seven, a duplicate in every way to Bill Sutton Sr. Three adopted, one natural. Or maybe they were foster children. No, Bill had said, "Sons. Daughters."

Oh, Liz wanted to talk with the Suttons, to get to know them better. They would be allies in the pro-adoption issue, she knew for sure.

On the way back to Betty's, Liz inquired of her mother, "Why didn't you warn me?"

"Some things are better found out for themselves."

When Rand arrived late in the afternoon, the children were full of details of their new friend, Mr. Sutton and his family. Rand went with them through the break in the hedge, to meet this special person, combination spaceman/honey bee man, and to take chicken soup and a chocolate cake Gran had made for them.

An intellectual man, Bill Sutton was also friendly, and Rand found no difficulty in maintaining a lively conversation with him. While Rand helped put a swing set together, they were discussing the World Series and the upcoming football season when Liz appeared to announce that supper was ready at Gran's; if he didn't come right away he had a choice between well done or cold.

"Just promise you'll come back." Was there an urgency in his voice? "Soon!"

Rand arrived back at Gran's house just as the steaks were coming off the grill. As the family sat down at the table, he commented to anyone listening, "An unusual family, aren't they?"

Gran affirmed his conclusion with, "A lovely family. I'm going to enjoy having them as neighbors."

"Can you imagine adopting so many kids?"

"Yes," Liz spoke. "I think it's great."

"You would." Rand spoke softly.

On Monday Liz made a cheesy-beefy casserole for supper and put together a duplicate for the Suttons. Truth was, she wanted a fine tune on this unique couple who had adopted not one, but *three* children. The fact that the children were all of different ethnic backgrounds did not puzzle her: She could love them all, too.

"Something to make your day easier," she said when Bea Sutton answered her ring.

"How nice!" she exclaimed sincerely, putting Liz at ease. "Better than hot dogs or bacon and eggs! Please come in."

"You're so busy . . ."

"Never too busy to spend a few minutes with a friend, old or new. Besides, I could use a cup of tea and a *sit* right about now. I've been unpacking books all morning, and dishes all afternoon."

"In that case—"

"In that case you'll join me, and I'll love it."

"I was going to say, I'll *help*."

"Absolutely not. And you just did." She indicated the casserole she held. "Thanks so much. It smells de-lish. You should have brought your mother. She's one special lady. Why don't I call her?"

"She left for Hartford this morning, to visit my sister Cassie for a few days."

"Oh, she told me she was going. Next time then. Come sit down. My husband is resting."

Liz was disappointed that he wasn't about, but soon found Bea to be more open when she wasn't dwarfed by her husband's giant personality.

"He tires easily some days. He works at the computer for hours at a time," she explained. "I think the most tiring part is sitting in the wheelchair."

"How long has he been confined to it?"

"Three years. And one month. And two days."

Don't make me ask, Liz ordered silently as Bea poured tea into mugs she had just washed. *Why is he confined?*

"I'm sure you're wondering why he's in a wheelchair. He was in a car accident that left him paralyzed. Someone cut him off. He lost control. Hit a pole. Totaled the car and almost himself. The culprit, drunk, drove off without a scratch."

"Is it permanent? I mean, have you . . ."

"Many times over. 'No more. No more tests, no more doctors, no more hospitals. *No more*,' he insists. Thank goodness his mind is fine. And his hands. He's able to drive a specially equipped car his company provided for him."

"He still works then?"

"They don't want to lose him. He's a dynamo. The car's in for service now."

"You've taken it well."

Bea's eyes met hers, and Liz realized there was far more to the woman than she could fathom in a lifetime.

"It seems so, doesn't it? I'm glad."

"So you adopted the children before the accident. That was good."

"Two. Two before, one after. That surprises you?" Bea queried, seeing Liz's eyes widen. "They're *our kids*. The oldest came last." Again Liz's eyes grew large. "We were negotiating for her when the accident occurred."

"And you went ahead . . ."

"I told you, they're *ours*. It would have been unthinkable to do anything else. As unthinkable as it would be to put Billy *up* for adoption just because his father *became* handicapped."

Quietly sipping her tea and nibbling on the shortbread cookies Bea had set out on a little paper plate, Liz was thoughtful.

"Did I say something wrong?" Bea asked, sensing a disquietude.

"Wrong? No. In fact, quite right."

Now it was Bea's turn to be puzzled. Her attention was diverted, however, and she said, "Bill, come have tea with us."

"Well, welcome!" he exclaimed to Liz. "My apologies for goofing off when we're privileged to have such an honored guest!" Expertly he swung his chair into position at the table. "Coffee for me, sweetheart. Now what is this quite-right conversation we're having?"

"I was telling Liz about our kids."

"Aren't they terrific? It sure would be dull around here without them," he proclaimed loudly. "So quiet."

Liz laughed. "I doubt *that*. They *are* wonderful though. Charie and Jimmy think so, too."

"Now there's a pair! You have others? Rand mentioned a Jeff."

"Jeff and Pam. Jeff is almost sixteen, Pam almost fourteen." She then explained Jimmy's status, his past, and what she hoped would be his future. "He's very special. It's like he's our own."

"Wonderful!" he boomed, and Liz wondered if he ever spoke in a normal pitch. "He's a fine boy, and he seems to fit right into your family. Go for it."

Liz had finished her tea and knew Bea was ready to resume her unpacking. She quickly and graciously made her exit with a promise to drop in again.

The next day was a gray wet one, and Liz consented to playing a game with Charlotte and Jimmy to allay their after-school restlessness.

"Oh, d—n!" Jimmy mumbled after scanning his Flinch hand.

"Where did you hear that word, Jim?" Liz asked.

"Jeff says it."

"Don't say it anymore."

"Should I tell Jeff not to, too?"

"I'll tell him."

Jeff appeared a few minutes later, wet and out of sorts.

"Jimmy is using words he tells me he hears from you, Jeff." Liz said un-accusingly, confronting him before Jimmy had an opportunity.

"Like the D-word," Jimmy insisted.

"Enough, Jimmy," Liz warned.

"You never heard *me* say that!" Jeff said, defensively.

"I did too hear you," Jimmy insisted.

"And when, I'd like to know?"

Jimmy's Home

"I was standing behind you when you were fixing your mini-bike, and that's what you said: 'oh, D-word.'"

"Stop!" Liz exclaimed.

"I'll wring your fat little head off your little neck and kick you all the way to the Glendale dump if you don't mind your business—"

"Both of you, stop. And stop using that kind of talk."

Charie advised, "You should just say darn, Jimmy. Not the other word."

"If anyone uses that word again they *will* be sorry!" Liz spoke sharply.

I give up!

Liz took Charie and Jimmy for their annual Halloween visits, first by car to Gran's, the Suttons, the homes of a few friends, and then to their cul-de-sac neighbors. Rand remained at home to parcel out the goodies she had prepared for the ghosts and goblins who rang their doorbell. "Now don't just hand them out, Daddy." Charie gave him the same lecture he used to hear from Jeff and Pam. "Find out who the trick-or-treaters are and if we know them. Make a list so we'll know if any of our friends come."

Finally, costumes were shed for another year, Charlotte and Jimmy were asleep, and Liz exhaled a sigh. She deplored this annual nuisance of who was going to wear what, where was the mask to this costume, the costume to this mask, hair coloring, the treat bags, the flashlights . . . They had been on their way out the door when Jimmy had tripped and tumbled down the steps, cutting his knee, tearing his costume, and getting angry at Charie for laughing at him.

"Well, you'd laugh too, Jimmy, if you saw a crumpled-up ghost falling down the stairs! Ghosts are supposed to float, to glide, like this!" she said, demonstrating her interpretation of ghostly characteristics. "You were a *ghost ball!*" She laughed loudly at her own humor. "With a red ghost blood spot on your knee."

"You won't feel like laughing, Charie, if I give you a crumpled-up face. And I don't mean your cockatiel mask!"

"And ghosts don't have any blood," Charie interjected.

"Shut up."

"Why don't you laugh too, Jimmy? That'd make it more fun," Charie added.

"Let's go," Liz said, after repairing Jimmy's costume with safety pins.

Pam was at Millicent's for an all-girl party and would spend the night at Persie's. "I met Persie's parents last week at the PTA meeting, and I know the girls will be well-supervised. You'd like them." Liz spoke to her nodding husband as they watched TV. The porch light had been left on for any straggling trick-or-treaters.

Jeff came in, helped himself to the two remaining treat packages and a half liter of soda from the fridge, and started for his room. He paused. "That's a lousy movie. The son attacks his stepfather because he's messing around with his sister, the mother tries to protect the son and everybody ends up injured, dead, or in jail."

"Thanks," his mother responded.

"'Night. You shouldn't watch it. Not your style."

"Goodnight, Jeff." Rand didn't answer because he was asleep. During a commercial, Liz, picking up Charie's cockatiel mask en route, went to the bedroom to change into her nightgown and robe. Holding the mask over her face, she looked in the mirror and grinned wickedly behind it. She had an idea. *Should* she? *Dare* she?

She started to get ready for bed, but after donning her new sheer nightgown, she took an old raincoat from the closet. "Whoops. Wait a minute." She ran to Charie's room and got a stick-on tattoo and put it low on her chest. Back in her room, she giggled to herself as she rummaged in the closet for boots, then slipped her feet into them, and, with Charie's mask in hand, quietly let herself out the back door. She shivered.

She was glad for once that Jeff would be using earphones and listening to his music while going to sleep and would not hear her ring the doorbell. She had to ring, then knock repeatedly before Rand stirred. When he finally realized the sole charge of answering the door was his, he shook his head and rose. Liz, chilled and excited, saw movement through the stained glass window beside the front door and she shivered again. Did she, shy reserved Liz, have the nerve? When Rand opened the door, there stood a trick-or-treater clad in mask, raincoat and boots. Then Liz opened her raincoat.

She scarcely had time to read his expression in the subdued porch light when Rand slid to the floor, moaning as his head struck the mahogany demilune in the hall.

"Oh no. Oh no. Oh no!" Pulling her coat close to her again, she ran to the kitchen phone and dialed the emergency number. "An ambulance, quickly! My husband fell! He's bleeding! He's unconscious! Oh, God, I hope he's not *dead!* He's not," she managed to say. "But hurry. *Hurry!*" She gave the address. "No sirens please."

By the time the ambulance arrived, Liz was fully dressed in jeans and sweatshirt, and trying to tend to Rand, administering ice to his wound and salve to his dignity, not to mention her own.

He had not spoken a word to her. He merely glared at her, appearing to have lost his senses. She moved away to make room for the medical team. *Oh, Randy, please don't tell what's behind all this! I'll be so mortified! Don't do that to me, please!*

After completing their routine checks, the EMTs brought in a stretcher.

"What do you think you're doing with *that?*" Rand demanded blearily.

"You need further testing, stitches, X-rays . . . You have a pretty good laceration there—"

"I am not going to the hospital. Not. N. O. T."

"You must—"

"I'm *not* going to the hospital with you, so you can just march that thing right out of here. When I go—*if* I go—I'll drive myself!"

When they left, Rand was seated on the couch; he was angry and had not as yet acknowledged his wife's presence. She brought a tray with herbal tea, a cup for each of them, and aspirin for Rand. When she finished hers, Rand had not yet touched his. She went to bed and heard him drive out, picturing him holding a towel to his head.

She was still awake when he returned. He engrossed himself in the late news and finally went to bed.

When he slid in beside her, she was still too embarrassed to look him in the eye, or even to initiate conversation. The darkness was a blessing, and he probably thought she was asleep.

After a long silence, he asked, "What did you do such a dumb thing for?"

Should she answer? She did. "I thought it would be funny." She wasn't laughing. She was close to tears.

"It wasn't."

"I know."

"Did you need stitches?"

"Staples," he corrected. "Four or five."

The bed began to shake, a little at first, and she was alarmed. Was Rand convulsing? What should she do? She wasn't informed about many medical procedures, and she was scared. Suddenly he burst out in a full-fledged howl, turned to Liz and enveloped her in his arms. "It was funny," he muttered, beginning to kiss her passionately. "It was funny, and I love you. You know what? I kinda like you, too. But it wasn't funny—*now* it is."

"How's your head?" she asked, gasping for air.

"I'll be all right. I have a headache."

"That's a switch."

Finally, when she lay beside him, sleepless, he whispered, "Liz?"

She thought he was asleep. "Hmm?"

"Keep the tattoo."

"Oh, the president's coming for dinner," Jeff mumbled, observing the elegant dining table with white damask cloth, burgundy-colored napkins and candles, and pink and burgundy silk bouquet. The candlesticks and flower bowl were white porcelain, as was Liz's best china.

"Not quite," Liz responded to her eldest, "but just as important. The Suttons," she explained. "Mr. and Mrs."

"Oh, the famous spaceman. Did he get his spaceship fixed?" Jeff spoke gruffly, somewhat sarcastically, giving his mother cause for concern. His mood swings were less frequent, but they surfaced periodically nevertheless. "He should be leaving for Wabbawiggyland soon. I hope he takes Charie and Jimmy with him."

Liz laughed in spite of herself. "Yes, he'll be driving it over tonight." She told Jeff about his special car provided by his company. "Dad may need you to help get the wheelchair into the house. Stick around, okay?"

"I have to go to the library," he growled unpleasantly.

"Can't you wait until they get here?"

"I suppose," he muttered. "Dinner for four. We lesser beings eat in the kitchen tonight, I guess. I'm right, right?"

"You love it," she chided, trying to kiss him on the cheek before he ducked. "Besides, we're dining at seven-thirty. You'd die if you had to wait. And we're having broiled salmon, asparagus . . ."

"Yuk, I'll eat now so I can leave."

"After they get here."

"I *said* I'd wait. I don't have to wait to eat, do I?"

"Fix your plate then," she stated, "and cheer up."

Jeff had come home and gone to his room with a dish of dessert; Pam, Charie and Jimmy were asleep.

Burgundy candles burned low and no one at the dining table seemed aware of the grandfather clock in the front hall as its Westminster chimes denoted quarter-hour segments. Rand and Liz, Bill and Bea sat; they talked; they sipped the fresh decaf coffee Liz had made long after dessert was over. A congenial group, its rapport was unique.

But although they had conversed about many topics, and the subject of children had surfaced many times, not once did Bill or Bea extol the merits, the joys, the *rightness* of adopting children. This had not fit into Liz's game plan.

Jimmy's Home

When the Suttons finally left for home, Liz sat for a few minutes before extinguishing the candles while Rand cleared the remaining dishes from the table. She put away the salt and pepper shakers and sugar bowl, then gathered the linen napkins. After filling the dishwasher and starting it, she put the pots and pans to soak and went to bed. The perfect evening had had one flaw: The Suttons had let her down. She felt betrayed.

Over the next weeks the friendship grew, however, and Liz often stopped in to say hello to Bea when she went to her mother's. One day it was Bill who answered her knock.

"Come in, Liz. Bea is running errands, but the coffee's hot. She'll be back soon. Join me for coffee?"

Moving quickly and competently, he took mugs from the rack; Liz filled them and sat across from him at the kitchen table.

"You have a fine family. We enjoyed our evening with you and Rand."

"Thank you. And thank you again. We enjoyed it, too. Are you pretty well settled now?"

"Is anyone ever really settled? Don't you always have that feeling that you're still finding places for things, still putting things away? A box full of things you've been hunting for . . ."

"And *throwing* things away. Things you shouldn't have packed at all. You're right, Bill. I guess life is that way. Never really settled."

She sensed that small talk was over when Bill finally asked, "How are plans developing for Jimmy's adoption?" At her surprised look, he said, "No, Rand has not commented on the matter."

"There's nothing new. I'm hoping we can accomplish great things before his mother decides she wants him. Or doesn't want him, and signs his release."

Bill unnerved her with his next words. "Does Rand want these great things accomplished, too? I sense not."

"We're working on that."

"Are you sure you know what you're working on?" he asked pointedly. "You may be building one thing up while you're destroying something else of equal or greater value."

"You're meddling." She tried to keep it light.

"I know."

Enraged, she flared, "What gives you the right—"

"—the right to speak the truth to a friend?"

She stood up and reached for her jacket.

"Liz, hold on. You're angry. I was afraid you would be," he continued with a touch of remorse, not for his words but for her response.

She had reached the door and stopped to face him, primarily to prove him wrong. Taking a deep breath and regaining control of her voice, she spoke. "You and Rand had no business discussing *our* business without me."

"Oh, ho!" he spoke loudly and with a calm affirmation. "I told you Rand and I have discussed nothing of the kind. He could have told you that."

His words were an affront, a rebuke, and the look she gave him was skeptical and contemptuous.

"But listen to this, Liz," he went on kindly, in a softer but more convincing tone. "Come sit down. Come," he repeated. She didn't move from the doorway. "Please, at least look at me." She refused. "Liz, I know this for a fact: Couples for the most part accept a child they have conceived themselves. At least they have an obligation to do that. But both parents have to *want a product of someone else's emotions.* Adoption has to be a two-party decision."

He wasn't at all sure she had heard what he said. The door closed softly behind her, and he was left alone.

CHAPTER EIGHTEEN

A few white snowflakes, like soft fleecy feathers, drifted silently in the pristine morning air. Here and there they fastened themselves to the window, then melted to leave miniature water spots on the clean glass. Liz stared out the window with a coffee cup warming the two hands she clasped around it. Her mind darted from one problem or project to another, seemingly reluctant to focus on one item long enough to peruse or plan. Christmas was just three weeks away. She was too busy in this too-busy season, too frustrated, too short on sleep . . .

"It's snowing," she said noncommittally to Rand, wondering how he could concentrate on the local news broadcast and yesterday's *Connecticut News Times* at the same time; he had already read it, but was annoyed that today's New York paper had not yet been delivered and probably wouldn't be. The voice from *Chopper 99* was giving the traffic report, warning about rush hour tie-ups on the "George" (the reporter's clipped name for the George Washington Bridge) and complete gridlock on the FDR Drive and all its northbound approaches caused by a five-car accident. An overturned semi on I-95 was causing major problems for inbound New York City traffic from both Connecticut and New Jersey. All this, and the snowfall was just beginning. The weather report would follow. Weather and traffic: how closely they were tied together. The chopper would soon be recalled because of the falling snow.

Rand was annoyed with her, she was well aware, and she was pushing it. She was forcing her interruptions. Her little grievance with Bill Sutton had infuriated him when he learned the reason for the long silence between the two families. More so when he found out that Liz had not only ignored Bill's attempted communication, but also had refused numerous invitations. Rand had found a true friend in Bill, and become one in return. Bill considered it not the least awkward to call occasionally upon Rand's muscle power, and he more than compensated in offering his brilliant knowledge of computers, the stock market, investment funds, and kids. They possessed many common denominators and enjoyed the luxury of late-night discussions, sometimes heated but always controlled. Rand frequently departed an almost dark Sutton house, waiting until Bill had transferred himself to bed and the lights had gone out before driving away.

It was preceding one of these departures that Bill had casually referred to Liz's silence. "I guess unsolicited advice is always unwelcome," Bill had told Rand, not really sure his offering to Liz had been unsolicited. Incensed, Rand had arrived home, awakened her accidently, and a confrontation had ensued.

"Go to bed," was all she had mumbled. After that they had hardly spoken for two days. Rand had then continued his friendly visits with the Suttons, risking Liz's hostility, and finding Bill a trustworthy confidant.

"Huh." It was not a question or an answer, but a sound. Rand's eyes were still focused on the paper.

"I was commenting on the weather," Liz spoke calmly. "It's snowing," she repeated dully without turning from the window. She didn't want to look at him. Sometimes she thought she didn't like him.

He switched to a New York station. The on-air meteorologist reported that a few flurries were visible in New York; the snow would be heavy at times with an accumulation of four to six inches, though there would be more in the outlying districts, and would taper off by early evening. Glendale never seemed to get much more than what was predicted for the City, so Liz wasn't sure what *outlying districts* were included. She hoped they got a lot less than six inches.

"Oh, I hope the bus drivers are careful!" Her comment was not heard, or at least not acknowledged. "I know you tell me I worry too much, but somebody has to."

"No, they don't," he mumbled.

"Maybe *you* don't."

"But you *do*."

"You could."

"Why?"

She ignored his question because she considered it inane. When she was sure he was back into his newspaper material, she stated, "I wonder what it will be like when it's time for the kids to come home from school. Oh, maybe they'll have early dismissal. I think I'll pick them up." She was purposely baiting him.

Fighting frustration, Rand spoke without looking up. "And put one more unnecessary vehicle on the road?"

"I'm talking about *my children*." She spoke quietly and deliberately. "Mine."

Without a glance her way, Rand turned the volume up on the radio. Now it was a commercial about learning a foreign language: French, Italian, Spanish—anything—complete with audio tapes.

"I do hope they'll have early dismissal if it gets bad. Why don't you get a local station so we can hear the area reports?"

He increased the volume again, keeping his eyes fixed on his paper. His manner said, "Why don't you be quiet?" He refilled his coffee cup, then poured another puddle of syrup for waffle-dipping and took another bite. She still made the best buttermilk waffles, even if he was annoyed.

"Mother and I were going Christmas shopping today." Liz spoke loudly to compensate, offering information he already knew. "Running errands, grocery shopping . . . Do you think it will get bad?" *How should he know?* She answered for him, but she wanted to antagonize him, disrupt his thinking processes. "We have so *much* to do. You know how it is at Christmastime. And I need stuff from the store: milk, coffee . . ."

This time Rand increased the volume beyond her capabilities to compete. It blared. She cringed.

The telephone rang. He was oblivious to the sound, she realized as the radio beside him drowned out anything short of an earthquake.

Liz, irate, circled the counter, leaned across the table in front of him, picked up the remote, and turned the radio off. Rand's angry eyes met hers. He was livid.

She smugly, confidently sat down opposite him as the phone rang again, this time in a silent room. Laughter, unbidden, unchecked, and too loud escaped from deep within her.

Rand rose to answer the phone, but the caller had given up. Feeling awkward and laughing with her, he sat down again. His laughter increased in volume until it matched hers.

Suddenly Liz's head went down on her arms, and, nearly hysterical, she dissolved into tears.

Rand's head shot up and he stared at her helplessly. Then snatching his coat from the chair beside him, he walked out into the snow.

The roast chicken was cold, the ice in the glasses had melted, and all but his dishes had been cleared away when Rand returned for dinner. After nibbling on cold chicken and broccoli, he put his plate with mashed potatoes, gravy, and cut corn into the microwave. Then after assisting Pam with a math problem, he romped with Jimmy and Charie, watched the end of a basketball game with Jeff, and went down to his basement workshop.

Late that evening when the household was quiet and Liz was preparing for bed, he opened the bedroom door and entered, closing it behind him. In one continuous motion he dropped to the bed and pulled her down beside him. Wrapping her in his arms, he held her firmly against him, his cheek pressed against her hair. He claimed her passionately, and Liz welcomed his touch.

"I love you," he whispered just before they drifted off to sleep.

Do you? she pondered. *Do you really? Sometimes I wonder what's with you, Rand. You stay out for hours, then think you can pick up life where you left off. You don't care about my cares . . . Sometimes I really do wonder.*

The new addition was well under way but had been put on hold again, except for token appearances by the builder, until after the holidays. It appeared that he was trying to appease them. Liz didn't hesitate to let him know how unhappy she was.

Jimmy's Home

"Gran's never going to move into it, you know, so what's the rush?" Jeff offered. "She'll never give up her nice house. So let me move in. I don't even have to wait until it's finished."

The unfinished small sitting room, kitchen, and bedroom were one-half flight up from the family room and were second floor to the garage. Liz, enthusiastic, and her mother, reluctant, had chosen colors for wallpaper, trim, and window dressings. "I'll help you, Liz Ann, but you know it's not going to be for me. Not unless I become handicapped in some way, and I have no intentions of doing that for ages to come. Let Jeff use the rooms. Or," she went on with a sudden thought, "it could easily have an outside entrance. Then you could probably rent it. If you finish the kitchen."

"Can't," offered Rand. "Zoning."

"Well, save your breath. And your money. I'm staying put. Besides, what would I do with all my antiques, my beautiful china?"

So that was the end of that. It looked like Jeff might get his wish. With conditions, of course. The unfinished sitting room could be a bedroom for Jimmy.

"Mommy, when's Christmas?" Jimmy inquired impatiently one morning when he came downstairs for breakfast. It was a frequent question, reflecting his excitement.

"Soon, Jimmy. All too soon."

"Why too soon?"

"Oh, because there's lots to do before Christmas comes."

"I wish it was tomorrow."

"Then we wouldn't be ready. No tree. No presents wrapped. No stockings hung. No gingerbread house or Christmas cookies made . . . And Gran has to make her date and nut pudding and potato candy."

"We'll just have to wait then, won't we?" he grinned. "And whoever heard of potato candy? But I can help you make Christmas cookies. Charie and I like to help you bake."

I know, Liz thought. *That's why I often do it while you're still in school.* The last time they "helped," Liz had berated Charie for eating a lump of raw dough, and she had spewed it back into the bowl. Liz had dumped the contents of the bowl into the garbage can.

The Sutton children liked to help, too. One day, back in the fall, when Liz had dropped in, Bill had been at the table making cookies. "Billy, get me three eggs. No, don't try to carry them all at once. You drop it, you clean it up. Betsy, I need sugar and flour. I'll measure. Just bring me the canisters. Bobby, you can get me the vanilla." Laughing and obedient, the children had delightedly carried out his every command. Theirs was a special household, no doubt about it.

"You can help me bake cookies, Jimmy," Liz told him with a wink. "That will be fun."

Liz returned home one day to find Charie at the kitchen table, attempting an emergency cleanup of cereal. The Lucky Stars were overflowing the huge bowl in front of her and covering the table. Most of them, however, appeared to be on the floor. There were two almost-empty, overturned boxes on the table, another on the floor. "Mommy, they overfloated! What'd you come home so soon for?" she shrieked. "I'm cleaning them up!"

"Yes, but *why* are you cleaning them up?"

"Because they *spilled!*" Her manner said, *What a silly question!*

"You know what I mean, Charie. Why did you empty three boxes of cereal?"

"These boxes are special. They have little games and stickers in them."

"Charie! Where did you ever get this idea? You know we wait until the boxes are empty, or almost . . ."

"Mom," she reasoned, "Gran showed me how to do it."

Before Liz could decide what to do about the ones on the floor, Mini and Sneakers appeared and began to take care of them.

Oh, Mom, she thought, *wait until I get ahold of you!*

Snow had covered the ground most of the month since Thanksgiving, and the early snowfall was contributing to the exhilaration of the approaching holidays. The air was crisp and cold, and its effect was invigorating. The decorations in town, the tiny white lights strung randomly on the small leafless trees lining Elm and Main Streets, twinkled through the snow-tipped branches.

Carolers sang their traditional repertoire in God's Acre, Glendale's triangular hillside green, which was surrounded by typical white New England churches of the postcard variety. Midway in the green a pine tree laden with an abundance of lights had just been set aglow in the wintry evening. A full-size crèche at the lowest spot where the ground leveled off made the scene complete. It was a lovely sight.

"I think the whole town turned out this year," Liz said to Rand, blinking away the snowflakes that brushed her eyelids.

"That proves they're all nuts," he shrugged. She poked him in the ribs with her elbow.

Nancy J. Sell

Except for losing Charie and Jimmy for most of an hour, then finding them window shopping at the toy store, the evening was delightful. Liz was sorry when it ended. They boarded the train, a spur line which dead-ended in Glendale, and rode it back to the Thorny Hill station where it then continued on. The train had been called "The Turkey Killer" for as long as Liz could remember. On weekdays express commuter trains traveled from near Glendale nonstop to New York City.

Snow was falling harder by the time they stepped onto the platform at Thorny Hill, and their feet crunched on the remains of the previous accumulations. After the train disappeared around the bend, there was no other light, no sound except for the scraping of a snowplow off in the distance, the whistle of the train, and an occasional car creeping along the nearby Parkway. The silence was broken again by the train whistle in the distance.

"Can you think of anything more lovely?" Liz asked no one in particular as they walked the mile or so back to their house.

"A few things," Rand responded. "When I look at this stuff coming down so beautifully, I think, 'How many hours is it going to take to shovel?' 'Will my fingers fall off from frostbite?' 'How many people will have heart attacks trying to clear their walks?'" *Maybe me . . .*

"You know you love it," she chided, putting her arm through his. He loosened his arm from hers and put it around her, pulling her close.

"Yeah, I do. It's beautiful," he said, and meant it, remembering their first walk in the snow that first Christmas he was a guest at her home.

The mile-long walk took more than an hour as they stopped to play: throwing snowballs, catching snowflakes on their tongues, and making snow angels. "Do you still smell the snow?" Rand asked her.

"Of course!"
"You're dreaming."

⌒

The Markhams' tree stood, still tied, in the corner of the new patio. Jimmy and Charie were eager to see it in place and decorated.

Liz followed a nonstop schedule of baking fruitcakes, a cheesecake for Don (her butcher friend at the supermarket), beautiful fancy cookies for friends and for people in Rand's office, followed by shopping, wrapping gifts, and decorating the house. The children grew more helpful each year, Pam especially, who had become general manager in charge of home decorations. Liz was glad to relinquish the major portion of this chore to her, especially as she felt a twinge of nausea now and then. She ignored it and chalked it up to exhaustion, maybe a flu bug. She tried to will it to go away.

Pam took Charie and Jimmy sledding and ice skating frequently, depending on favorable weather conditions for either, and this proved a great help for their mother. They made a *gi'antic* snowman and snowlady, and a fort where their leaf house had been. Rand said they needed a matching fort so they could have a real snowball fight, so they set to work on the second one with verve.

After supper that night, Rand and Jeff chose up teams, and with the spotlight from the house illuminating the battlefield, they enjoyed a rowdy fracas. Several neighbors joined in. Poor Mr. and Mrs. Snowman, unable to defend themselves, were demolished. Liz watched from the window, glad the teams were even without her.

The Christmas season was marred by one distressing incident. Rand and Liz always made an appearance at the office Christmas party, arriving late and leaving early, often taking in a late movie or driving on into the City to see the tree and decorations in Rockefeller Center. Last year they had attended the Christmas Spectacular at Radio City Music Hall.

Liz did not enjoy office parties.

"Couldn't you try to go, Liz? I know you don't feel well, but if the evening's too much for you, we'll come right home."

But feigning sleep, she didn't move.

Rand went on. "My car in still in the garage, so I'm taking your car. I'll be home before long."

Liz mumbled something as Rand left the room. He went to the party alone.

Arriving a little late, Rand pulled into a parking place in an already crowded lot. He turned off the motor, put his head back, and closed his eyes. He had seldom attended a party, a play, or any other social activity without Liz. He reached for the key to restart the car and paused, then retreated. He wanted to show Liz he depended on her not at all. But he did depend on her. Who was he kidding?

Two other cars pulled into nearby spots, one of them close to his. One couple passed him after pausing to lock up, and patted his front fender. Rand raised a hand and signaled his intentions, then followed them in.

Bebe, approaching him from behind, slipped an arm through his. "Aha! The family man *sans wife* tonight. How different. How delightful!"

Rand's hand came out of his pocket to disentangle himself from Bebe, the clinging vine. He scowled at her. "No less the family man, my dear, just because I'm alone. Liz is sick."

"Nevertheless, I'm going to keep an eye on you. And keep the mistletoe handy." She patted the sprig she had tucked into the low-cut V of her black velvet dress. She wore red shoes, a matching rose in her hair, and carried a red clutch purse. Her ensemble was striking, and she looked gorgeous. "I've heard that a lot lately. Liz is sick. Sick of you?"

"Probably. But she's stuck with me." His scowl returned. He tried to ignore her. He helped himself to hors d'oeuvres as Bebe handed him a glass of punch. He knew the champagne was not for him.

"Too bad! She can get unstuck. Hey, we're really celebrating tonight, aren't we? A night off the wagon?" She indicated the glass in his hand with an impish smile.

Annoyed, he shrugged. "Why not? It's not the spiked stuff."

"I should have said, '*What* are we celebrating tonight?'"

He raised his glass. "Here's to Liz, to Christmas, to office parties, to Bebe . . ."

"And to our Family Man, Randolph Markham. No, *J.* Randolph Markham. And the J is for? Oh, well, such a nice name. So distinguished . . . Such a nice man. What a hunk! Oh, I know. *Jeffrey Randolf Markham.*" She had already had too much to drink. "And to mistletoe!" She snatched it from her bosom and, in attempting to hold it over Rand's head, fell against him, clutching her arms around his neck. Her moist red lips were against his cheek, as she attempted to kiss him, snapping a selfie at the same time. Again he untangled himself and wondered why he bothered. *Kinda' nice*, he said to himself. But sipping his drink and wiping his cheek where he knew her lipstick had been imprinted, he left her, moving on to another group and hoping she would do the same. Realizing Bebe had slipped him the wrong punch, he put his glass down.

It was late when Rand decided to leave. A few people remained. He should have avoided Bebe as he headed for the door. "As they say," he said aloud, "one for the road." He held up another drink one of the men had thrust into his hand. Guilt plagued him, but he promised himself no more. Ever. Again, he put his glass down.

Bebe approached him as he walked toward the door. "Remember, I'm keeping an eye on you," she whispered.

With that, she again drew some mistletoe from her cleavage and tried to reach over his head to kiss his cheek. He gritted his teeth but faked a quick smile.

"I hope you didn't bring your picture-taking device." Rand spoke of her ever-present state-of-the-art cell phone.

"Of course I did, I wouldn't go anywhere without it. It's my entertainment!"

They chatted briefly, then Rand said, "I'll see you later," as he left her to join a small group of men.

"Count on it," she spoke while turning away.

Out of the corner of his point of vision he spotted her aiming her phone at different individuals, sometime singles, sometimes groups, sometimes special people, many of them men. She returned to Rand and with him cheek to cheek, took another picture.

Rand was getting ready to leave, but unfortunately Bebe stopped him to ask for a ride home since she lived in Riverdale, "almost next door to Glendale," she reminded him. "I know where you live." Rand spoke harshly; he was annoyed at her for putting him in this spot, and at himself for the same reason. Reluctantly he agreed to drop her off knowing she was too drunk to get home safely. The people she had arrived with had already left, and the attendance was dwindling. And now it was snowing.

When they pulled up to the condo complex where she lived, Rand put the car in park and glanced at Bebe. "Well, here's where you get out." Rand wondered if she would find her way after the drinks she had consumed. She looked at him and sweetly said, "Aren't you going to see me to the door? I thought you were a gentleman."

"Get out, Bebe. Out!"

"I need help. My key might not work right. I might fall down and not get up. I'll die in the cold. Don't you dare leave until I get in the house!"

Rand, steaming, opened his door and slammed it. When he pulled the passenger door open Bebe looked up at him with dreamy eyes. "Out," he repeated.

"Help me!" she cried.

Rand grasped her wrist, drew her to her feet, and steadied her stance. "Give me your keys," he demanded. She reached back into the car for her purse, not realizing her phone had fallen to the floor as she had grabbed it, and took out her keys. She released them to him, but took advantage of the closeness and brushed her lips across his cheek, stopping at his lips. Rand immediately pulled away from her.

After making sure she was safely in her condo, he dropped her key on the floor inside the door and left. "I made it," he said out loud, drawing his own keys from his pocket and checking for his cell phone. He thought about giving Liz a call to let her know he was on his way but tabled the thought because she was likely to be asleep. He headed for the car, thankful there had been no witnesses to the awkward display.

A cruising police car passed but didn't stop. "Oh boy," Rand breathed a "thank you" to the winds. He opened his car door, got in, and closed it. Twenty minutes or so later, he was parking Liz's car in her garage. He was annoyed at himself for not realizing sooner that Bebe had slipped him the spiked punch. "Well, I'm

Nancy J. Sell

home." He pushed a button to close the overhead garage door then headed for the front door.

Rand reached up to the ledge above the front door where the spare house key was kept. His searching fingers examined the entire edge. No key! He checked a second hideout under a rock in the front garden. Rand groaned, this time more graphically. He was locked out of his house!

He pressed the doorbell and cringed as the musical *ding-dong* echoed through the quiet house. He rang it again and again, each time in closer sequence. His aching head made him impatient.

A light went on in their bedroom. Then he saw shifting shadows against the leaded stained glass windows on either side of the big front door. He suppressed an impulse to put his finger over the peephole as he sometimes did. Liz wouldn't think it was funny this time. She had probably hidden the keys, too.

"Welcome home, Rand."

"Trick-or-treat!" He weakly added "Hi" when she didn't respond.

"Must have been quite a party to keep you out so late."

Stepping inside and closing the door behind him, he groaned again. "It was."

"That's obvious." She faced him angrily.

"Liz," he sighed, "could we save it until morning? I've had an upsetting experience, my head is killing me, I'm freezing . . ."

"My husband, who never drinks, comes home smelling of alcohol and with lipstick on his face, and I'm to pretend I don't see it."

"I'm not drunk."

"And what kind of games did we play at this party tonight, Spin the Bottle? That's outdated."

"Go to bed," he snarled.

"Good idea."

She ascended the stairs with Rand slowly following. When he reached the door to their room, his pillow hit him full in the face and the door was shut firmly and securely in front of him. He heard the click of the lock as he reached for the handle.

"Who cares?" he loudly addressed the closed door. "The fireplace is warmer anyway! Warmer than *you!*"

As Rand stretched out on the floor before the fire he had rekindled, he wished he had stayed home.

Several days later, Liz, when feeling better and the snow had stopped, was making a short trip to the grocery store. She spotted something of interest on the floor of her car. Examining the item, she found it to be a cell phone. *No, mine is in my purse*, she thought. *Or maybe I left it in the kitchen. I wonder whose it is; they're probably looking for it.* Turning it on, she discovered that the security had been disabled. She looked at the pictures and gasped. Bebe and friends, Bebe and someone, Bebe and another man. Bebe and . . . Bebe and . . . Bebe . . . she flipped through the pictures until they appeared to be near the end of the party. Then Bebe and Rand! They were kissing! "No!"

On Monday Rand went to the office and submitted his resignation.

CHAPTER NINETEEN

"You can't resign, Rand," Leo Maxwell, his boss, lectured. "I won't let you." He had just put some important items on hold for this confrontation.

"Who says I can't? I just did."

"I won't accept it. Take a vacation. You've got more than ample time accumulated. Take the wife to the Caribbean for two weeks to make peace. Go to Alaska this summer. I'll even buy your tickets. Give yourself time to think it through."

"I'll take a rain check on the tickets. But I don't need time," he contended, reflecting that Liz would be livid to hear herself described as an impersonal object: *The Wife*. Anyway, he wasn't about to take *the wife* anywhere when they hardly spoke to each other at home. "I'm tired of this zoo," he continued. "I'm taking today off, what's left of it. Then I'll need two, three weeks to finish up my projects, prepare for a replacement, clean my office out . . ."

"Don't do it, Rand," Maxwell reiterated as he backed out the door. "I need you here!"

Max waved at Bebe as she passed by; he held up a phone number she had requested.

"Gotta run," Max said, "but don't do it."

Rand sat at his desk doing nothing for a full fifteen minutes before the storm in his chest cavity subsided.

He didn't tell Liz about his conversation with Max. She was extra kind, extra understanding, extra patient with her family. Rand knew she wore a mask; she was hurting. She wasn't kind, understanding, or patient with him.

"Liz, would you let me tell you what happened the night of the party?"

She smiled in her new condescending manner and said, "No explanations are necessary."

"Certainly they are."

"They are not! It's done! I saw the pictures! Just forget it!"

"I can't forget it! The pictures don't tell the true story. Please let me explain."

"Don't you understand? It doesn't matter."

"It matters. You know it does."

"To you. Not to me. Not anymore."

"I want it to matter to you. I want you to understand."

"I do. And it's done."

A week before Christmas, Rand and Jeff brought in the Christmas tree, and after they all fussed over which side should be the front, Rand carefully strung the lights on the tree so they were evenly spaced. In an attempt to please Liz, he placed them meticulously. The white lights of the star on top just barely cleared the ceiling.

When he finished, he pulled out some mistletoe, held it over his wife's head, and planted a warm, lingering kiss on her lips. He knew she would not fuss in front of the children, but her whole manner was set in a firm line, unyielding.

"Now I have a surprise for all of you. Everybody, stay. Don't go." Rand fussed with a contraption that connected the tree lights to the electrical outlet. Turning to face them, he ordered, "Everyone sit down and look at the tree. Jim, Charie, everybody. I know you're too excited to sit still, but this will take only a minute." He sat too.

When they were settled but still fidgeting, he commanded, "Look at the tree!" Rand clapped his hands once. Instantly every light on the tree responded.

They squealed with delight. "Oh, Daddy, you're a magician! Do it again!" Charie exclaimed. "I'm going to get that mistletoe and give you a kiss!"

"You do it," he told her. She started to get up. "No, I mean clap your hands." Her palms smacked together, and the lights went off.

"*On!*" Jimmy shouted, clapping loudly.

With much laughter and clapping, they experimented with the new entertainment. Finally, Liz said congenially, "If we don't get the rest of the decorations on the tree, we'll be up all night finishing it. Let's go, kids."

Rand and Jeff disappeared; it was the unspoken agreement that installing the tree and stringing the lights was a father and son job; ornaments were the responsibility of everyone else. Liz and the girls began putting on the multi-colored decorations. Jimmy tried to help, but Liz wished he had gone off with the boys. Still, he was enjoying the proceedings, wanting to help but at a loss.

"You're doing a great job, Jimmy." Liz mentally crossed her fingers. "Did you ever help decorate a tree, Jim?"

He shook his head from side to side, deliberately and sadly. "Nobody would let me. Mrs. Blair said last year that I might break some of her ornaments. Then she broke one. I laughed and she got mad. She said that word you told us not to say. I won't say it, at least not out loud."

"Don't say it to yourself either, or sometime it might just pop out." She smiled. "Here, let me show you. Take a box in your hand and put each one on carefully, one at a time." The box was too big for his hand, so she placed it on a chair near the tree. "When this box is empty, start another one. Pam and I will do the high ones, and you and Charie the low ones." Charie had her own box that sat on a step of the ladder Rand had used to place the star on top of the tree.

Jimmy was awkward at first, but Liz wasn't concerned about breakage, as the very choicest she put on herself. Twice she lost one to the trash can, which put Jimmy at ease. The two little ones soon wearied of the job, however, and became absorbed in the annual TV production of Dickens' *A Christmas Carol*.

When the tree was finished and resplendent in holiday finery, Jeff and his father reappeared to approve the spectacle. Liz then had them sit in a circle and presented each one with a gift: a well-chosen special ornament she had purchased with great care. For Jeff she had picked a Santa on a minibike. "Mom, I'll keep it forever," he said, tongue-in-cheek. For Pam it was a pixie with a funny hairdo. "Love it," she said. Charie's was a teddy bear that looked like Bearsh; and for Jimmy, a robot with movable appendages. She had been at a loss for Jimmy until she saw the robot and thought, *Maybe someday, Jimmy, you'll be a real boy, or at least be accepted as one.* The Christmas heart she had bought for Rand was gift-wrapped, still in a bag in her dresser drawer.

Nancy J. Sell

After these were opened and hung on the tree, Rand dished up ice cream. "Who wants hot fudge?" he asked, and of course almost everyone said, "Me!" Liz said, "Not me!" They sat on the floor looking at their handiwork while they ate their treat. Rand had made them into sundaes, complete with whipped cream and a cherry on top. A fire burned on the hearth, thanks to Jeff who had agreed to comply under duress.

Liz felt a measure of warmth and security. They were so dear, each and every one of them. Yes, she loved Rand, too, with all her heart. But right now she felt more comfortable with him at a distance. If only he would give in and let the matter of Jimmy be settled.

The awesome thought that was gnawing away at her during the past few weeks—she wished she could ignore it. She had tried, oh, how she had tried! But she would not reveal her suspicions now. Maybe not for a long time. Truth was, she could eat only a couple of bites of the treat Rand had fixed. "Guess I'm just too tired." Rand finished his, then reached for hers and poured hot fudge on it.

The last week had been a whirl of activities. Besides the holiday preparations at home, there were parties and programs at school, a Sunday School party, and a pageant at church in which Jimmy had been the only male participant in his group. Unplanned, he had become an angel with a crooked halo, and with a black-and-blue egg and three stitches on his forehead from a fall he had taken into a cement step.

Rand had been at the wheel of the car when they returned from the program at church. He had been quiet, thoughtful, even while they were visiting at Gran's for a treat afterward, and Liz suspected that, although he had gone reluctantly, he had enjoyed it. The program had been touching, and she had felt a moment of emotion. They were reminded that Jesus came to earth as the

Jimmy's Home

Saviour, to die for them. That message resonated with Liz, and she wondered if it had with Rand as well.

As they turned into their drive, Jimmy and Charie, and Liz, too, were roused from their drowsy state by Rand's exclamations. "What in the world . . . !" he exclaimed as he jolted the car to a halt, jumping out almost before it relaxed. The Christmas tree, visible where it stood in the bay window, flashed on. Off. On. Off. Rand ran for the door, key in hand, and stopped midway. Returning to the car, he excitedly told Liz and the children who were wide awake now, "You've got to see this to believe it. Come. Hurry."

The flashing of the tree and Mini's barking were simultaneous. "Woof," on. "Woof," off. "Woof," on. "Woof," off.

"Oh, no," Liz exclaimed, joining the three in their laughter. "Jeff must have forgotten to put Mini in the basement!"

The phone was ringing as they entered the house and continued for the next half hour or so as, one by one the neighbors called. "What's going on over there? Is everything all right? Weird!"

"I'm going to call Gran to tell her!" Jimmy announced.

Charie stomped her foot. "I wanted to!"

Liz and Rand had invited friends, adults only, for an informal gathering and dinner buffet. Liz wished she had canceled it before the invitations went out, but she had mailed them the day of the office party.

Each guest was instructed to bring a white elephant grab bag gift. These ranged from an ugly brown candy dish to a child's potty chair to an unused monstrosity that no one could identify or claim. Rand was trying to exchange the potty chair. "Oh, no, you don't!" Liz warned. "I want it for a planter!"

"Hey, I wish I had thought of that before getting rid of it!" Bea exclaimed. "I almost donated it to charity."

After the hilarity, Rand asked them to tell something about a special Christmas past, or what this Christmas meant to them. Liz extinguished the lights; the fire flickering on the hearth and the candles on the mantel were the only sources of illumination.

"Your turn, Randy. You must have something special. Let's hear it."

Rand spoke softly. "I'm thankful for a very special family and a special woman to love. I pray I will be worthy of them."

When it was her turn to speak, Liz stated simply, "I'm happy to be able to share our Christmas and be a family to a boy without a real home. He needs to know what love means. I'm trying to show him, not only our love, but more importantly God's love." She avoided Rand's eyes. She had to say it. "I hope we'll be able to do it for many more years."

They sang Christmas carols a cappella, and finally, slowly and reluctantly, their guests started to leave. "It's been wonderful, Liz. Rand. We wouldn't have missed it for the world." Nina and Norman spoke sincerely.

Liz flushed. She almost hadn't asked them. Mitzy and Stan were not on their guest list.

Bill and Bea Sutton were the last to leave after lingering another half hour by the fire with their host and hostess. "A memorable evening." Bea spoke sincerely. "Thanks for inviting us."

"Liz," Bill said, holding her hand firmly and meeting her gaze directly, "I'm glad to be here."

After they were gone, Rand helped Liz clean up. He knew she waited expectantly for comment on her Christmas wish, but he didn't mention it.

Jimmy's Home

"You did a fine job, honey. You know how to put a party together. Those bacon water-chestnut thingies were great. The big hit of the evening."

She smiled without comment, and again Rand saw the mask, the wall, an intangible, subtle barrier that prevented them from getting close.

"Why don't we finish this in the morning?" he asked.

"You go to bed. I'll work on it until I unwind."

He helped until nothing was left except emptying and reloading the dishwasher. Then silently embracing her, he kissed the top of her head and went to bed.

The next morning Liz was up early to get a head start on her baking; not even Charie was up, and she liked being alone in the early part of the day. But she felt ill.

After letting the animals out, she began making pie crusts. They would be stored in the freezer until Christmas Eve day. Rinsing her hands at the sink, she glanced out the window and was dismayed. There lay Mini, guarding the motionless form of Peter. Or was it Potter? She put boots over her slippers, a coat over her robe, and hurried to Mini's side. Gently she lifted the rabbit, made a bed for him in the warm kitchen, and placed him in it.

That night the rabbit died. *Oh no! The rabbit died!* An omen! An old wives' tale, she was sure.

Charie and Jimmy grieved for two days. And they argued.

"Charie, you're always leaving the cage door open," Liz reasoned, enforcing Jimmy's cause. "So even though Jimmy's rabbit died, it's not his fault. It's only fair to give him your bunny."

"I'll buy him one with my own money," she lashed back. "But he can't have my Potter!" She bravely fought tears. "*Please*, Mommy," she added softly.

Liz wished she felt better. She had no doubt now as to the cause of her illness. And of course the rabbit died. An omen, she knew. Perforce, she kept moving, and the activity helped. The last two days before Christmas were much too busy, but oh, how she loved the holidays! The activity kept her mind from other things, too, things she inevitably would have to face. But not now.

She assigned chores and, surprisingly, they were accomplished with minor complaints and great enthusiasm. When she felt well, everyone responded well. However, the opposite seemed true, too.

Several times she saw Jimmy studying the tree, gazing intently at the colorful, exquisite ornaments, sometimes reaching out a gentle finger to touch one. Liz did not remind him of the rule about not touching; in fact, she did not acknowledge that she had seen him. His face was so bright, his expression so tender, she could imagine his mental tour to faraway places as he pondered the small but vast world of make-believe.

On Christmas Eve, after the children were in bed, she was about to do some last-minute wrapping when Rand drew her down to sit beside him on the floor by the fire. "I've got things to do." But she silently yielded, in body only. He then presented her with a silver and red gift-wrapped package.

"Ooh," she exclaimed, "even the wrappings look expensive!" She had seen him with the present in time to retrieve the Christmas Heart from her dresser drawer. She had serious misgivings about giving it to him.

Rand stretched out and put his head in her lap as she opened it. She wanted to push him away, but it was untimely.

"I wanted to get you something to hang on the tree," he explained, looking up at her adoringly, "but I decided to get something to hang on you."

"Rand! It's beautiful!" She held up a fine gold chain from which hung an oval diamond pendant. She wiggled her lap from under his head and maneuvered until her face was close to his. It was an aggressive move on her part, the first in a long time, and she was cautious, careful. "You're so thoughtful. Sometimes."

"Would you love me if I weren't? Sometimes?"

"Well, assuming you still love me." He encircled her head with his arm but exerted no pressure. She didn't answer, so he continued looking up at her. "And other times?"

She wished she hadn't started this. "Let's not spoil the moment."

"Other times I'm thoughtless, right?"

"You said it, I didn't."

"I know I am. I don't mean to be." He turned to look into the fire. "I am sorry, Liz. Forgive me?"

"That's not a simple question to answer."

"Sure it is."

"Life is always so simple to you."

"Don't make it so complicated."

"Let's talk about it another time."

"Okay," he agreed without shifting his gaze from the flames. "If you'll set a date and time for our talk. Be specific." After a long silence he reminded her, "Date and time." He spoke into the quietness again. "I love you, Liz. And I like you, too. But I can't live like this. I want to talk about that party."

"I don't."

"I was set up, you know. And I want you to know every detail about that night . . ."

"I really don't want you to tell me."

"Nothing happened . . ."

"Sure. You know that."

"I know it."

"How can you know it when I smelled alcohol, I saw traces of lipstick, and you drove Bebe home? Don't forget, I found her phone in my car and saw pictures from the party."

Rand sighed as he moved away from her, resting his head on his crooked arm. "I know it, Liz, that's all."

"Open your present," she stated flatly.

He opened it slowly, thoughtfully, and quietly read aloud the inscription on the heart-shaped ornament:

This Christmas Heart is my gift to you,
A gift with my love, our love to renew.
A Christmas heart, so rich with joy
Is lasting and real, without alloy.

His voice broke, but he continued:

Its fullness expresses only in part
The genuine love of my loving heart.

When Rand turned to look into his wife's face, his eyes were red and moist. He drew her hand to his face and, turning back toward the fire, he kissed each finger, then held her palm against his cheek. He wanted so much more, but in spite of the sentimental expression of her gift, he knew she was out of reach. He knew it. He was surprised she had given it to him, considering the atmosphere between them.

"No," she insisted, pushing him gently as he tried to kiss her. "I might get scurvy."

His fist crashed to the floor, and Liz cringed inwardly. "*Cute!*" he snarled. "But not funny, Liz."

Jimmy's Home

Liz lay motionless beside him on the floor. Finally, as the living room clock struck twelve, she eased away from him and went to bed.

Long before they stirred from their beds on Christmas morning, she heard Jimmy and Charie in muffled animation as they discovered their stuffed stockings and exclaimed in delight over the contents.

Liz got up and ran water into the sink while she vomited into the toilet. It was a difficult sound to muffle, but she succeeded. Rand always slept with his head under the pillow after the first streak of dawn brightened the window, so he did not hear her retching.

The opening of gifts, the gathering of friends and family at Gran's for her wonderful turkey dinner, the reading of the Christmas story by Liz's brother Stephen, the playing of new games and, again, the singing of carols filled the entire day. It was noisy and delightful.

Rand used every opportunity to reach for her, to hug her, to caress her, knowing she would not resist in front of her family. Liz wore her new diamond pendant and received much admiration of it. Rand smiled contentedly.

"You guys must still love each other, huh?" her brother Robert queried with a grin. Rand gave him a high five.

The day was over too quickly. Jimmy and Charie were almost asleep as they ate sandwiches of leftover turkey Gran had sent home with them. "Everyone should have some leftovers," she had insisted, and no one had complained.

Pam had already fallen asleep on the couch, but would be up again in an hour or so, for she hated to have the day end. She would review each moment, each gift she had given, each received, each comment, and she would treasure each and every facet of the day.

The two little ones examined their gifts again, item by item, and chose some special things to take to bed with them.

The building of memories, Liz thought as she drifted into oblivion at the close of the long, lovely day. *That's what it's all about.*

She dreaded the morning.

CHAPTER TWENTY

"Have you told Rand you're pregnant, Liz Ann?" her mother asked several days later. She had stayed with the children for two consecutive evenings while Rand and Liz attended post-Christmas parties, spending the nights rather than going home each time. The children were on vacation until after New Year's and loved having Gran there to play their new games with them.

Startled by the question but hiding her surprise, Liz countered her mother's bluntness with, "What makes you think such an absurd thing?"

"I heard you vomiting."

"There are other causes for vomiting. I've got the flu bug."

"Not this time."

"You're assuming too much."

"Have you told Rand?" she reiterated.

"What's to tell?"

"You know very well, Liz Ann, and don't deny it. Have you told him?"

"No. And don't you."

"I wouldn't think of it. But why haven't you?"

"I don't want him to know. Simple."

"Why haven't you told him?" she pressured.

"Mom, please. This is between him and me." Liz made an effort to keep the words soft, but she felt rotten and wanted to tell her mother to butt out.

"You're not being fair, honey."

"And how do you define *fair*? Tell me. I'd like to know."

"I know what you're up to, but you're not being fair to Rand. It's his child too. I assume," she added softly.

"Mother!" Liz flared, but she willfully, deliberately, ignored the dig. She refused to further acknowledge the comment, thus giving it credibility. Besides, it was unlike her mother. "I'll tell him when I'm ready to."

But she had no intention of breaking the news to Rand or the children. Not for a while. How would they accept this, especially Jeff, who would be nearing seventeen when she presented him with a new sibling? Charie would be ecstatic, Pam a question mark. But Rand was her prime concern. After his initial shock, he would be happy, she thought. But she couldn't risk telling him. The timing could not have been worse. All arguments in favor of making little Jimmy a part of the Markham family would go down the drain with the revelation of this unwelcome announcement. She would withhold the news indefinitely until it came out of itself, until it was obvious.

Mrs. Bradshaw's monthly visit fell on the second Friday in January. She was due at 3:00 p.m. By mid-afternoon, Liz was usually feeling brighter and was able to assume an air of alertness to conceal the tiredness that plagued her.

Jimmy was ready and waiting for the agency lady when she arrived. Liz had fixed tea. The visits were so routine now that Charie and Liz always joined Jimmy and Mrs. Bradshaw for their little tea party.

When they finished their cookies and tea, however, Mrs. Bradshaw asked the children to go play. It was obvious she wanted to talk with Liz alone.

"I didn't want to burden you with added pressure during the holidays, Liz. I know you're anxious about this."

"I am."

With mixed emotions, she told Liz, "Jimmy is now released for adoption. His mother has signed the papers."

Liz's spirits plummeted, and she was struck silent. "I knew you'd be telling me that," she uttered after a lengthy pause. "But I was hoping it would be later, much later, rather than sooner."

"It was inevitable she would make some decision soon." Mrs. Bradshaw spoke softly, as if thinking aloud.

"I knew it was coming, but I'm crushed. At the same time I'm relieved she hasn't decided to take him."

"I am too. I know her, don't forget. I'm afraid she wouldn't be good for him. She has virtually ignored him for six years!"

"Oh, Jimmy . . ." Liz interjected, fighting tears.

"I would not be in favor of her taking him, even if she wanted him. Unfortunately for some, the law favors the biological parents, and my opinion wouldn't count for beans. Most often that's good, but not in this case."

"Where does that leave me now, Sylvia? How much time do I have?"

"One month. That's all I can promise."

Liz paled. *"One month?* Please . . ."

"You *must* decide. I had to fight for that. You know, there are so many couples waiting. One couple already is being considered, although they have not been informed of that as yet. Your decision *must* be within one month."

Liz wept inwardly. Only one month left to convince Rand. How could she? *Impossible!* She didn't want this news. She wanted to continue as they had, that comfortable unfettered routine . . .

Sylvia continued, "After that . . ."

"Don't talk of 'after that.' It must not be."

"I have to. You *must* prepare yourself."

She emphasized *must* again, and Liz was annoyed.

"There will be a series of meetings of the couple and child, a luncheon, an outing, et cetera. Then the child, Jimmy, will visit the new home."

"It sounds like dirty politics. A lure . . ."

"In each case the child's well-being has priority over everything else, you know. Anything we can do to ease the transition for him will be done."

"Of course," she managed over the lump in her throat.

"Friend to friend, Liz, you know how I feel about leaving him here. I'm behind you all the way."

"I know," she sniffed.

"But I'm helpless."

"I know," she repeated, "and I appreciate your efforts and interest. What's the maximum length of time before . . ." she hesitated, finding it difficult to talk.

"Before he actually leaves? If he leaves? Two to three months. We want him to feel comfortable in his new situation before taking him out of his old. And there's a lot of paperwork, of course. Liz," she continued hesitantly, waiting for Liz to meet her gaze. "Your home may be the best place for Jimmy . . ." She paused awkwardly as if trespassing on private property. "But the alternative may be best for *you*."

"Not true," she quickly defended. "I'm just a bit under the weather right now."

She was numb. She needed a miracle; she had to find it, even if she had to create it herself. Jimmy belonged here and nowhere else.

"Randy, this is his home," she argued again.

"No, Liz."

"It's Jimmy's *home*. I love him as if he were ours, Rand, flesh of our flesh. He *is* ours. *I can't give him up!*"

You have to, his look said. Or was it, *you're nuts?* "I don't think you've heard a word I've been saying for the past ten months," he said through tight lips. "You're talking about a six-digit financial commitment, not to mention mental, emotional, and physical drains. I cannot accept this for me or for you." *And I've got this wretched pain in my chest . . .*

"You certainly could if you wanted to."

"I don't want to. No. No," he repeated as if affirming it to himself and sealing it.

"Why should this be one-hundred percent your decision? I'm the one who will put in the most effort."

"Is that *right?*" he interjected sarcastically.

"My vote should carry the most weight."

"Spare me." He was weary and angry. "This isn't an election, Liz. It's not up for a vote. It's supposed to be a mutual objective on each of our parts to do what's best for each of us and for all concerned. But—"

"All concerned but one."

Jimmy's Home

"Jimmy's *not* our responsibility. Not physically, morally—not in *any* way."

"You're a cold-hearted, mule-headed—"

"Apparently this is going to be one-hundred percent my decision or one-hundred percent yours. I don't see any in-between, Liz."

"There could be."

"Not if I'm to stay in the picture."

"You mean *I* have to vote. Between you and Jimmy."

He nodded, not wavering from her gaze. He met her look without a word, without a blink.

"You're rotten clear through," she said, accusingly.

Their voices increased in volume until they were shouting at each other. Not a day passed that they didn't argue heatedly over Jimmy's destiny. She was becoming frantic.

All other conversation between them ceased.

The snowplows had been through during the night and piled white mini-mountains high on either side of the narrow road. Later, other equipment would be sent out by the town to cut back the banks and widen the pavement. Some of the snow would have to be trucked away. School had been canceled this morning, so Liz had no need to worry about the children waiting for the buses on such hazardous rural roads. There were no sidewalks, and small clusters of kids usually gathered in driveways along the bus route.

"Isn't it beautiful!" she exclaimed to Jeff as they waited to turn onto the road from their driveway. The main roads were clear and almost dry by now, they had heard on the local news. It was late afternoon, and Liz and Jeff were headed for the Department of Motor Vehicles for Jeff to take his test, and he was driving. Their relationship had taken a decided turn for the better, and the summer vacation had marked the turning point.

"Mmmm. I guess," he answered abstractly. They waited at the stop sign for several cars to go by before they turned onto the rural route. She was glad to see the blacktop showing as the sun and salt melted the remains of snow left by the plows.

"You're a good driver, Jeff." He was a natural, almost self-taught.

"I know," he spoke seriously, confidently, but she noticed a quiver, the slightest beginning of a pleased smirk at the corner of his mouth. "Thanks. Have you ever noticed, Mom," he went on as the traffic light at the next corner turned green and they headed south toward the Parkway, "how many people turn right on red when the signs says not to?"

"You're also very observant."

They traveled a full minute in silence, then he continued, "I observe a lot of things."

"Like what?"

"A lot of things other people don't see. What kind of profession would be good for someone who notices things?"

"Doctor. Reporter. Novelist. But to be good at most anything . . . at *life*, you'd have to be more mindful of the beautiful things around you, like the snow in winter, the flowers in spring, the flowering trees." Her voice trailed off. "The beautiful people we love. What else do you observe, Jeff?" Liz was delighted to be having a real conversation with her son.

"Like how things are with you and Dad."

She winced and felt the blood drain, then rush to her cheeks. It was an unexpected confrontation: Jeff, usually so private, was also respectful of other people's privacy. Silent again, this time for several awkward minutes, she finally asked, "What about Dad and me?"

"Like you're not a unit anymore. You're two separate people. Almost like actors on a stage."

Liz, startled and angry, did not reply. She had to weigh her emotions, her responses carefully, and she was not sure she could do that now. Furthermore, she was not about to discuss her marital situation with her teenage son.

"Do you mind me saying that, Mom?"

"Well, I guess not," she lied. "Actually, I do, Jeff, but if that's what you're thinking, feel free."

"Tip of the iceberg. Can I tell you what I think is wrong?"

"I think Dad and I can handle any problems we may have without your expertise . . ."

"I have to say it, though, before it's too late. I think . . ."

"You may need to be corrected."

"I'll risk it. Here's the thing. I think you're *not* handling it."

"Jeff," she said, chiding him . . .

"Remember when you told me Dad was the best, and I'd better take good care of him? Don't you think that advice goes for you, too?"

"Jeff," she repeated, attempting to conceal her indignation.

"Let me say it, okay, Mom? I'd hate to see you and Dad split. In fact, I couldn't hack it. Jimmy. I think the problem is Jimmy."

Having said that much, Jeff visibly relaxed. "I really like the guy, Mom. Jimmy's a neat little kid, and I'll be pretty bummed out if the time comes for him to leave. But if I had to make a choice, can you guess what I'd pick? I mean, if I had to pick between—"

"I know what you mean. You really care what happens to Dad and me?" Liz was buying time to recoup. "Sometimes you give us reason to wonder."

"Are you kidding? I hate what Dad does to me sometimes. You, too. But I know, when all else fails, I can come home to where sanity still reigns. And sometimes there's even peace and quiet."

Jeff honked at the car in front of them when the driver failed to move immediately after the next light turned green. "I know you probably don't appreciate me talking like this, Mom. But Dad's not going to give in, and we don't want you—us—to lose everything."

"Don't you think *I* need taking care of, Jeff? Am I the bad guy in this? Not so, my son . . ."

Jeff slammed on the brakes as he turned into the parking lot of the DMV. An employee in uniform jumped out of the way, then turned to wag a reprimanding finger at Jeff.

"With your luck, Jeff, that's probably the inspector you'll get for your test."

He groaned, then parked in a designated spot. Liz, unable to relax while Jeff was being tested, mulled over their conversation. Humbled by Jeff's concern, she pondered her options and came up with no solutions.

An hour later, the same inspector handed Jeff his report. "Go get in that line," he said, indicating the closest one. "Just be careful," he warned with a scowl on his face and a twinkle in his eye, "turning into parking lots."

"Hey, Mom! I'm free!" Jeff exclaimed, smacking his palms on the steering wheel. "I'm going to frame this!"

"You're going to carry it with you, even when you're not driving. It's good identification."

"I can fly solo now! I'm free!"

"That's what you think."

"You don't mean someone's going to tag along all the time?" He was dismayed.

Jimmy's Home

"No, Jeff. But we don't want you to forget whose car you're driving."

"Whew! What a relief! You know I can take care of the car all right. Flat tires. Dead batteries . . ."

"And yourself."

"Of course."

"And the gas tank."

"Ouch. That's a problem. You know, what I really need is a motorcycle."

It was inevitable, she supposed, since he and Rand had discussed it from time to time, but she hoped that topic would be tabled for a long time to come, especially since Rand wanted one too.

Was she the bad guy? How would Jeff have responded? She wondered.

Charie and Jimmy were having a campout on the new playroom floor. "You kids were supposed to put these games away," Liz reminded them as she put a pile of boxes on the shelf in the closet.

"We forgot," Charie crooned remorsefully. "Thank you, honey," she added with a giggle, playing the mom. "'Sides," she explained, "we want to play with them in the morning."

"I think Jeffy's happy he passed his test, don't you, Mommy?" Jimmy asked. "Now he can take us to town, and to the gym, and stuff like that."

"How about The Favorite House of Pizza?"

"Oh no, not there."

"You're right," Liz agreed. "Have a good campout." She continued, "and don't wake up too early."

Charie held out a hand to stop Liz from leaving. "Mommy, I have to tell you somethin' 'portant." She sat cross-legged in her sleeping bag and waited until Liz nodded for her to continue.

"What?" Liz obliged.

"I and Jimmy saw Pammy smoking out 'hind the garage today."

"Did you, dear? But Mommy told you never to tattle." *Not again*, Liz thought: They had gone through this same routine with Jeff. But each had a deep loyalty to the other.

"Never to tattle unless it might hurt someone . . . if what they're doin' is wrong. And smokin' hurts," she explained, poking her finger down her throat until she gagged, "down there." Her eyes got red and watery.

"Aren't you s'prised?" Jimmy asked incredulously from inside his sleeping bag, completely covered from the nose down. "Aren't you going to yell at her?"

"I have to think about it first. Does Pam know you two busybodies saw her?" she asked, looking at Charie.

"Oh, no. She didn't see us."

"She was with Mill'cent and Persie, and they were peeking around the garage to see if anyone was coming," Jimmy explained. "Course Mill'cent and Persie were smoking, too."

Liz, trying to treat the matter lightly, asked casually, "Where were you two?"

"Inside the garage, sitting on the steps. Looking out the window. That's where we hide from monsters."

"It was kinda dark in there, so they couldn't see us."

"How about letting this be our little secret for now. Can you two keep a secret?" She knew they could. Whether or not they *would* was another matter.

"Are you going to tell Daddy?" questioned Charie.

"We shouldn't keep secrets from Daddy."

"But we do, Mommy. You know we do when it's his birthday, and when it's Christmas, and when we have a surprise for him," she reminded, hugging Liz so tight her mother had to tickle her to free herself.

"Goodnight, you two. Have a good campout."

Liz was troubled. Pam was increasingly less recognizable as the easy-going, delightful daughter they had known for thirteen years. She was rapidly becoming a stranger to them. The climate between Pam and her brother was uneasy, also, sometimes uncomfortable, and Liz heard them in frequent aggravated but subdued interchanges. Persie had an obvious crush on Jeff, but Jeff's feelings toward Persie bordered on contempt. Liz was troubled, but she was unable to face another dilemma.

A few nights later, Rand was watching the news on TV while he read the newspaper. Liz had just related to him the saga of the garage sitters.

"Pam?" Liz looked up from the book she was reading when she heard her daughter in the kitchen. "Come here for a minute, dear."

"One sec," she replied as she returned the ice cream to the freezer. "If it could wait, I'm almost finished with my homework." Her face was pleasant, her tone cheerful, a deviation from the present norm.

"Your mother and I would like to talk with you for a minute, Pam. It won't take long." Rand put aside his newspaper and pressed the mute button on the remote control.

Pam assumed a deep resonant voice. "Sounds serious! What did I do now? Got it!" she smiled. "You're going to let Persie do my hair."

"Pam," Rand stated bluntly, "we understand you've started smoking."

"What?" she returned almost too quickly; her expression turned cold. "Me, Dad? Where did you get that idea?"

"That's unimportant."

"To you, maybe."

"It is unimportant, Pam. But is it true?" he asked.

"Of course not. Where . . ."

"Behind the garage?"

"Of course not." She began to sound edgy, defiant.

"With Millicent?" Liz questioned. "And Persie?"

"Mom," she said, defensively, "I said no. Are you going to believe me, or the person who's telling you such stories?"

"Of course we trust you, Pam," Liz pulled a reverse and mentally crossed her fingers. "I'm glad it's not true."

"You know how I feel about it, Pam. It's just an unhealthy habit," Rand spoke, fully aware of the difficulty in giving it up. "And expensive. And unfragrant."

"Goodnight," Pam mumbled. "I'm going to bed."

"I thought you had homework," Liz spoke brightly in an attempt to retain open communication.

"As soon as I finish my math," she added.

Alone again, neither of her parents spoke. Each returned to his or her previous activity, each more fully captivated by the subject of Pam.

Before many minutes had passed, a teary-faced Pam appeared.

"It's true," she confessed. "I'm sorry."

Rand pulled her down to sit beside him and hugged her. "That's my girl, Pam. You know, almost everyone tries it, so we're not concerned about that. What really hurts is that you lied to us."

"I said I'm sorry."

"Good." Rand smiled as she got up, not sure exactly what her apology referred to, but had a good sense as to when to let things go. "The subject is closed forever."

Liz was silent. *I'm not sure about forever,* she thought. She had a gut feeling that this was the beginning, not the end, of a problem.

Jimmy's Home

This particular subject might be closed, but it would certainly lead to others. Her smile was a mask to display for Pam.

Sylvia Bradshaw called almost a week later with the tidings that she would be taking Jimmy out for lunch on Saturday.

"Something special?" Liz questioned, her heart jumping. "You could just come here."

"This will be difficult for you, I know. But it's got to be. I want him to meet some people."

"Maybe he won't like them."

"That's a possibility. I'd prefer you didn't inform him of anything except that I'm taking him to lunch. Would you do that?"

"Certainly. You leave me no choice." Liz agreed, but began thinking devious thoughts. "Can I come along?"

"Not this time. Maybe another time when matters are getting more settled."

Rand had called her a manipulator. Well, she was. Anyway, maybe Sylvia would have an emergency. Maybe these people would have an accident. Maybe Jimmy would be sick . . .

But on Saturday Liz was so sick she couldn't get out of bed. "Bye, Mommy," Jimmy spoke to her from the bedroom doorway. "Mrs. Bradshaw is here, and we're going now."

Liz could do nothing but grunt a response. Even that much effort sent her running for the bathroom where she had nothing to heave, but wished she did. She told Rand she had a migraine again.

Liz slept all morning. When Jimmy returned, she had progressed to the sofa and was sipping ginger ale. Sylvia left Jimmy at the door, and he was exuberant over the outing. "Some friends of hers came and had lunch with us, Mom. A real nice lady and man. They thought I was nice, too."

"Who were they?"

"Mr. and Mrs. Wilcox. She called him *darling*, and he called her *my sweet*."

"What did they look like?"

"Oh, I dunno. She was sorta pretty but not very. He looked okay. But they're nice. She invited us to her house sometime. Mrs. Bradshaw and me. They have a big TV that takes up the whole wall. And a boat, and a swimming pool, and they live on a pond where you can go ice skating in the winter, and fishing in the summer. And pretty soon Mr. Wilcox said we'd be able to find polliwogs..."

"Blackmail!" Liz muttered to herself. "Jimmy," she interrupted him, not wanting to hear any more, "why don't you go help Pam clean up the kitchen. She could use a little help today since I can't do much."

The truth was, Pam, noisy at her job, was working in anger. She resented having to help with housework, she hated her siblings at the moment, and she was extremely upset with her parents. Liz deplored her daughter's dramatic personality changes, and, ill as she was, they grieved her.

"Why should I have to clean the kitchen?" she shouted in disgust. "That's your job."

Liz swallowed a retort and stated sweetly, "It's also my job to teach you how to do it."

"You already taught me. I know how to clean house."

"Prove it."

"How many times?" she bit back, and Liz thought she sounded like her father.

"What's happened to you, Pam? You've changed..."

"Nothing. I'm me. I haven't changed."

Jimmy's Home

"Something."

"I haven't changed. This is me," she reiterated. "Will the real Pam Markham please stand up. And I did. Ta-da!" She curtsied.

Liz winced. "We never laugh and have fun together anymore."

"That's because I've just decided I'm not going to be 'good ol' Pam' anymore." With that declaration, she had stalked off to the kitchen.

Jimmy ran off with verve to join Pam, ready to relate the news from his luncheon with Mrs. Bradshaw, and to extol the wonders of his new friends, Mr. and Mrs. Wilcox.

Liz agonized over their conversation, went to the bathroom and vomited, and went back to bed.

Jimmy searched her out to inform her that Pam wouldn't let him help.

"Why?"

"She said I talk too much."

"Do you?"

"No," he slurred indignantly. "Course not."

Charie came in, and at once they started to argue. "Be quiet, Jimmy. I'll tell Mom what Pammy said."

"I'll tell her if I feel like it. I already told her anyway!"

"Why don't you just get out so I can talk to Mommy?"

"I don't have to, do I, Mom?" He sat on the edge of the bed and started to bounce.

Weakly Liz ordered, "Go play. Both of you. You're making me sick."

Hours later, she was aware of Rand, on his way to the shower. "How do you feel?" he asked when he realized she was awake. She didn't answer, but rotated her wrist, turning her hand back and forth. "I'm going to call the doctor," he informed her.

"You're not."

"I am if you're not. How long do you plan to wait before you get help? You're getting dehydrated."

"I'll be all right."

"When?" At her silence he continued. "I'm beginning to have strong suspicions as to the cause of this sickness, Liz."

Perforce she remained calm, facilitated in part by the lethargy that gripped her. Did he know she was pregnant?

"I think you may have had a bug to begin with, but it's turning into a Jimmy sickness."

"Then that should tell you something," she spoke hardly above a whisper. He went into the bathroom, and she waited for the bathroom door to slam but it didn't. In fact, he didn't shut it.

"If you don't call the doctor in the morning," he announced loudly from under the spray, "I'm going to."

"No, you're not." She knew he couldn't hear her, and she also knew she had no alternative; Rand would make that call.

When she talked with Dr. Rinaldi the next morning, she told him she was pregnant. "But no one else is to know yet. Not Rand—"

"You should see your gynecologist, Liz."

"I will. But could you prescribe something for me so I can keep some food down?"

"Who is your gynecologist? Dr. Mantell?"

"Yes."

"I'll call him for you."

"Dr. Rinaldi, Steve, I'm so weak from not eating . . ."

"He knows your history, Liz. I'm sure he'll have the pharmacy deliver medication for you, or he may give it by injection. He may admit you for tests. He'll want to see you, in any case."

"Thanks," she stated resignedly. "I'll call him."

"I've known you for a long time," the doctor continued, "long before you were my patient." They had been neighbors before he had become the most sought-after internist in town. "Is there some reason you don't want Rand to know?"

She spoke flatly, listlessly. "Yes."

A week later Liz found herself excluded from another of Jimmy's special luncheon appointments. It rankled her even though she was too weak to join them, even if she had been invited. Her absence from these socials, and Jimmy's elation when he returned from them made her helplessness more dispiriting.

"Are you feeling any better?" Rand asked when he returned with Jimmy from one of Jeff's high school basketball games.

"A little." She had not called Dr. Mantell. Having eaten a cup of the chicken soup her mother had brought when she came to fix supper for the family, she was now able to retain a little nourishment, so she felt she might survive. "How was the game?"

"Good."

"How was Jeff?"

"One more foul and he would have been benched. He'll be good if ever he learns to control himself. He's an aggressive player—just what the team needs more of."

Rand put his arms around her, but she was too listless to respond. He sighed resignedly and released her, asking, "When are you going to snap out of this, Liz? It's gone a little far, don't you think?"

"You really care? Let me know when you start to."

"When did I ever give the impression that I didn't care?" he asked softly and sincerely.

"Most of the time lately."

"Oh, no! You're not going to lay that one on me! *You're* the one who doesn't care. About *anything* around here."

"And what is that supposed to mean?"

"Just what I said. You don't care two hoots about Jeff's game—"

"I do. But you don't care two hoots about me, about what I care about . . ."

"When did I ever stop caring? Would you answer that?"

"It's not too apparent."

"I don't need this, Liz. I don't need your being sick all the time for no logical reason. I don't need your stubbornness. I don't need this confounded pressure—"

"*Stubbornness? Mine?* Excuse me! Am I hearing correctly? Now let me tell you what *I* don't need." Eyes met and glances locked, and the silence was static with emotion. Finally Liz spoke. "You." Neither of them flinched. "I'm not sure I love you anymore," she continued. "And I don't like you right now either."

Rand took out a suitcase, packed it quickly, and left.

CHAPTER TWENTY-ONE

That was on Friday night, and by Monday Liz, feeling better, was anxious. If only she could recall her harsh words; they should have been left unsaid, however true they were. Is life better with or without him? That was the question usually posed. She *needed* him, but that wasn't the stuff that held marriages together.

On one of her trips to the basement, she noticed her kaleidoscope in the trash can. She picked it up and held it to her eye; it was still broken. She doubted it was fixable, but she placed it on Rand's workbench.

Feeling more settled physically than she had in weeks, she washed, dried, and folded laundry and ironed Rand's shirts so they would be ready for him when he returned. As she put the clean clothes away, she wondered if he had bought a new supply; he had neglected to take most of his toiletries, too. But a week later she noticed they were gone; he must have stopped by when she was out. Or asleep.

Jeff and Pam offered no comment, merely gave her blank, bewildered stares. She volunteered no information. Emotionally drained and physically spent, she was unable and un-wanting to listen to teenage advice.

"Mom, have you talked to Pam lately?" questioned Jeff in annoyance one evening before going to bed. "I think she needs you. You know, she's weird lately. It's Persie. *She's* the weird one. She gives me the creeps."

Liz surmised that Jeff was attempting to communicate something to her, but when she tried to talk to Pam, the door between them was shut. Pam feigned busyness, boredom, and independence, and Liz gave up.

"Mommy, I miss Daddy," Jimmy told her the next morning. "When is he coming home?"

"Soon," was her only comment. "Maybe," she added.

"When's soon? And why maybe? He still lives here, doesn't he?"

"I wish he didn't have to go on business trips," Charie complained, looking annoyed at Jimmy.

"Oh, me, too," Jimmy agreed.

I miss him too. Oh God, how I miss him! Liz formed the words in her head but left them there.

"Liz, you're a fool," was her mother's sentiment.

"I didn't ask for your opinion."

"So I noticed. But I'm giving it to you anyway."

"So I noticed."

"There's more at stake here than the welfare of one little boy."

"One little boy is just as important as the other factors."

"I don't deny that."

"We'll work it out. We need time."

"Seems to me time is in limited supply."

"How so?"

"You've pushed a little too far."

"I had no choice."

"Certainly you did."

"Hobson's choice. I have free rein to choose, but there's only one selection."

"I won't say any more."

"Thanks. I'll count on that."

"Unless you ask, but I'll be praying."

Another weekend was upon them, two since Rand's departure, and Liz had not seen nor heard from her husband. She knew he saw the children, and attended Jeff's basketball games. Then, an hour before the children were due in from school that next Friday afternoon, she came face to face with him as she came from the laundry room with a basket of clothes. Neither spoke. After an awkward silence, Rand took the stairs two at a time, came down carrying a suit, a tennis racquet, a pair of sneakers, a gym bag, and he left.

Jimmy was to leave for two nights, to visit his new friends, Mr. and Mrs. Wilcox. He was so excited his saliva bubbled when he talked. "I need to take my ice skates, 'cause the pond is frozen just right, Mrs. Wilcox said."

"I want to go with you, Jimmy." Charlotte was adamant. "That's not fair for you to go visitin' without me."

"You do things without me sometimes, Charie. Besides, Mrs. Wilcox is *my* friend, not yours."

"You're supposed to share, Jimmy. I share my Gran with you."

"I'll ask her if you can come."

Liz intervened. "Not this time, Charie." She knew the answer, and she couldn't bear the house to be too quiet. "Why don't you invite Frannie over for a pajama party? She's a good friend."

Charie responded by running to the phone and dialing her friend's number. Frannie's was the only one she had memorized. "What's Mindy's number, Mom? I want to invite her, too."

"Just Frannie this time, Char." *One is enough. All I can handle.* And Frannie lived closer.

The pajama party was a success. It kept Charie occupied and Liz busy enough to ward off depression. The party lasted for the duration of Jimmy's absence with no overlap, so Charie was ready for his return.

He was exuberant. "You should see their house, Mom! It's so cool! They have a 'cuzzie, a swimming pool, and a tennis court, and . . . and . . . !" he exclaimed. "And Mr. Wilcox was there the whole time. He has an office that I couldn't go in. That's where he works every day. His name is Jim, too! Neat, huh? And he played catch with me, and basketball. And in the spring we're going out in the rowboat, and he's going to teach me to use the paddles."

"Oars," she corrected. "Do you like Mr. and Mrs. Wilcox, Jimmy?" She almost said, "Better than us," but she checked herself.

"Yeah," he drawled, his eyes shining. "And I'm going to oar the boat."

"Row the boat."

"And I had my own bedroom with lots of boy things in it. I asked them if they had a boy who lived in that room, but they said no. They want to get one." He took his ice skates to the basement. When he returned he asked, "Isn't Daddy home yet?" When Liz shook her head, he wanted to know, "When is he coming?"

"Soon."

"When's soon?" he queried again. He ran off to play, not waiting for an answer.

When's soon, Jimmy? I wish I knew. I only know it's after now.

Liz eased herself onto the sofa and gradually curled her knees toward her chin in an attempt to alleviate the pain in her lower abdomen. Charie and Jimmy had left on the school bus five minutes before, and she had managed to watch it come to a halt, the door swing open, and the two little ones board. Jeff and Pam had left much earlier in the car. Then, bracing against the walls and furniture, she had staggered to the sofa.

Holding the portable phone to her ear, she pushed the proper buttons to reach her mother. *One, two, three, four*, she counted the rings. *Oh, please be there!* she cried in anguish.

"Mom . . ."

"Liz Ann, what's wrong?" Her sleepy voice became alert.

"Call Dr. Mantell," she said, straining as the pain became unbearable.

"I'll call an ambulance."

Liz pressed the off button quickly to clear the line.

She heard the ambulance and cursed it, cursed the siren. *I'm not dying! Maybe not.*

Betty arrived moments before the ambulance and unlocked the door. "I think she's having a miscarriage," she informed the emergency medical technicians.

Liz was being wheeled into an examining room when she heard Dr. Mantell being paged; then she heard Dr. Rinaldi's voice beside her. "Dr. Mantell is in the hospital," he assured her, taking her hand. "You should have seen him, Liz. You should have been under his care."

"Spare me," she pleaded.

A nurse put a thermometer in her mouth and fixed a blood pressure cuff in place.

Jimmy's Home

Dr. Mantell entered talking. ". . . an ultrasound." As usual, he had begun his statement at a distance with the assumption that everyone concerned or otherwise was listening.

Dr. Rinaldi said, "I'll look in later."

"Stay." She held his hand tighter.

"I have an in-service, Liz. You're in good hands. I'll be in to see you, I promise," he responded reassuringly in answer to the pleading in her eyes.

"I suspect an ectopic pregnancy, Liz," Dr. Mantell explained to her. "I want an ultrasound first. Then we'll go in with a scope. Just a small incision under anesthesia. As soon as we know what the problem is, I'll medicate you for pain. All indications are that it's an ectopic."

An hour later, Liz lay on a stretcher outside the delivery room. She had been medicated in the emergency room by Mo, the same nurse who had cared for Jeff last summer.

"Pre-op meds, Mrs. Markham. You'll be delightfully relaxed but not asleep until you're in the OR. You'll be fine, just relax."

Betty had blown her a kiss as she passed by on the stretcher. "Don't worry, honey. I'll take care of everything at home." She had supplied the admitting information. "I'll be there for the children . . ."

Rand will never need to know about this, Liz speculated drowsily. *I'm so glad I didn't tell him.* She stared at the monotonous white ceiling tiles and the evenly spaced recessed lights.

"An ectopic pregnancy," Dr. Mantell had explained without her asking, "commonly called a tubal pregnancy, is caused when the embryo attaches itself to the inner wall of the fallopian tube instead of the uterus." She knew all this already, but she listened. Her brain felt detached from her body. "When the fetus begins to grow, it causes a great deal of pain." She knew that, too. *Even death, if not remedied.*

Nancy J. Sell

"Then I'm to have an abortion."

He looked at her nonplussed. "The pregnancy will be terminated, true. The fetus aborted. But we don't call it an abortion. You know, there's really no option. The baby can't develop there, and it's a life-or-death situation for you *and* the baby, or just the baby. And we don't want to lose both of you."

She thought: *Let's let it be both*. But she couldn't stand the pain.

"Why haven't you been to see me?" Dr. Mantell inquired. "And where's your husband?"

She wept, and he didn't press for answers. Despair engulfed her. She had lost Rand. She was losing Jimmy. She had lost touch with Jeff, Pam, and Charlotte. Now she was losing this life, this new beginning, this baby that, despite the negatives, she wanted. *At least I've still got you, Mom.*

"Time to go, Mrs. Markham," the nurse said, checking the IV bottle and Liz's wristband before wheeling her into the operating room.

She was remotely conscious of the coldness of the sterile room, the plainness, the casual manner of the staff.

"I'm Dr. Hanes. I'll be assisting Dr. Mantell."

Liz saw dark eyes between the blue mask and the cap. "Where is he?" she asked, looking into the nonperson's eyes.

"I'm here, Liz." Dr. Mantell's voice came from her other side where a masked nurse held his gloves.

"Is this OB?"

"Don't you recognize it? You've been here before. Three times."

"Four," she corrected. *One dead, don't you remember? Now another one. And now it's my turn, too.* She didn't much care except that Rand would find out.

291

Jimmy's Home

The hum of the recovery room became increasingly more tangible as Liz surfaced from the dark depths of an anesthetized brain and body.

"What's your first name, Mrs. Markham?"

"Liz," she answered without wondering why they didn't look at her wristband. "Elizabeth." She mumbled around the word. "Liz Ann. Elizabeth Ann Markham," she slurred, then vomited.

"That should bring her blood pressure up," she heard the nurse comment.

After being transferred to a bed in a pink room, she immediately gave in to numbness: caring but not caring; feeling but not feeling. She was semi-roused each time a nurse or an aide checked her blood pressure and temperature.

Pink is for girls. My baby must have been a girl.

When Liz opened her eyes again, the room had grown dim with the fading light of a quiet wintry afternoon. She watched the IV fluid drip into the tubing until her eyes grew too heavy to stay open. She was roused again by a nurse hanging another small bottle and attaching it to the tubing. She referred to it as a piggyback to another nurse who had appeared.

"Your mother called to see how you're feeling, Mrs. Markham. She left while you slept, I think to pick up a kindergartner. She said everything is fine at home and not to worry. She'll be in to see you tomorrow when the kids are in school."

She chattered while she worked. "Do you want something to eat? How about a cup of tea? How many kids do you have? Ages? Boys? Girls?"

Liz mumbled answers and wished she would go away so she could sleep again.

Betty had called Rand's office as soon as she arrived home from the hospital and was given another number where he could be reached. Though she was momentarily puzzled about that, she put it aside. "She's in surgery now, honey, so there's no need to hurry to the hospital. Rand, you are going, aren't you?"

"I—I'm not sure, Mom. I think Liz would rather I didn't."

"Baloney. She doesn't know what she wants."

"You're wrong there."

"Well, she doesn't know what's good for her."

"I'll call you back in about fifteen minutes. I have a few things to tend to, and I need to think."

Five minutes later Rand was back on the phone with his mother-in-law.

"Would you do me a favor?"

"Of course."

"Call the kids' schools and tell them I'll pick them up. I'll need their exact dismissal times."

"Charie is home, Rand. She was dismissed at noon. Are you going to the hospital?" she asked bluntly. *I don't care if he does think I'm meddlesome*, she thought.

"I . . . don't think so."

"That's not the right answer."

"We'll talk later, okay? I could use a listening ear."

"I'm good at that, Rand. And if you ask me, I'll even give you my opinion."

He laughed. "I already know that."

"I'll have Charlotte ready and waiting for you."

Charie especially was confused by his absence from home, so she was delighted to have her father to herself in the middle of the day. He had been with them at unpredictable hours during the past week, and in places other than where he was supposed to be.

Jimmy's Home

Pam was waiting with them in front of the high school when Jeff came out.

"What's up, Dad?" Jeff looked perplexed. "I'm supposed to be at basketball practice in fifteen minutes."

"I won't hold you up. I wanted all three of you together to tell you."

"Oh, no!" Jeff was aghast. "You and Mom aren't splitting up for good."

"No. At least that hasn't been mentioned."

"Something's happened to Mom!" Pam shrieked.

So Pam still belongs to us, Rand thought. "She'll be all right, Pam," he assured her. "But yes, something has happened. She's in the hospital." He explained as much as he knew of their mother's condition.

"Oh, Daddy!" Charie cried, "Mommy and I *wanted* another baby! Oh, Daddy!"

"Dad . . ." Jeff cleared his throat and started again. "Does this mean . . . ?"

"I understand she'll be fine, Jeff. There's usually no danger with something like this if it's caught in time."

"That's not what I meant. You and Mom . . ."

Rand gave him a direct look and spoke sincerely. "I wish I had an answer for you." He knew the truth now would ease later hurts and added, "Don't get your hopes up."

"You are going to see her, aren't you?" asked Pam.

"Of *course* he is, Pam!" Charie exclaimed in astonishment. "Why wouldn't he, Pam?"

Rand shook his head from side to side. "I don't think so. It's a hard decision to make."

"Can we decide for you? We'd like you to." Jeff paused, "I'd like you to."

"We," corrected Pam. Her irritability of the past months had all but disappeared in the face of this adversity.

"Me, too, Daddy," offered Charie. "Give her a kiss for me, Daddy. Oh. I want to go with you!"

Rand shook his head again. How could he be truthful and spare them at the same time? Jeff went to basketball practice, and Rand took the girls home where Jimmy was waiting for them. Betty had continued to take charge.

"Thanks for your help," Rand smiled at his mother-in-law as he patted her shoulder. "I was pretty overwhelmed."

An ambulance, its flashing lights cutting through the late afternoon darkness curtained with heavy snowflakes, blocked the doorway over which the red EMERGENCY sign stood out in illuminated block letters. A man, unnoticed in the confusion, entered through a smaller door and sank into the nearest chair in the emergency waiting room. He leaned forward and rested his head on his crossed arms, a position that eased the pain in his chest and facilitated breathing.

"May I help you, sir?" an anxious emergency room attendant finally asked. "I didn't see you come in. Are you here to see a patient?"

"I need a doctor."

With no further ado, he was assisted to an examining room and helped out of his upper clothing and onto an examining table. "This is Dr. Sprague, a cardiologist, Mr. Markham." Rand was wired to an electrocardiogram machine. The nurse continued, "Who is your regular doctor? I'll have him paged or call his service."

"Dr. Sprague will do fine, thanks."

Jimmy's Home

Sometime later, Dr. Rinaldi spoke softly, not wanting to waken him if he were sleeping. "Rand?" The tests were done, and he had been left in the quiet examining room to rest.

Rand groaned. "I didn't want to see *you!*"

"Oh?"

"I mean, I was hoping to keep this private."

"How severe was the pain?" Dr. Rinaldi questioned him.

"Pretty awful."

"I just read your chart. You've been having these pains for a year?"

"Almost."

"How frequently do they occur?"

"They used to be occasional, like once or twice a month. Easy to forget in between, you know? Now they're once or twice a week... You know I already answered all the questions."

"Why didn't you come see me? Answer that one."

"I thought about it."

"What's *with* the Markhams these days? I don't know you."

"We're weird. Disconnected."

"I've noticed. Disconnected for sure. Your EKG and other tests are normal."

"*What?*"

"Your heart appears to be fine, but Dr. Sprague is going to order a monitor for a few days just to be sure."

"I can't believe it. Why the pain?"

"Have you been under a lot of stress lately, a lot of aggravation? Your work?"

"Yes, right. My work."

"I'm going to prescribe Valium for you, Rand. Just take it when the pain starts. Take it then, but only then. I'm also going to prescribe a long vacation in the Caribbean for the two of you after Liz recovers."

"Are you treating?" Rand chuckled. "And all these months I've been thinking heart surgery."

"You're a jackass for not having it checked out."

"Good word."

A nurse brought the dose of Valium the doctor had ordered. He stood to go after handing him the prescription order.

"Thanks, Doc. You just took a load off my mind."

He saluted. "I'd like to see you and Liz together sometime soon, in my office. The two of you. Together. Or I can stop by your house."

"Why?"

"Just . . . to talk."

The hospital corridor was dim and silent except for his footsteps as Rand exited the elevator and walked through the connector to the new wing. He had dozed for a while after Dr. Rinaldi left him, and it was late.

His mother-in-law had clued him in as to Liz's location. She had, in fact, given him full details, leaving nothing to chance. He would have no difficulty finding obstetrics anyway; it was familiar territory.

"Rand," Betty had asked again after their brief talk, "are you going to the hospital?"

"No," he had replied.

"Wrong answer again. What do your children want you to do? Have you considered that?"

Jimmy's Home

He had raised his eyes to hers, giving a silent answer.

"Then isn't that reason enough to go? Rand, you must for their sakes. And your own."

"I have to consider what Liz wants, too."

"And forget about four others? You've scaled other mountains together, and managed the valleys, too. Go see her, Rand. At least go. Know that you've done all you can before you give up."

"How did I rate? Other guys complain about their mothers-in-law." Rand had patted her hand. "But I've given up. I don't plan to go." He'd given her a weak smile and left.

But here he was, tackling the longest part of the journey. As long as he was in the hospital, he'd just peek in on her. She'd probably be asleep.

"Dr. Mantell?" he addressed the young doctor approaching in the dim corridor. "Randolph Markham."

"Ah, yes. Mr. Markham. Your wife is doing fine."

Rand listened while the gynecologist explained Liz's problem and the surgical procedure to correct it. "I understand she's been a pretty sick girl from the beginning. What I don't understand is, why she waited so long for a checkup. We might have discovered it sooner."

"I didn't know she was pregnant," Rand spoke candidly.

"But she did."

"Apparently Liz didn't want anyone to know."

"Why?"

Rand felt like telling him to mind his own business. He shrugged helplessly. "I suspect for many personal reasons that are too involved to discuss now. But we do have a sixteen-year-old son, almost seventeen, you know. It won't be too many years until we start thinking about grandchildren."

Dr. Mantell shook his head. "Pooh! Many women her age are having babies. And she wanted the baby, I gather. She was pretty upset." Rand didn't answer. The doctor looked at his watch. "I'm keeping you," he smiled, "and you're keeping me. Go see her."

Liz slept. When she awoke, the room was almost dark. Rand stood at the window with arms spread wide, his hands braced on the window frames, his forehead against the pane. She was troubled and closed her eyes. She sensed his movement to the chair beside her bed, and feigned sleep. She slept again.

Of course she wanted the baby! She's Liz, isn't she? Rand thought as he pressed his head against the cold window pane and stared at the almost-empty parking lot below. He had let her down. He hadn't helped her through a tough time.

But I didn't know she was pregnant! For better, for worse . . . sickness . . . health . . .

Now the damage was irreparable.

I love you, Liz. His mind formed the words, but his lips were silent as he turned from the window and moved to the bedside. *If only we could go back. But what would we change? The impasse is too great. I'm afraid it's too late. We'll never find the way. Dear God, help us!*

Goodbye, Liz. I can't continue this charade.

Opening her eyes again, Liz found herself looking into Rand's dark tired eyes. Her lids dropped as she tried to collect her thoughts with a still-foggy mind. She had forgotten he was there, and she could no longer pretend to be asleep.

"I didn't think you'd come," she finally offered after a long uninterrupted silence.

He counted fifteen IV drips before answering. "I didn't think you'd want me to." The silence that followed was heavy with resentment and accusation.

"I didn't."

He found it difficult to speak. "Because you meant what you said? Or because you didn't want me to know you were pregnant?"

Her eyes grew misty, and she squeezed them shut. "I had an abortion," she stated softly.

"No. You didn't."

"I was pregnant, and now I'm not. I didn't have a miscarriage, so what do you call it?"

"Not an abortion."

"What, then?"

"A tubal pregnancy. The egg, the embryo, started developing—"

"Don't. I know all about that."

She was quiet, motionless, and he thought she slept again until she asked, "What time is it?"

He looked at his watch, leaning forward so the night light shone on it. "Twelve thirty."

"You'll be too tired to go to work in the morning."

"Tomorrow's Saturday." He didn't tell her he wouldn't have been going to work anyway. "Do you want me to leave?" He hardly saw the movement as she shrugged her shoulders. He stood to go. "Goodbye, Liz. I hope you get well quickly. I hope you'll be happy."

As he reached the door, she whispered, "Rand." Not certain he had heard correctly, he turned to her silently and waited. Their glances locked, and neither could turn away. "Did Mother tell the children?"

"I did."

She was surprised. "What did they say?"

"They were concerned about you, that's all." He started to add, *and us*, but he caught himself. "And us," he continued, since she had to know it already. "And Charie was disappointed. She said to give you this." He blew her a sad little kiss. Liz's eyes filled with tears, and though she tried to control herself, she began to shake with sobs. He watched from the doorway, waiting until she was quiet again.

"Goodbye, Liz," he reiterated when she seemed controlled.

"Can . . . we . . . Sometime . . . can we . . . talk?"

He moved to her side and looked down at her. "Just what is it you want? *What*, Liz! I don't know anymore. I don't know *you* anymore." They stared at each other, unwilling and unable to say the necessary things, the things to start them down a mutual path. "What do we have to talk about?"

The door opened and a nurse entered, easing the tension but prolonging the misery. She asked, after hanging a new bottle of IV fluid, "Mrs. Markham, would you like something to help you sleep?"

Liz shook her head negatively. "Yes. Not yet," she said, and they were alone again.

"Do you want to talk now?" Rand asked thoughtfully, sitting down again. Leaning toward her slightly, he rested his elbows on his knees, his head against his clasped fingers. "I'm not sure I know what to talk about. You'll have to tell me." His voice was husky, and his words came in a strained whisper. "And we'd better wait until you're up to conversation."

She turned on her side and reached for his hand, drawing it close to her heart. Rand, baffled, looked at her in surprise as her face contorted. She sobbed.

He half stood, half sat on the edge of the bed and touched her other hand.

Looking into his face with brimming eyes, she freed both of her hands from his light touch and reached for his face. Bewildered, Rand bent over her and pressed his wet cheek against hers.

She circled her free arm around his neck; Rand's arms went around her, and together they wept.

"Oh, Liz," was all he managed to say. "Oh, Liz! If only . . ." She slept again.

CHAPTER TWENTY-TWO

Early morning light brightened the room and the subdued sounds of hospital routine greeted her when Liz awakened again. The faint smell of coffee from breakfast trays reached her as the door opened, but it had no appeal. Her mouth felt chalky as she received the thermometer from the nursing assistant whose cool hands reached for her pulse.

Something was wrong. Rand was gone.

"My husband," Liz formed the words around the electronic instrument in her mouth, "he left?"

The young woman put a finger to her lips in a *shhh*, then pointed to the next bed. Rand, fully clothed and covered with a white hospital blanket, was sound asleep.

"Daddy! Daddy! Daddy!" Charie cried ecstatically when she looked up to see who had just come in. "Oh, Daddy!" she exclaimed as she jumped into his arms. She hugged him as he sat down with her in the rocker she had just vacated. She put both hands on his cheeks and pulled him toward her, then kissed his fish-face lips. She gazed into his face, suddenly sad. "You didn't bring Mommy home."

"She has a little fever. Maybe later today the doctor will say she can come home, or for sure tomorrow."

"I miss her."

"I know."

"I missed you, Daddy." She touched his nose with hers and gazed into his eyes.

"Oh, Charie, I missed you so much."

"Not as much as I missed you."

"Prove it."

Rand was aware of his mother-in-law, newly arrived in the kitchen. "Did you wake Grandma up?"

"No. Well, I didn't mean to. I got in bed with her," Charie replied.

"Oh. Why?"

"I don't like to be by myself. I was lonely."

"It's okay, Randy," Betty offered. "I was ready to get up."

"Where's everybody else?"

"Jeff's gone to help Mr. Schmidt with something," answered Charie. "He called last night and wanted you to help him, so Jeff went. Jimmy's at the place where he'll be 'dopted. He's coming back later today. Pam's still asleep. Gran's fixing bacon and eggs for me. Want some?"

"Sure. If there's enough."

"You caught me just in time. I'll fix enough."

"She heard us!" Charie whispered.

Rand laughed. "That's okay. We're not telling secrets."

"Oh, Daddy!" Charie interrupted, asking, "Did you give Mommy my kiss?"

"I did."

"Did you give her one of your own?"

"I did." *Sort of. On the cheek.*

"Did she send one back to me?"

"She did. With her eyes."

"You silly! You can't kiss with your eyes!" She giggled.

"Wanna bet?"

"Show me."

"Next time I will. I have to find one."

"'Kay."

"Want to help me pack a few things for Mommy to wear when she comes home? Something warm and comfortable."

"I know," Charie exclaimed, ready to get at it. "Her pretty blue sweat suit she got for Christmas. It matches her eyes."

"Good idea. But let's eat breakfast first."

"Can I go with you to see her?"

"Nope."

"Why?"

"'Cause then everybody will want to go."

"So? We won't tell them where we're going."

"Listen, let's go eat, 'cause I have other things to do too. You stay with Pam, okay? Then Grandma doesn't have to stay."

"She wants to."

"I'm okay, Randy. I'll leave supper oven-ready for whenever you want it. I'll stay until after lunch."

"You're so good to us. Charie, what can we do special for Grandma?"

"Take her out for dinner!"

"Deal! But let's make it a real sit-down dinner where there's flowers on the table, and candles, and real napkins and tablecloth . . . You know, fancy stuff."

"But then I have to mind my manners," Charie complained. "Chew with your mouth closed, take your elbows off the table, sit up straight, don't lick your knife, no double dipping . . . What's double dipping?"

"You know, when you lick your knife or spoon and put it back in the dip, or in the peanut butter. That's why you have to practice those things at home. Then you don't have to think about it when you're eating out." Rand laughed. "I know. Mommy might not feel like it today. Or tomorrow."

"You're right. We'll make it a family date, sometime soon."

CHAPTER TWENTY-THREE

Sunday morning dawned beautifully clear and bright, the kind of late-winter morning whose stimulation set one's pulse racing. A light snowfall was beginning as Rand mounted the church steps.

Faith Chapel. That's what he needed: faith in the living God. A faith that would bring hope for him and the future of his relationship with Liz. Somehow this had escaped their carefully planned routines. Life together with Liz had sounded so promising, he had mused while helping Charie and Jimmy with breakfast.

Where had they gone wrong? Had they gone their own separate ways and not considered each other and what was right for them, as a couple, as a family? Had they not considered God's will for them? But shouldn't his decision, as head of the family, been the deciding direction of the adoption issue? So many questions, but no conclusions. The answer was perhaps obvious now, in that Jimmy would never be part of their family.

God, show us. Lead us. Is it too late to pick up the pieces of a broken heart? So where do we go from here? Show me, God. Show me.

Flickers of pleasure greeted him as he moved into the pew his mother-in-law occupied. Charlotte and Jimmy sat between them, and Charie hugged his arm, resting her head against it; Jimmy moved to his other side and did the same.

Rand's thoughts drifted in and out of his surroundings: the program, the hospital, his home, his work that he had agreed with Max to resume with varied schedules, not to include Bebe. Three voicemails and a house call from Max with offers of new routines had convinced him to return on a trial basis. The promised cruise to Alaska was an added bonus.

He enjoyed the singing of the choir as he scanned each face, then focused on the small bald circle of the young but capable director's head. As the choir finished and the sermon began, Rand's mind wandered as he started counting the hairless heads of the male populace in front of him, then the women in blue dresses, the ones with curly hair. He was beginning to count the children who traipsed in and out, probably to and from the bathroom, when the pastor's words caught his attention. Rand wished they would stay put. He was trying to listen.

Rand left with the words of the final hymn, "Holy, Holy, Holy, Lord God Almighty," fading with each footstep. He didn't wait to be sociable; he wanted to ponder what he had just heard. He wanted to think about his time with Liz, where they were headed. Enough was enough.

There was more to it than believing in God, he knew. Commitment. That was it. One had to come to God, acknowledge sinfulness, accept Christ, the willing sacrificial Lamb God had provided. Christ's birth, death, and resurrection weren't an accident, they had been *planned* by the Almighty. Rand knew that, but had left it out of his life for too many years. "God's way," the pastor had said—"*no other way.*" He quoted John 14:6: *"I am the way, the truth, and the life: no man cometh unto the Father, but by me."* And Rand prayed, "Jesus, I come."

Nancy J. Sell

It was snowing hard when Rand arrived home with Liz late Sunday afternoon. Each one welcomed her as if she had been away for a month. Rand took the single red rose he had bought in the hospital gift shop for her, and put it in the usual skinny vase.

"Oh, Mommy," Charie cooed, "I missed you so much. I wanted another baby for us, you know."

"I did too, Charie."

"Maybe we could just keep Jimmy," she said in a whisper that was heard by all.

Rand winced. Liz frowned. Pam gasped. Jeff just gawked. But Jimmy grinned. All knew it was too late to reverse the wheels of progress, not unless something were to befall his new family.

"But I'd rather have a baby that can't argue."

"Well," Rand said in an authoritative voice, "change of subject. I smell the chicken dinner Gran left for us. Pam must have started it in the oven. Table set? Drinks poured? Then let's eat. C'mon, Liz, you can try to eat." Though progress had seemed to be made in their relationship, the conversation regarding Jimmy had not helped. Liz was hurting, and Rand knew it. He was hurting too.

"After we eat, let's play a game," Charie suggested.

"Or do a jigsaw puzzle," offered Jimmy.

"Well, I'm not so sure Mom is up for anything so strenuous. How about if I go to the Suttons' and borrow one of their new movies?"

"Hey, great idea! I'll call and make sure they are home."

"You kids clean up the supper stuff, Mom will lay on the couch, and I'll go get the movie."

"You need me to help you, Dad," Jeff spoke.

"You're probably right, Jeff. Liz?"

"But it's snowing, Rand. Why don't we find something here?"

"We'll be okay."

"Dad?" Jeff started as they drove away from the house.

"What, Jeff?"

"Are you . . ." he hesitated, "back to stay?"

Rand swallowed hard. "I don't know, Jeff. I hope so. I just don't know."

"We need you, Dad. I need you . . . Can I ask you something?"

"Sure. Not sure I'll answer . . ."

"I know there's still something wrong between you and Mom. Besides Jimmy . . ."

"You're perceptive, Jeff. I can only tell you, I hope it's fixable."

"Well, if you need a place to sleep, you can have my bed."

Rand laughed. "And where will you sleep?"

"On the couch. Or on the floor."

"Thanks, son. That's a very kind offer. I'll let you know."

They returned with three movies to choose from. Rand lifted Liz's feet from the couch, sat down, and put them in his lap. He often massaged her feet, so he thought with an audience she wouldn't object.

Charie disappeared and returned with massage lotion for her mother's feet.

"Here's the deal, guys. We watch until nine o'clock, and then you all hustle off to bed."

"Eight o'clock," Liz intervened. "That's bedtime for Charie and Jimmy on school nights."

"Uh-oh. Well, tonight's special. How about a compromise? Eight-thirty?"

"If they brush their teeth and do whatever before then," Liz insisted.

"Okay, guys?"

"I have a little homework to finish too," Pam informed them.

At eight-thirty Rand shut everything down. "I have an idea. Tomorrow will probably be a snow day, so why don't we call it The Markhams' Snow Day? So. Let's finish watching the movie." He looked at Liz for a reaction. She frowned at him, but kept silent.

When the movie ended a half hour later, he reached a hand down to help Liz up to a sitting position.

"I need to get some water to take some meds," Liz told him.

"I will get it for you," he offered in a soft voice.

Liz had gone to their room, so Rand followed with the water. He held the glass while she got the pills, then helped her out of her sweat suit and into her nightgown. She was shivering, so after she got in bed, he lit the fireplace, then pulled the covers over her and sat beside her. Neither spoke, but their gaze held until her eyes filled with tears. She reached up to him, and as he leaned into her touch, she sobbed. She put her hands on his cheeks, wiped the moisture from his eyes with her thumbs, and cried.

"I love you, Rand," she whispered. Though he could barely understand her words, he knew what she was saying. "I never stopped loving you, you know."

"I know, Liz. I know that. But I wanted to hear you say it. I *needed* to hear you say it."

They clung to each other until she whispered, "Come to bed."

"In a few minutes, I will. I want to check on the kids, check on lights and locks, make sure everything is turned off and closed up for the night."

Rand knocked lightly on Jeff's door and heard a mumble from within. "Jeff?"

"Huh?"

"You can stay in your bed."

"Cool, Dad," he mumbled.

"We can all sleep in. It is still snowing hard. I have no doubt school will be canceled. We'll shovel snow when you get up." He heard Jeff groan as he walked down the hall.

When Rand crawled into bed beside Liz, he wasn't sure how awake she was, but he pulled her into his arms. "Are you awake?" he asked after a while.

She jiggled her fingers softly against his cheek.

"Do you agree now that I was set up at that Christmas party?"

"No."

Rand groaned inwardly.

She was quiet for a while, and he thought she had fallen asleep. "But I forgive you," she whispered softly.

With a contented sigh and a smile on his face, he settled down to sleep.

The next morning, Liz peeked at the digital clock: 6:30, then put her hand on Rand's pillow. He was gone.

She closed her eyes and debated whether she wanted to get up or stay in the warmth and comfort of the bed. At 7:00 she slipped into her robe and slippers. In the process she noticed an object hanging on the wall by Rand's side of the bed. *The Christmas Heart.* She smiled. *How like him to hang it there.*

She found him dozing in the big chair in the family room, supposedly listening to the news. She took the remote and turned off the TV, and as she brushed his arm, he opened his eyes.

"Do you want coffee?" she asked.

"I want you," he said, opening his arms to her. She cuddled down in the circle of his arms and snuggled her face in his neck. "I want to tell you what happened to me."

"Something good, I hope."

"I made things right with God."

"Oh Rand, what a lovely thing to hear! I've had many thoughts about my relationship with the Lord lately. I made a commitment to Him when I was a child, and somewhere it fell by the wayside for too many years. Recently I recommitted my life to Him. Now here we are rejoicing in the Lord and each other."

They sat quietly, both deep in thought until Rand asked, "Do you remember the first time I put my arms around you?"

"Of course. How could I forget? You started an honest-to-goodness snowball fight when you did that."

"I started it! You're the one who sicced all the little rug rats on me. How do you figure I started it?"

"Oh, Randy, I loved having your arms around me."

"You sure kept it a secret. Do you remember the first time I kissed you?"

"Of course. You mean the test run, or the one for real?"

He chuckled.

"That same day. That first Christmas you spent with my family. First the test one to see if you should keep going. The real one was one minute later."

"And you loved it when I kissed you, too, didn't you?"

"Mmm hmm. I just didn't want you to know it. I wasn't into kissing guys on a regular basis, you know. And I was nervous about being so close to you."

"Well, I'm glad you got over that."

"Me too."

He pulled her close. "You're so thin, Liz."

"I haven't been able to eat much."

"We'll fatten you up."

"Yeah, right."

They sat in silence for a long time, eyes closed, content in each other's closeness.

Jimmy's Home

"Rand, there's a bug on my knee. Or maybe a mouse. Smack it!"

Charie, who had snuck into the room, erupted in peals of laughter. Rand put his arm out to her, and she climbed on his lap to cuddle with him and her mother. "I love you, Daddy."

"I love you too, honey."

"I love Mommy, too."

"So do I, Charie. So do I. Liz, I'm so sorry I wasn't here for you. You know those promises I made twenty years ago: for better or for worse . . ."

"I didn't exactly want you to be here . . ."

"That doesn't excuse me, you know."

Charie put her finger on his lips, then pinched his lips shut when he tried to talk. She giggled. "Daddy's got a fish face."

Meanwhile Jimmy appeared, rubbing his eyes and yawning. He found the TV remote where Liz had left it.

"No TV now, Jim. We're having a special family time. You can come up here with us." Rand patted the arm of the chair.

"No, he can't!" Charie intoned. "He's not family now."

"Well, either he stays and you go, or both of you stay."

She hid her face in her father's chest as Jimmy climbed onto the arm of the chair and leaned into the people pile.

"Wow! Where's the camera?" Jeff asked as he entered the family room, then went to get it.

Pam wandered in minutes later. "Looks like a good day for a snowball fight," she remarked.

School was canceled for the day. The Markhams' Family Snow Day turned out to be a wonderful idea. They would hope for one every year.

CHAPTER TWENTY-FOUR

The snowdrops were daring to poke their delicate white heads through the unwelcome late snowfall, and the crocus shoots were in evidence in the sunny bare spots of the lawn the day Mrs. Bradshaw came to take Jimmy to his new home.

It was a Saturday, and Rand had offered countless logical but unnecessary reasons why he had not left for his trip to the town dump. The Glendale dump was something special, and Jimmy and Charlotte loved to go with him to treasure hunt. They had more important things to tend to today, however; Charie was helping Jimmy pack. And they argued.

"You can't take that, Jimmy. It's mine."

"Mommy said I could have it, so now it's mine."

Liz intervened. "I'll get you another book, Charie."

"Same one?"

"Of course."

Pam was to go shopping with Millicent, but she stayed.

Liz's hospital stay was four weeks past, and her recuperation had been quick and thorough. The attention from her family, the breakfasts in bed, the fresh flowers (sometimes one, sometimes a dozen red roses) almost every day, the loving concern, had accelerated the healing process.

The sheer delight of having Rand home again overwhelmed her, and his tenderness touched her deeply. She savored the warmth of his body against hers as they lay close in the darkness of their room. There was no passion: that would wait. They shared so much: the hurts each had nurtured, the hopes, plans, and dreams that had been tabled, and the promise for the future. And sometimes they were quiet, comfortable, just enjoying the closeness.

Although she felt weak and listless for a few days after her release from the hospital, Liz began to rebuild damaged relationships with her offspring. They were delightfully responsive. The time was special for all of them; they were giddy with the joy of reunion. All was not well yet, but all seemed to be improving.

Betty arrived just before lunch on this day Jimmy was to leave. She had served willingly and well while Liz was ill, and in her quiet manner celebrated the resettling of her loved ones into their proper places. Everyone knew the reason for Gran's visit today was to see Jimmy off, and to support the hurting that was yet to come.

Jeff arrived in time to eat, so Gran set another place. Sylvia was expected for lunch, so as soon as she arrived, they sat down to eat the homemade chicken soup and crackers Betty had brought from home. Jimmy's bags sat by the door, Tedley was atop the pile with Bearsh keeping him company.

All too soon it was time for tearful goodbyes. Jimmy sadly hugged each one and was hugged in return. The sadness on his part was superseded by anticipation of more good things to come. Liz was unable to talk as she held him close, and as soon as Rand closed the door behind them, he reached out to encircle her in his arms. But she had headed for their bedroom.

Snatching Charie's eight-by-ten stick picture of *Jimmie* from the wall, Liz crumpled it in her fist. Dropping to her knees beside the bed, her arms outstretched above her head, her hands clutching the comforter, she cried.

She sensed Rand's presence and wished he would leave her alone. Her body shook with her own private grief.

He sat beside her on the floor, his back against the bed. After sitting awhile with his elbows on his knees, his head on his folded arms, he reached an arm in front of her and drew her to him. She resisted at first, then yielded, and he held her close while she sobbed great wrenching sobs.

CHAPTER TWENTY-FIVE

The days following Jimmy's departure had been, as Gran would have said, "Deep water" for Liz. Her highs and lows were a strange mixture of contentment over Rand's return, delight in the fragrance and visual beauty of a new spring season, and the agony of a grieving heart. She had lost another child. But there was no grave to visit, no forced finality.

"Come on, everybody!" Rand announced a few weeks after Jimmy's departure, "Let's go on a camping trip. We'll all take Friday off and leave early in the morning. You have to choose between White or Green."

Jeff groaned. "White or green *what?*"

"Why, mountains, of course. I've always enjoyed both—great skiing and scenery up there—so maybe you won't have to choose. We'll see both."

"Oh, Dad—"

"Don't be the pooper of every party, Jeff. I thought we could take a look at some colleges while we're up that way. Dartmouth is not far from White River Junction."

"You don't expect me to qualify for *Dartmouth!*" His voice squeaked.

"We can *look*, Jeff."

"Rand, I'm not sure . . ." Liz interjected.

"You won't have to do a thing, honey. You can be the queen of our hearts, and we, your royal subjects, will dote on your every desire."

She remained skeptical. "I'll stay home. You go, Rand. Take the kids. They'll love it."

"Honey," he continued, "I want this to be restful for you. I promise you don't have to do a thing except look beautiful. It will be good for everyone. We are all missing Jimmy. And if we're lucky," he said confidentially to her alone, "we'll find some time to ourselves. In fact, we'll *plan* it!"

But the camper was still in winter storage, and Rand found it too difficult to get it ready on such short notice. "We'll stay in a motel. The most luxurious one we can find. My treat."

"I'll stay home," she reiterated.

"Nothing doing," he insisted.

"I'm tired."

"You're going to rest."

"We'll need reservations . . ."

"Nah. Not this early in the season. Vacations haven't started yet. Don't be a fussmusser."

Liz shook her head at his logic. But it might be nice to get away for a long weekend. She would hold Rand to his word regarding her royal status.

After a leisurely trip, they arrived in northern New Hampshire at dinnertime. "Let's get our motel first. Then we can go out for a good seafood dinner. Don't worry, kids, they'll have landlubber meals, too. Chicken fingers probably. We can relax while we eat, maybe even look around, take in some quaint shops," Rand planned aloud. But at nine o'clock, they pulled into the last motel they hadn't yet tried. A worn *Vacancy* sign gave a weak welcome.

"*Mount-ain Re-sort*," Charie read aloud. "Daddy, I want to stay somewhere else."

"Should be named, *Last Resort*," Jeff grumbled, wishing more than ever he had remained at home.

"Well, it's probably nice inside," Rand reasoned. Liz gave him a sidelong glance and groaned inwardly as he exited the car and headed for the door over which hung a red neon *Office—Vacancy* sign. "It'll do for tonight," he said as he returned and leaned on the car window. "They just had one room left." He avoided Liz's eyes. "Let's unload, use the bathroom, and find someplace to eat."

Their fast-food supper of hamburgers, french fries, and soda pop would have been more palatable had their moods been more cheerful. It was almost midnight when they finally retired.

"Quitcherbellyaching," Rand mumbled into the darkness. He lay close to Liz in the narrow bed. Charie and Pam shared another three-quarter bed, and Jeff, on the floor, was rolled up in a sleeping bag that they had brought along, just in case. They had reinforced the torn window shades with blankets and towels, chased spiders from the metal shower stall before using it, thrown an occupied mousetrap out the door, and checked the bedding carefully before getting into it.

"Did we bring some bug spray? I don't think I like the floor," Jeff had mumbled as he slid into the sleeping bag and covered his head.

"You're still the queen," Rand whispered audibly to Liz, causing her to shake with laughter, and then as her reaction was so often these days, her laughter dissolved into tears. "I love you, Liz." His whisper was for her alone. "Stop laughing."

"Stop whispering," Pam muttered.

The next morning, Jeff refused to get up for breakfast. He had crawled into the girls' bed as soon as they had vacated it, and he had no intention of leaving it. "Bring me a doughnut or something," he mumbled into his flat feathered pillow. "And cartons of milk and orange juice."

"No breakfast if you don't come with us," his father mandated. Jeff answered by putting the pillow over his head. When they returned, however, Liz saw Pam slip a bulky waxed bag to her brother; Charie passed a carton to him after they were packed up and had started on their way. Liz smiled to herself as tears welled up again. Rand had noticed the sharing of food too, and said nothing. She knew he was amused, and in a strange way, touched.

As they neared the Canadian border, Rand became anxious about gas and pulled into the first station he saw.

"Kind of matches The Last Resort, doesn't it?" mused Jeff as he roused himself from sleep and got out to pump.

Liz headed for the ladies' room. When she was ready to leave, she grasped the door handle and pulled, only to find the handle in her hand and the door still shut. "Randy!" she called over and over. "Pam! Charie!" Sitting on her heels, she peeked through the hole where the handle belonged, and saw a puzzled Rand and Jeff, standing by the car, peering around, up and down the road, obviously looking for her. "Randy! Jeff! I'm in here! Pam! Charlotte! RANDY!" she screamed. "I CAN'T OPEN THE DOOR!"

An 18-wheeler parked nearby with its motor running drowned out her voice.

Liz began to cry again. What did they think? That she had lost her marbles and disappeared? She thumped on the door until her fist hurt, but no one heard her. Peeking through the hole again, she saw Rand talking to the attendant who shook his head.

Charie appeared in her limited span of vision, and Liz thought she was about to cry, too. They all vanished, and Liz banged on the ladies room wall, thinking they might hear her in the office.

Looking through her peephole again, she saw her husband and children get into the car. Rand looked worried. The car disappeared, another took its place, and Liz began to sob. "Rand," she called again in a voice muffled with tears. "I'm in here."

"Daddy! Daddy!" suddenly she heard Charie's voice. "I found her! I found her! She's in the girls' room!" Liz wept again with relief: Oh, they must have moved the car to make room for the next customer! Of course they wouldn't leave her.

Liz sat down on the toilet seat and snuffled as she listened to the attendant, with Rand and Jeff, working on the door. Finally it opened, and she was in Rand's arms, sobbing and laughing. "Oh, Mommy!" Charie exclaimed, throwing her arms around her mother's legs, "I'm so glad I had to go potty again!"

Later, when they pulled into a trailhead to take pictures of a large moose, Charie squealed, "I wish Jimmy was here!" Liz cried, then laughed. Rand, with his hand at her waist, drew her just a little closer and kissed her forehead.

Back on the road, as they continued south, Charie commented, "I'm glad Jimmy's not here. We'd be squished!" Liz laughed again, then cried. Rand took her hand and squeezed it.

"Well, if you didn't have this pillowcase full of junk with you," grumbled Jeff, holding Bearsh upside down, "there would be plenty of room."

"Give me Bearsh! He's not junk," she explained emphatically. "And neither is anything else I brought. *You're* junk."

"Should have left me home then."

"Next time we will."
"Quiet please," muttered Pam.

The trip had a refreshing, renewing effect on Liz, but there was something missing: Jimmy. It would take a long time to adjust to his absence, to the knowledge that his absence was permanent, and she ached for him as she had ached for her third child, buried near her grandfather so long ago. She *would* adjust, but she would never stop missing Jimmy, not completely. There would always be a special place in her heart for him.

CHAPTER TWENTY-SIX

Liz opened the window to the damp early-morning fragrance of hyacinth and magnolia blossoms. The daffodils were in full bloom, the tulips yet to follow. The moment seemed untouched, uncluttered, almost holy in its beauty.

The beautiful flowers were past their peak, however, and caused her a brief moment of depression as she thought about how many years it had been since Jimmy's departure from their home. But as the magnolias and hyacinths faded, she knew the forsythia would bloom again, and then the dogwood trees. Azaleas, rhododendrons, and lilacs in their brilliant display would follow, and then the lovely state flower, the Mountain Laurel. Each annual appeared and faded in predictable, scheduled order, giving new hope to the living, new life to sagging spirits. And so life went on.

Laurel. It was the name given their darling little granddaughter. She was the delight of their lives. Jeff and Sally often left her with them for an afternoon, an evening, sometimes a weekend or longer. Laurel adored her grandpa, and when she was with him, no one else existed. She was as at home with Liz and Rand as she was with Jeff and Sally, and Rand was in his glory. Liz appreciated

Jimmy's Home

the way her daughter-in-law *belonged*. Sally was as much a part of the Markham family as Jeff was of her family. Now a new baby was on the way.

Mini's favorite tree stump that had held Liz's bird feeders in winter and flower pots in summer was gone; but then so was Mini. Rand had buried him two years before in a far corner of The Woods that the Markhams had purchased ten years before to make room for an in-ground swimming pool. Potter was buried where the old tree stump had been, with Peter beside him. His body had been exhumed and replaced so the two could rest in peace together, so Charie said.

Liz picked up the kaleidoscope that sat on the table beside the window and held it to her eye. She had never seen such a beauty. As she turned it, the colorful crystal fragments drifted in liquid, continuing to move after she stopped turning it. It was exquisite, and a source of constant fascination to her.

Rand had presented her with a huge gift-wrapped box on his second visit to the hospital after her OB surgery, and in it was this new kaleidoscope. It stood on a tripod of carved cherry wood, and it was expensive. She knew its value, for she and Rand had admired it while browsing in a gift shop before her other one had been broken. His thoughtfulness was a touching thing, and Liz had held him in a long embrace with her cheek pressed close to his. How good it had been to be close to him again. Now she turned the kaleidoscope, stopped and waited for the colors to settle into a lovely pattern, then turned it again. She never tired of it.

She heard footsteps behind her and expected Rand's familiar touch, but the arm that encircled her waist and the head that rested on her shoulder were Charie's.

"I'm as tall as you now, Mom."

"I know. Overnight."

"Seems like it, huh? But I thought I'd never get there. Are you sad, Mom?"

"Only that you grew up so fast."

"About the wedding, about Pam leaving?"

"Oh, a little. It's kind of a happy-sad mixture."

"I know. I'm going to miss Pam. I wish she didn't have to move so far away!"

"Nowadays people are hopping all over the globe, Charie. Maybe Pam and Eric won't stay in California. I know they'd both be happy about transferring back here." Eric had taken an enviable position with a large computer firm, and was appointed to the San Francisco office.

"Is that one word or three? *Now a days,*" she emphasized each syllable in answer to Liz's puzzled look. "You don't say thenadays, or onceadays. Why do you say nowadays?"

"Oh, Charie," Liz laughed, "you always were a word bug. That's a good question though. Thenadays. *Once . . .*"

"Anyway, I wish they would stay here."

"I do, too." A brief silence fell between them.

"Have you told Dad yet?"

"California is a nice place to visit, my ladies," Rand spoke as he put an arm around each of them. "Especially San Francisco. Told Dad what?"

"Yeah, if we get invited!"

"We will. Even if we have to invite ourselves. But we'll go, I promise. Told Dad *what?*" He spoke louder, with feigned annoyance.

"Who's got all the moolah?" Charie asked, rubbing her thumb and fingers together, and purposely ignoring his question.

"We'll go in hock," her father replied with a wink. "Told Dad *what?*"

"Later," Liz informed him.

Rand left, pretending hurt, and Charie exhaled. "Whew! That was close!"

"I know," Liz giggled nervously. "No, I haven't told him. What do you think he'll say?"

Charie shrugged an *I don't know*. "But I can hardly wait to find out."

"Do you know whose birthday is today, Charie?"

"Somebody's somewhere."

"Jimmy's. He's eighteen."

"Oh, his, too?" she asked indifferently, yet mustering interest for her mother's sake. His was a closed volume as far as she was concerned. She remembered being sad when he left, she remembered her mother's grief, but she also remembered it being a special time of family restoration. "I wonder where he is, what he's doing. He was a nice kid. When we weren't fighting."

Liz wondered, too. Often. He had been a frequent visitor the first year after he had left them. "Guess what!" he had exclaimed. "My name is James Wilcox, the Third! But my middle name is William. My Dad's is Timothy." Then he began to interest himself in other things. Liz suspected his new parents of severing the tie that bound him to them. She was hurt, but time's healing balm eased the pain, though she continued to keep a tender corner of her heart for him.

"I wonder if he's going to college somewhere, and where."

It was a process, but her resentment toward Rand had faded, too. She never thought she could conquer it, but with God's help she had come to the conclusion that the choice was hers: nurture that resentment and destroy her marriage, or look the problem in the eye, accept the outcome, and bury it. She made the difficult, the right choice. Their feelings for each other, their loves and their likes, had grown richer and deeper. As a result, the children had rallied in a new way, too. Peace had not automatically reigned, but the pieces had gradually fallen into place.

"Did you send him a birthday card?" Charie asked, reminding Liz of her presence.

"What? Oh, yes, I did, honey. I've never missed a birthday or a Christmas."

"I wonder why we haven't heard from *him?*"

"Maybe he never received them. That's a possibility, but they've never been returned."

"They probably got put in the garbage. I wonder what he looks like now. My guess is an ugly toad." Liz gave her a sidelong glance and frowned. "Who are you kidding?"

As she looked back now, the changes in their lives seemed rapid, awesome.

Rand had attended church with Charie and Gran every Sunday for several weeks before Liz joined him. He never said a word, never asked her to go with him, never criticized her for staying away. It had been apparent to Liz that God had become an important part of his life. She had seen changes in him: a regeneration rather than a reformation. Pam had begun to attend once in a while, too, then regularly when she met a boy named Eric. Jeff's attendance was still sporadic, but improving.

At the time, the changes in their lives had been slow and subtle but complete.

EPILOGUE

The doorbell rang, and Liz dried her hands on the kitchen towel to answer it for the third time within the last half hour. Probably another gift. She had so much to do, and with the wedding just two weeks away, fifteen days to be exact, she could use a full-time door monitor.

It was another wedding present, and she placed the beautiful package with the others that had arrived this morning. She paused to admire the lovely gifts already opened. Pam and Eric would be able to entertain in style in their tiny three-room apartment. She wondered where they would put all the exquisite china and crystal, and what they would serve in it. Hopefully they would have larger quarters soon. The apartment belonged to friends of Eric's who were letting them use it for six months while they were in Europe.

I am the mother of the bride, she told herself again. *If I can just retain my wits and hang loose and not fall flat on my face, I'll be fine.*

She had no sooner put her hands back in the dishwater when the doorbell rang again. Nina Schmidt, on tiptoe, tried to peek at her through one of the leaded glass panes of the front door, then entered without waiting for Liz to open it.

"Hi, honey. I know you're going crazy with the big day just around the bend. I came to help. I do everything but windows. And ovens. Unless they're self-clean. Tell me what to do, or I'll just find something on my own."

"You're so thoughtful. I just don't know . . ."

"Sure you do. How about me cleaning up this messy kitchen while you do something else? My stars, Liz, it's messy. Now don't argue," she chided when Liz balked. "I *know* you've got other things to do. And if you don't, you can go take a nap."

"I could finish cleaning the living room windows," she smirked at her friend, "since you won't. *And* clean the oven. Except that I just did it. And then get the draperies hung."

"Then do it. And I'll tell you what else I'm going to do. Did. I prepared your supper. You have a choice: my house, or to-go."

"Nina, you're such a good friend."

"You're not such a bad one yourself. Someday you can do the same for me. Now what about supper?"

"We're all eating at such crazy times right now, it might be better if we ate here."

"Well, they can come to my house piecemeal." She looked at Liz. "Okay. I'll bring it here. I'll bring disposables so you won't have any cleanup."

"You're great. Thanks. It means so much."

The rift between them was so far in the past that neither Liz nor Nina ever thought of it anymore. The situation had come to verbal blows; then Mitzy became angry at something Nina had done and joined what she considered a more elite circle. With tears and hugs, Liz and Nina had apologized to each other and their friendship was renewed, strengthened by the pain of adversity.

After Nina finished the dishes, she emptied the dishwasher. She mopped the kitchen floor, then folded laundry and put clean sheets on the two beds Liz had not yet made up.

"I hate to tell you, but those things don't stay done."

"Good. Then I'll know how to do them next time."

Liz wondered if she worked so aggressively in her own house. She thought she must. Nina left at noon and was back at five o'clock with their supper.

Rand and Liz lingered over coffee and Nina's lemon meringue pie when the doorbell rang again. It was so good to *sit*, and Liz winced at the sound of the bell. She wished the caller would go away.

Charie was dressing to go bowling with a group of young people, among whom was Drew Davenport, a special interest of the moment. "She can do better than that," was Rand's comment when Liz told him. "Her taste is appalling."

"You're prejudiced."

"Charie," she called. "Answer the door. It's probably Drew. But he's awfully early," she told Rand. "He's trying to impress her. And us."

Rand addressed Liz's back as she headed for the door. "I am." Charie had not responded to her beckoning.

"You am what?"

"Prejudiced. But impressed," he called.

The young man standing on the front steps was not Drew. The vaguely familiar look about the mouth and the big brown eyes caused Liz to squint as if to better scrutinize the visitor, to bring the vision into perspective from a page of a closed book. She inhaled and waited as if her heart, the clock, and the world were on hold.

He grinned shyly. "I brought this guy in case you didn't know me," he said, bringing a worn fuzzy bear from behind him. "His name is—"

"Tedley!"

He was still grinning, that same light-up-the-face grin Liz knew she would never forget. "*Jimmy!*" she exhaled the word with her breath. "Jimmy!" she repeated. She felt awkward.

Then recovering and laughing at herself as tears surfaced, she exclaimed, "Oh, come in! I'm so rude! Jimmy, you've grown so tall," she gushed as she shyly put her arm around him and started to kiss his cheek. Jimmy, laughing, gave her a lingering bear hug and returned her cheek kiss. "And Tedley," she continued breathlessly, "you haven't changed a bit!" He laughed with her.

"Rand!" she called, "come see who's here." As he appeared in the hall, she declared, "Rand, *Jimmy's* home! Jimmy came *home!*"

"Where is everyone?" he inquired after Rand had greeted him with a warm handshake and hug. Jimmy too had overcome an initial reticence and seemed more at ease. "They haven't all moved out, I hope." As he spoke, his eyes moved to the stairway where Charie had descended to the turn. Her carefree run reduced itself to a halting, hesitant stop as she caught sight of the young man talking with her parents.

"Charie's here," Liz said unnecessarily. "Charie, come down and say hello to some old friends."

Charie's eyes went from the old bear to the young man's face. "Jimmy?" she silently mouthed the word. "Jimmy!" she whispered and smiled hesitantly, shyly.

"We're just having coffee and lemon pie," Liz offered, sensing Charie's sudden withdrawal and seeking to ease the awkwardness of the moment for her. "Come join us and tell us what you're doing here, how long you can stay, and anything else you can think of."

His family had moved to Maryland eight years before. He had nurtured dreams of returning to Connecticut and had applied for enrollment at the University of Connecticut's main campus in Storrs. The fact that it was more costly for out-of-state residents didn't matter, Liz decided as she thought about the expensive new little blue car sitting at their curb. He would be taking two summer courses that were to start next week.

Charie, who had unobtrusively phoned Drew to cancel her evening plans, began to relax and take an active part in the conversation.

"Things have changed around the old neighborhood," Jimmy remarked. "I thought I'd get lost coming up from the turnpike."

Rand suggested they take a drive to show Jimmy that Glendale, at least, had not changed. New buildings under construction had been carefully planned to retain the elegant country look. Liz remained to finish up some lists she was making for the seating of wedding guests while Rand, Jimmy, and Charie left in the Markhams' car.

"Who belongs to the classy blue car?" Eric asked when he and Pam came in an hour later.

Jeff asked the same question when he and Sally appeared unexpectedly en route home after an evening with friends. Liz had offered to babysit, but they turned her down, claiming her schedule was already too busy, and they had left Laurel with Sally's parents.

"A surprise," Liz informed them.

"Hmmm. Maryland plates," Jeff mumbled. "Don't know anyone down there."

When the sightseers returned, Jeff and Pam were delighted to become reacquainted with Jimmy, and there was much handshaking and hugging by all.

"So how do you feel about becoming grandparents?" Jimmy asked, having noticed Sally's condition.

"Delighted," Liz answered. "But we're old hands at it," she explained, giving Sally's abdomen a light pat. "We have a lovely little Laurel we want you to meet when Jeff and Sally bring her over."

"How does Liz *ever* feel about babies?" Rand asked. "*Any* babies: rabbits, dogs, cats, raccoons, people . . ."

"Are you still crabby, Jeff?" Jimmy asked, then went on to explain, "Charie said once you were too crabby to be a father."

"No," Jeff answered.

"Yes," Charie countered.

Jimmy asked about Gran, about Mini, Potter, Sneakers. "Does Gran still say Sat-ah-dee?"

"Of course."

And so began a series of *Remember Whens*, as first Jimmy drew from their memories, then they from his.

"I never forgot the fellow at the beach down south—what was his name? The one whose father drowned trying to save him . . ."

"Greg," Jeff inserted. He never forgot either.

"I've wondered, more lately, what he's like, how that trauma affected him."

"*Our* lives were greatly touched by it," Rand offered. "His must have been, too."

"But we're kind of a touched family," Pam spoke.

"Sometimes a little nutty!" Sally interjected with a grin.

"Really, what I mean is, we're sensitive," Pam attempted to explain, frowning at Sally. "We feel for others. Empathetic, that's what we are."

"It would be interesting to know him now," Jimmy concluded, then went on. "Remember when we went to New York to go to that Christmas show . . . ?"

"Oh, no!" Rand moaned. "We were all supposed to forget that!"

Liz, who had contentedly listened to the chatter, spoke. "It was a lovely evening . . . until it was time to go home. Whatever possessed you, Rand?"

He had driven them down the parkways where they had turned south toward the city limits. "We'll park here and save the big parking fee in Manhattan. The kids will get a kick out of the subway ride, too."

"I don't like it," Liz told him as they locked the car.

"Shush up," he said affectionately. "This here's my turf, you know."

"And you survived. Miracle."

After spending an hour or so at the top of the Empire State Building oohing and aahing, and then enjoying the huge Christmas tree, the decorations, and the ice skaters in Rockefeller Center, they had been enthralled by the Christmas Spectacular at Radio City Music Hall. After a late snack of hot chocolate and doughnuts, they reluctantly headed for home. The little ones were almost asleep on their feet.

The policeman Rand stopped to ask for information regarding a subway back to the car was incredulous. "You parked *where?*"

Rand, trying to appear casual and knowledgeable in the face of the policeman's shock and his family's appall, repeated the location.

"Well, if your car is still there, and if it still has tires and parts necessary for its operation," the policeman continued. Rand swallowed hard and avoided eye contact with Liz. "I'd suggest you try one of these gypsy cabs, see if you can get one to take you there."

"Okay," Rand said, bringing them back to the present, "the car was still there, intact. Let's be honest. Who was scared that night? Not me."

"Liar. I was. So were the kids, the ones old enough to know enough to be! Jimmy," Liz changed the subject, "remember when you and Charie saw Pam and her girlfriends smoking in back of the garage..."

"Oh, so they're the ones who squealed. You rats!"

Jimmy grinned. "You were a naughty girl, Pammy."

"You don't know the half of it. Someday I'll tell you all about Persie, someday when Eric isn't around and we have more time. She was a shoplifter, a foul-mouth gossip, the makings of a real tramp."

"Be nice," her mother warned.

"I'm *being* nice! She was exciting to be with, but I also felt sorry for her."

"You mean there's more to tell when Eric *isn't* around?" Jeff asked. "Like how much influence she had on *you?*"

Pam avoided his questions. "Enough, Jeff." Then she added, "Those were tough times for me."

Liz gave her a quick embrace. "For all of us. You were a pill then. A real pip."

"Oh, I've got one," Charie, quiet until now, spoke up exuberantly. "Remember when Mr. Stewart was digging for the addition, and you flushed the toilet, Jimmy? And out the open pipe the water came, right on him!"

"Hey, wait a minute! You flushed it first, Charlotte Markham! Which means *you* doused him with the worst! Then I was trying to tie a sign on the handle so it wouldn't happen again. Mine was purely accidental! And just clean water!"

"But *you* made him get mad and leave!"

"And I'm the one who had to call him back," Rand reminded them.

"You were just doing your Daddy Duties," consoled Charlotte.

When the laughter subsided, Jimmy asked about the spaceman.

"Mr. Sutton passed away suddenly last summer. A stroke. What a loss to his family. To us. To all his friends. We miss him. He was so special." Liz looked at Rand, who had lost his truest friend. Tears had streamed down his face at Bill Sutton's graveside service.

"Charie, remember how we used to gargle with punch?"

She nodded. "And you used to choke all the time. One time you sprayed my face." She smirked guiltily.

"Uh-uh! You're the one who used to choke! I knew how to gargle when I was two. One. Maybe even before I was born!"

They asked Jimmy about baseball, polliwogs, and school. Rand asked, "Where are you staying tonight?"

"Here, if you ask me!" They laughed, and he stammered, "I mean, I know you're busy with wedding plans . . ."

"We wouldn't let you go if you wanted to!" Liz assured him. "Gran's apartment is empty. Our guest apartment. It's full of stuff for the wedding, but we can find the bed for you."

The evening had passed, and Jimmy was again bedded down in the Markhams' home. Liz was tired, but her spirits were lifted. The change of pace and the stimulation of the evening had helped rejuvenate her.

Before he left for UConn on Sunday afternoon, it was decided Jimmy would stay with Jeff and Sally when he returned for Pam's and Eric's wedding.

"Daddy, Jimmy wants to take me to the senior banquet at church the weekend after the wedding," Charlotte informed Rand, pushing his newspaper down from the top. "Mom says to ask you." Jimmy had returned the weekend after his surprise visit. Jeff and Sally had assured him, when he called, that it was no problem at all for him to stay with them for an extra visit. They would simply go about all their planned activities. Besides, this confirmed their suspicions as to what was emerging as the real reason for his additional visit.

"What about Drew?" Rand asked, stalling for time to savor this new suspected development.

"He isn't going. He'll be away."

"What does your mother say about it?"

Charie repeated with an edge of impatience in her voice, "She said to ask you, Dad. I already said that." She knew her father was stalling for the purpose of deliberating.

"I think they're making eyes at each other, Liz," he had said the night before, always aghast at the possibility of his baby falling in love.

"So? You made eyes at me once."

"I still do," he said, pulling her down to his lap. He pressed his nose to hers and crossed his eyes. "But that's different. We're talking about Charlotte, our baby."

"Face it, Rand. Our baby has grown up. She's seventeen."

Now Charie pressed. "Dad?"

"What about Drew? Not fair to embarrass him that way..."

"He won't be there, remember? He's away. I said that."

"Oh. So someone will tell him."

"So? I'm not committed to him."

"That's good. Keep them all guessing."

"So?"

"I'm thinking."

"You are not."

"Am."

"Not. You're stalling."

"On one condition then. You come straight home after, and you wake me up if I'm asleep to tell me you're home."

"*Daddy*," she drawled. "We'll probably stop for ice cream or something. And besides, that's two."

"Two what?"

"Daddy, what a filibusterer you are! Two conditions."

"There's one more. No kissing. He might turn out to be the right frog."

Her giggle sounded like it held tears as she threw her arms around him and buried her face against him. "Trust me, Daddy. No kissing," she promised. "Probably." She wiped the moisture from her eyes on his shirt and whispered in his ear, "Besides, you'll always be my best boyfriend."

"I hope not," he whispered back.

"Randy, are you nervous about the wedding tomorrow?" Liz asked her husband as they were preparing for bed. The weeks previous had been a blur of activity, and they were tired.

"What a question. Of course. It isn't every day a man gives such a treasure away to heaven knows what."

"You mean 'who' not 'what.'"

"I mean *what*. He's probably an animal."

Laughing, she made a fist and socked him gently on the shoulder. Rand thought the world of Eric. "You're prejudiced. Eric is a fine boy. The finest. And you're being very protective. My parents probably felt the same way about you," Liz challenged.

"Never."

"Anyway, we're not losing a family member, we're gaining one. That sounds original, doesn't it? Randy?"

"Hmm?"

"Have you ever loved anyone else?"

"Physically or emotionally?"

"*Randy!*" she squeaked. "I'm serious."

"Hey, I'm serious, too!" He was quiet for a minute before answering, "I almost fell into a relationship with another woman once," he muttered in a stage whisper. Aloud he asked, "Before I met you, or after? Before doesn't count."

Her head was bowed, but he could see tears glistening through her lashes. Putting his finger under her chin, he tilted her head up and looked lovingly into her eyes. "I had girlfriends, you know that." She blinked, and the tears rolled down her cheeks. "You want me to kiss and tell?" he continued, then nodded negatively. "No, my darling, there's never been anyone else. You were all I could handle. I'm a one-woman man."

She laughed and wiped her eyes as he added, grinning, "There was a time, however, when I might have done some looking around. There was this cute little trick I knew . . . She was Greek . . ."

"Oh, *Randy!*" She spoke with difficulty as she tried to regain control. "It was rough for a while, wasn't it? We really came over some rocks and through hard places." She stood and wrapped her arms around him.

"But I never stopped loving you, Liz." He didn't tell her how close he had come to giving up everything when they had temporarily parted ways. "By the way, are *you* nervous about the wedding?" Rand asked.

"Not much. Not now, anyway. I'm determined I'm going to be calm and enjoy all the goings-on. I see so many mothers fall apart during their daughters' weddings. I want to be a model mother of the bride."

"Well, I never told you this, but you were a model mother of babes, mother of middle schoolers, mother of teenagers, mother of pets. So why wouldn't you be a model mother of the bride?"

She snuggled into his neck. "I love you for saying that. But I failed so miserably so many times."

"In your own eyes. I did, too. It's going to be a wonderful wedding."

"I just want them to be happy. That's the most important thing, Randy."

"They've got a lot going for them. Let's get to bed or we'll *both* fall apart tomorrow."

"By the way," he asked before turning off the light after they had climbed into bed, "have you told Dad *what?*" He hadn't forgotten Charlotte's comment and had brought it up a number of times in the past weeks. "Liz?" he prodded.

She hadn't forgotten it either and knew this was pressing. It was a matter to be discussed no later than tonight.

"Liz?"

She threw the covers off and, turning on the light, she crossed the room to her dresser and pulled out an envelope from under her mirrored tray. She handed it to him.

Puzzled, he slid the paper from the envelope. It was a wedding invitation reply.

Liz read it silently from memory for the umpteenth time as she knew Rand read it anew from the response card. *Mr. & Mrs. Jeffrey Randolph Markham, Sr. will attend*, was written on the reply. She had invited Mr. Jeffrey R. Markham Sr. and guest, not knowing there was a new Mrs. Markham Sr.

Rand's eyes flashed. They met hers, and she couldn't look away. Neither of them flinched. Finally Liz detected a softening in his, and then a flicker of a warming. When he reached for her, she slid between the sheets and moved into the circle of his arms. Rand turned off the light and they lay in silence for a long time.

"You're not angry?"

"No. Well, at least I'm working on it."

"It's time to mend the last fence."

"You're asking a lot, Liz. Too much."

"It shouldn't be that difficult."

"I still don't trust him with my ladies."

"But I'm right. Right?"

"As long as I don't let you out of my sight."

"But there's a new Mrs. Markham now. Did you know that?"

He grunted an affirmation. "I just noticed. Poor woman."

"Randy?" She asked after a long silence. She was sure he was unconscious.

"Hmm?" he asked sleepily.

"There's a new spark to Charie."

"You noticed, too?"

"It's fragile, but it's there."

He didn't answer.

"Randy, don't go to sleep."

"I'm tired."

"I want to say something."

He rolled over and threw his arm across her. "Say on."

"Are you sure you're awake?"

"I'm awake."

"You were so wise, so *right* in your decision not to have Jimmy stay with us when I wanted to adopt him."

"Oh?"

"They never could have grown up in the same house."

He moved close to her again. "I agonized over hurting you so much."

"You never told me."

"I thought you'd never *ever* forgive me for saying no."

"But I did forgive you. Somewhere along the line. I'm not sure just when. And," she paused to inhale deeply, "I was wrong too, you know."

"Not for loving and caring so much." He embraced her tenderly. "It's over the dam. Let's go to sleep now, okay?"

She sighed. "Rand?"

"Now what? We're supposed to be sleeping."

"Tomorrow's the beginning of another new beginning."

He squeezed her hand. "Let's remember that for every tomorrow. What's that old saying about the sun shining on a happy bride?"

"I think we're in for a sunshiny day for all."

"I love you, Liz. And I really like you, too. Now *go to sleep!*"

She smiled into the darkness for a long time after Rand had fallen asleep.

www.ingramcontent.com/pod-product-compliance
Lightning Source LLC
Chambersburg PA
CBHW030902080526
44589CB00010B/108